SHADOWRUN COMPANION

FASA CORPORATION

TABLE OF CONTENTS

SHADOWRUN COMPANION
(UPDATED FOR SHADOWRUN, THIRD EDITION)

Original SR Companion Authors
Zach Bush
Jennifer Brandes
Chris Hepler
Chris Hussey
Jonathan Jacobson
Steve Kenson
Michael Mulvihill
Linda Naughton
Brian Schoner

Revised Edition
Text compiled and produced
by Michael Mulvihill and Robert Boyle

Product Development
Michael Mulvihill

Editing
Robert Boyle
Sharon Turner Mulvihill

Shadowrun Line Developer
Michael Mulvihill

Editorial Staff
Editorial Director
Donna Ippolito
Managing Editor
Sharon Turner Mulvihill
Assistant Editor
Robert Boyle

Art & Production Staff
Art Director
Jim Nelson
Cover Design
Fred Hooper
Cover Illustration
John Zeleznik
Black and White Illustration
Doug Alexander, Janet Aulisio, Tom Baxa, Joel Biske, Brian Despain, Fred Hooper, Mike Jackson, Larry MacDougall, Jim Nelson, Mike Nielsen, Paolo Parente, Matt Wilson, Mark Zug
Layout Design
Fred Hooper

Corrected Fourth Printing. First Printing by Fantasy Productions 2001

Published by FanPro LLC • 1608 N. Milwaukee • Suite 1005 • Chicago, IL 60647

Find us online:
info@shadowrunrpg.com
(email address for Shadowrun questions)
http://www.shadowrunrpg.com
(official Shadowrun web pages)
http://www.fanpro.com (FanPro web pages)
http://www.wizkidsgames.com
(WizKids web pages)

INTRODUCTION

The *Shadowrun Companion* is a universal rulebook—its focus is greater than a single theme or topic. This book covers multiple aspects of the *Shadowrun* game and universe, providing new and expanded information for both gamemasters and players. In addition to offering more flexibility in character creation and campaign design, it provides new optional rules and creative ideas and solutions to common problems that plague game play.

Many of the ideas presented in the first edition of the *Shadowrun Companion* were incorporated into *Shadowrun, Third Edition*. It was thus necessary to revise the *Shadowrun Companion* to reflect the new rules and to include fresh material.

The *Shadowrun Companion* takes players through the life of a shadowrunner, from character creation to character retirement. The *Character Creation* section helps you create more well-rounded characters by offering hints and help for creating a complete background story. We also include a point-based approach to character generation, with options for creating otaku, ghoul, shapeshifter and metahuman-variant characters. This section also introduces Edges and Flaws, a mechanic that offers a wide variety of personality traits to help players make each character unique.

The *Skills and Training* chapter focuses on using the Athletics Skill and many of its specializations, including swimming, jumping, running and even being an escape artist. Rules for training to improve both Attributes and skills are also included.

Player character contacts have always been an important but under-used part of the *Shadowrun* universe. *Contacts and Enemies* suggests ways to expand the role of these non-player characters (NPCs), from creating NPC personalities to exploring the distinction between what a contact knows and what he's willing to reveal, to staying on a contact's good side and maintaining confidentiality. Players also can network their contacts through Friends of Friends, an option that adds new depth to characters' sources for information. This section also describes several non-traditional contacts, including the Shadowland BBS. *Contacts and Enemies* provides rules for creating enemies, non-player characters with a more sinister reason for interacting with player characters, and tips for how to effectively present such NPCs in the game.

The *Advanced Rules* section offers optional rules for Karma. These variations include favors and markers, and guidelines for character advancement in an amoral (Karma-less) campaign. This section also offers a system for creating workable statistics for famous NPCs, threats and other opponents of shadowrunners. Following this material are state-of-the-art rules, which allow gamemasters to control the technology curve in their campaigns; rules for DocWagon; and more security systems to use against runners on a run.

Running the Game offers gamemasters a framework and outline to use in designing their own scenarios, adventures and campaigns, including baseline payments for various shadowrunning activities. *Alternate Campaign Concepts* shows gamemasters how to develop and run alternative campaigns and includes examples of player character groups such as DocWagon EMTs and Lone Star teams. This section also provides rules for creating street gangs and designing gang-member characters, suggests campaign hooks for drawing street gangs into a *Shadowrun* game, and describes five Seattle gangs in detail to demonstrate the possibilities of running gang story lines.

DEVELOPER'S SAY

The *Shadowrun Companion* is one of my favorite books.

When this book was first introduced, it created options for and interest in areas that no one really thought existed, such as alternate campaigns and metavariants. It introduced one of my favorite characters—Lord Torgo—and it included Edges and Flaws and Enemies; each of which have made the games I run much more fun and exciting as a gamemaster. It also appealed to those fans who asked me all kinds of questions regarding rules, theory, gamemastering and problem-solving.

The *Shadowrun Companion* was the first salvo in my quest to invigorate *Shadowrun* by opening up new horizons for the game world. Thankfully, it succeeded. It satisfied both new players who were presented with a number of new options for their characters, their gamemasters and their campaigns, and long-time fans who were provided with rules and revisions that they had been requesting for years. As I stated in the original *Introduction*, the *Shadowrun Companion* was not intended to be *Shadowrun, Third Edition*, but rather a way to provide answers for all the fans in a quick and efficient manner.

In retrospect, we did an even better job than I had expected. When it came time to create an actual *Shadowrun, Third Edition*, we ended up using about a third of the information presented in the original version of this book. Luckily, we are working with a vibrant universe and receive continuous input and opinions, so there are always new ideas to include and old rules to be refined. In other words, this revision of *The Shadowrun Companion* contains even more of these options than its previous incarnation. Instead of "fixing rules" (which was the point of SR3), we were able to incorporate and update information that had previously appeared in sourcebooks that are now out-of-print.

So, as it stands, the *Shadowrun Companion* is now updated and ready for action in the shadows … .

As always … Have Fun! Play *Shadowrun!*

CHARACTER CREATION

This section provides suggestions designed to help *Shadowrun* players generate a wide range of interesting, fully realized and fun-to-play runner characters. In addition to options for varying the character-creation system, this section provides optional rules for creating shapeshifter characters and for playing additional metatype variants.

THE CONCEPT

Who do you want to play? This is the most important question to answer before you begin to create your character, because your character can incorporate almost anything you can imagine. You can model your character after a figure in a movie, book or play; after someone you know personally or an individual currently in the news; after a historical or mythic figure; or even after yourself—the choices are endless.

Think about what sort of person you might enjoy "being" when you game—a fresh-faced innocent just out of Corpville, a jaded street punk who's been rolling people for food his whole life, a disillusioned hard-boiled ex-cop, and so on. What motivates your character—does she simply lust after money? Does he want to bring The Revolution to the oppressed people of the Sixth World? Is she a psychopath who loves mindless violence? Does he just want to get by?

MORE THAN AN ARCHETYPE

Like most roleplaying games, *Shadowrun* tends to force players to spend an inordinate amount of time calculating their characters' game statistics. Agonizing over Attribute choices, trying to squeeze maximum efficiency out of every Skill Point and deliberating for hours over the purchase of each piece of equipment—players put a lot of effort into designing lean, mean fighting (or decking, or spellcasting or driving) machines. Finally, they push the mountain of sourcebooks and scrap paper aside and proudly present a completed character sheet to the gamemaster, who looks it over and asks, "So, what's this guy like?"

"Uh, well," the player says, "he's a street samurai, you know? Um ... kind of tough, fearless, honorable ... you know, a street samurai."

Or, "She's a typical decker, kind of geeky, really cocky about her decking skills and nervous about everything else."

Or, "My cat shaman? He's, uh … (sound of pages flipping) … 'sly, rather vain, and holds lots of secrets.' Yeah, that's it."

Why are so many players willing to spend so much time on their characters' guns, gear and statistics, but so little on their personalities? Combat may be exciting, but players could certainly experience the same vicarious thrill of blowing things up by visiting the local video arcade. Roleplaying games offer much more than the thrill of combat. They allow players to take on roles, to become actors in stories of their own creation. That's why the basic concept of a character is important. Background, motivation, personality—these things make characters interesting. And the more interesting and distinctive you make your role, the more you—and everyone else in your game group—will enjoy play.

A character's place in a team of shadowrunners is determined by his personality at least as much as his abilities. Characters who bear striking similarities in game terms may be wildly different in outlook and effectiveness, depending on their personalities and the way their players portray them. Consider one of the most basic character types, the "guy with lots of combat-oriented cyberware." The *Shadowrun* core rules alone offer four variants on this basic theme: the street samurai, combat decker, weapons specialist and mercenary. All these characters possess several of the same important elements: wired reflexes, smartlinks, excellent physical stats and at least one Big Gun. In fact, you could substitute the street samurai statistics for any of the other characters' statistics, and the change would make very little difference. So what distinguishes these characters from each other? Each follows a different mindset, takes a different approach to the world.

The street samurai is an urban predator who balances honor, loyalty and reputation against the need to survive on the mean streets. The combat decker is trained to steal data under hostile conditions. He could hack in remotely like other decker dweebs, but he prefers the excitement of being on site, where the bullets are flying and his life is on the line. The weapons specialist is an expert who prides herself in efficiency and a job well done. Cold and calculating, she's driven to provide her services and so to prove herself better than the rest. The mercenary has two goals: earn her nuyen and stay alive to spend it. Sure, she'll take risks, but only when necessary. Every step of the way, she has her eyes fixed firmly on the bottom line. She may agree with your cause or your politics, but she never works for free.

It is these personality differences—not the sample character name at the top of the page, not the game statistics—that distinguish these four similar character types. The preceding examples offer only the broadest, most stereotypical characterizations, but even these bare-bones personality outlines provide better character-building frameworks than statistics alone.

So when you create your next new character, try spending some extra time on the twenty questions beginning on p. 10 of this book. You may want to add more detail to your character's background as he or she develops a stronger, more distinct personality during gaming sessions, but these guidelines offer enough of a framework to give you, your group and your gamemaster a few strong "hooks" to make your character come alive. Regardless of which questions you choose to

answer for your character, ask yourself why the character made each decision. Why did your former wage mage leave her cushy research job to run the shadows, where she gets to sleep in coffin motels and dodge bullets? Why did your decker sink his entire life's savings into a single, three-pound hunk of electronics? Why did your street shaman choose the path of Gator? (Here's a hint: the correct answer is not, "To get +2 dice for Combat and Detection spells.")

START WITH THE STORY

Players can take the concept of story-based character creation one step further by designing the character's background before determining his or her statistics. Rather than beginning the character-creation process by saying, "I want to play a rigger," and then designing a background that fits the abilities you want him or her to have, create the character's background first and select his or her game abilities based on the character's life story. The following example shows how two runners based on the same premise can develop into very different characters through their backgrounds.

Imagine that you want your character to be a female human rigger who developed an interest in vehicles at an early age. The logical place to start is by determining how a young kid might get involved with vehicles in the first place. Suppose that Character A is the daughter of a high-ranking corporate military officer, and was fascinated by the t-birds and helicopters she saw every time she visited her father's base. At home, she spent most of her free time playing flight-sim games and watching military vids. When she took her corporate aptitude tests, she rated in the top percentiles for vehicular skills, spatial visualization and electronics, thus making her a prime candidate for the corp's Airborne branch. With her father's blessing, she entered corporate military training.

Character B, on the other hand, grew up on the mean streets of the Barrens. For her own protection she joined her brother's go-gang, where she had to learn to ride—and fight—to stay alive. The go-gang did the occasional minor job for a local Yakuza clan, and Character B's raw talent and hunger for success soon caught the attention of the oyabun. He recruited her to run low-priority errands for the clan, and her solid performance eventually led him to rely on her for jobs requiring greater levels of responsibility and trust. After a year or two, the Yakuza recruited Character B as a low-level soldier.

Once you establish the foundation for the background, consider some of the early changes the character may have undergone. For example, every would-be rigger eventually needs to acquire some cyberware, if only a vehicle control rig. Turning points such as these offer good opportunities to explore your character's thoughts and motivations. How does your character *feel* about having a computer implanted into her brain? Character A would probably feel few qualms about such a step; working in a high-tech environment, surrounded by experts with easy access to all the top-notch cyberware they need to do their jobs, she would probably be eager to go under the laser and jump-start her career. Character B, on the other hand, might well dread having the rig implanted. But if the Yakuza—at this point, her only route out of the gutter—made it clear that her continued employment depended on her accepting cyberware, she might feel compelled to undergo the surgery despite her fears. As a result, she might never really embrace her tech and perhaps even refuse to consider further implants.

After creating your character's early life story, decide how your character became a shadowrunner. Character A, for example, would need a pretty dramatic reason to turn against the corporate world of her youth. Perhaps her father refused to follow an order that he morally opposed, and corporate officials court-martialed him and ousted him from the ranks in disgrace. Or perhaps another corp tried to "recruit" him, and his parent corporation killed him rather than let him defect. Either event would shock and disillusion Character A, and she might well turn to the streets out of bitterness and a desire for revenge.

Character B, on the other hand, grew up close to the shadows as part of the go-gang, and her stint as a Yakuza courier kept her on the street. Perhaps running against the corps was a natural reaction when a corporate strike team wiped out her brother's gang in response to some petty vandalism or as a distraction for some covert operation. Her decision to run the shadows might just as easily be a result of heavy recruitment by shadowrunner friends or a misguided belief that living the "glamorous" life of a shadowrunner represents a move up in the world. Character B's presence in the shadows takes on a completely different dimension if the Yakuza did not approve of her choice.

Now that you've figured out how your character ended up in the shadows, you can go to the rulebook and build her statistics. The most logical allocation for Character A would be Priority A for Resources, Priority B to Skills and Priority C for Attributes. She would probably be carrying a substantial amount of military cyberware, most likely including a headware radio, crypto circuit and similar communications gear. Her skills would focus on military-style helicopters, planes, drones and t-birds and include Tactics and perhaps Leadership, but only minimal self-defense skills, because she wasn't trained to operate outside her vehicle. Her primary contacts would be corporate and military.

Priorities for Character B, the ex-go-ganger, might sensibly be distributed as Attributes A, Resources B and Skills C. The only cyberware she might have is the vehicle control rig, with perhaps a spur, smartlink or other personal defense cyberware to help protect her on the streets. Her Vehicle Skills would center on cars and motorcycles, based on minimal exposure to larger and more expensive vehicles. She would, however, possess better personal defense skills than Character A, because she grew up depending on herself rather than her squadmates for protection. Her contacts would include gang, Yakuza, and other street-level people and organizations.

After selecting your character's game statistics, you can define her personality, based on her life history. This may not seem important, but your character's personality will determine how she acts and reacts to different situations. For example, Character A's military background would probably give her a disciplined, by-the-book mentality—she might even be a bit too strait-laced and rigid at times. As a runner, she would want clearly defined objectives, and would probably be reluctant to change objectives in mid-run. She would likely have little tolerance for looting, inter-team bickering and other unprofessional behavior—she would expect the other team members to show the same professional discipline that she does. She would also be ready to either give or follow orders.

Character B's unsupervised childhood on the streets would likely leave her independent, strong-willed and stubborn. Though less disciplined than Character A, Character B would be more flexible, able to adapt to changing situations on the fly. She would be far less likely than Character A to wait patiently in the van piloting drones while the run takes place.

THE SKY'S THE LIMIT

The background-first approach to character creation illustrates one of the basic strengths of the Shadowrun character system—it is not limited by character classes. While other roleplaying games provide distinct sets of character classes that can be combined only in a limited number of ways, the players' own imaginations are the only limits in the Shadowrun character creation system. In the preceding example, Character A combines aspects of the rigger and mercenary Sample Characters, while Character B adds parts of the ganger Sample Character to her rigger nature. Because Shadowrun characters are not limited by class, they can have any sort of skill or ability that players want and gamemasters allow. In fact, the best Shadowrun characters, like the most interesting people, combine many different "roles" to create a well-rounded whole.

The Sample Characters in the Shadowrun, Third Edition (SR3) rulebook and supplements represent some of the major types of characters in the game world. They are examples, nothing more. They allow inexperienced players to jump into the game and start having fun without spending a lot of time on character creation, but they are essentially one-dimensional characters—which usually makes them less interesting than complex characters created by players. So don't hesitate to go beyond the archetypes and familiar stereotypes when creating Shadowrun characters—variety is the spice of life, and a unique, rich character will make the game more fun for everyone.

Consider, for example, the possibilities of a detective character who also happens to be a mage. Think about the potential of a secret-seeking Snake shaman who's also a newsfax reporter, a Shark shamanist hit man, or maybe a decker who enjoys his Three Musketeers reality filter so much that he actually becomes a competent swordsman. Let your imagination run wild. An imaginative background story opens up a multitude of possible combinations—and it's more fun than simply designing a character around a particular set of abilities.

The background-first method of character design can also suggest dozens of adventure hooks you can use to involve your characters in games. Say your group includes a mage who has a kid sister, for example. The seemingly ordinary corporate extraction that your group just got involved in may seem a lot more interesting if the targeted biotechnical engineer also happens to be working on a cure for the mysterious disease that's killing the mage's kid sister. Or maybe your playing group contains a street shaman who has claimed an area of the Barrens as his own little urban protectorate. When a megacorp buys the area and the wreckers move in to make way for new condos, will the shaman fight to defend his turf or try to move "his people" out? Will the other characters on his team help him?

These types of adventures can provide a refreshing change of pace from the usual fixer-generated jobs and give player characters a chance to affect their game world more directly. By creating rich backgrounds for their characters, players don't have to rely on their gamemasters alone to come up with interesting runs. The personalities and motives of the characters themselves and the events of their lives can spawn adventures and help foster more varied, less predictable play.

SOMETHING TO CONSIDER

Gamemasters determine every character's relationship to the rest of the *Shadowrun* world once a game begins, so players and their gamemasters should work together when players create new characters. Cooperation helps prevent players from surprising gamemasters with character elements they may not want in their games, and lessens the chances that a gamemaster will disallow a character that one of his players has created.

FINISHING TOUCHES

After completing the game statistics, you can put the finishing touches on your character by creating a biographical sketch. Then the gamemaster can introduce the character into game play.

A biographical sketch combines all the bits of background you've created for your character. Tell the gamemaster as much as you can about the character. This is your chance to go crazy. It's your character, so he or she can have whatever history you want—no rules, priorities or numbers to worry about. Once again, the *Twenty Questions* below offer a good place to start with this part of the creative process.

As soon as you are finished fleshing out your character, the gamemaster can find a way to introduce the new runner into game play. A story line that lets the character demonstrate his strengths and weaknesses makes for an interesting, believable introduction, especially if the story also provides opportunities for the personalities of the other characters to shine through. The story should also include situations that force the characters to work together. For suggestions on ways to introduce new characters into an established group, see *Integrating New Team Members*, p. 88.

TWENTY QUESTIONS

When creating a character, we recommend you ask yourself the following twenty questions to flesh out the details. We have assumed that certain basic considerations—sex, race, magical ability and so forth—have already been decided. Such character elements are important to the creation process, and should have been decided before you started your character.

The questions below appear in no particular order, so feel free to begin with a question that triggers an immediate response and work back through the rest at your leisure.

BACKGROUND

Where is your character from?

This question serves to give you an instant background for your character. It also sets up a framework by which many other questions can be answered. Be specific. Don't just give a city or country, give an exact location. For instance, two characters growing up in Seattle could easily be from completely different areas; one may be from the hard-boiled Barrens and the other from the pleasant corporate structure of the Renraku Arcology (before the bad times …). Use *New Seattle* and other available source material to help narrow down specific neighborhoods and locales.

Does your character have a family?

This is an important question that almost always gets left out of game play. A family can be very important in defining a character. Does your family make demands on you and your time? Do you shadowrun in secret so that they don't even know, or are you estranged from them to the point that you never talk? Were you raised to believe one thing but have now turned against that code? Are any of your relatives working in opposition to you (such as an uncle in Lone Star), or does your lifestyle put them in danger?

Another consideration is the question of whether your character has ever been married or had children. If so, where are they now? Is your character currently seeing someone? Several someones? Is he or she a runner as well? How does your career impact your relationship?

Does your character have an ethnic background?

The answer to this question goes hand-in-hand with the questions above. Your character's ethnicity should have a large impact on their cultural upbringing. Were you raised in a foreign country, or were your parents immigrants? Were you raised in a culturally rich environment, or was your lifestyle largely assimilated? The UCAS has been a cultural melting pot, and your ethnicity likely impacts your personal history and outlook, as well as how people perceive you. Despite the effects of the Awakening, ethnic racism and prejudice still exists in some areas, although it takes a back seat to views toward metahumans.

APPEARANCE

What does your character look like?

Create a quick description of your character's physical appearance, including height and weight and the color of skin, eyes and hair (if they even have any). Are you a taller-than-average dwarf, or a troll so short you look like an ork? Are you athletic and in shape, or are you underweight and scrawny? Your physical description includes both your character's natural appearance and any body modifications such as cyberware, tattoos, piercings, scarification and so on. What about that green mohawk … or those trademark custom cybereyes? Are any of these characteristics distinguishing? Do you remind people of a famous sim star, or scare people with your steely glare?

What does your character dress like?

Now that you've described your physical body, it's time to dress it. What's your character's style? Does he have any? Are you the height of fashion or are synth-cotton sweats and a black "Skuzzy and the Gonzos" T-shirt the only things you ever wear? Do you "dress down" for street work or "snazz up" for social engagements? Your character's Resources and Lifestyle may certainly affect these options. A Salish-Shidhe tribesman will dress up very differently than a Barrens street rat or a character raised in wealthy Magnolia Bluffs.

Does your character have physical quirks?

While *Edges and Flaws* (p. 17) can help you pick some physical quirks for your character, there are a number of other habits or distinguishing features to choose from. Is your character known for hair or fingernail chewing, or scratching themselves in very unflattering places? Was your nose broken and never set correctly? Where did your character get all those scars? There are a number of suitable physical handicaps that have little or no game application, such as limps, twitches, stuttering or even missing fingers.

SKILLS, ATTRIBUTES & RESOURCES

Where did your character learn their Active Skills?

Since these are the skills a shadowrunner uses the most, it should be determined where your character learned to deck, wire explosives, fire guns, cast spells and so on. When was your character trained? By whom, and under what circumstances? Is the character still tied to these names or places in any way?

Where did your character learn their Knowledge Skills?

These skills give depth and history to your character, so it's important to ask why your character has a fine understanding of elven wines or how they learned psychology. Each classification of Knowledge Skills (Academia, Background, Interests, Sixth World and Street) carries with it a story of how the character would be exposed to such information. Descriptions of when, where and how they learned such things, as well as the teachers and circumstances could spawn stories and insights into your character.

Where did your character get his goodies?

Your character begins the game with a set amount of resources (gear, cyberware, contacts and so forth). How these resources became available to your character is part of your character's history, from each piece of cyberware to each individual bullet. How did your character earn the nuyen to get that implant? Does she owe someone for the "favor" or did "daddy pay for it?" Maybe the character has an extensive background in military or security service and is only now hitting the shadows. Each piece of gear can have a story linked to it. Perhaps that Ares Predator was the one your father the mob boss gave you, or your older brother wore that armored jacket the night he was killed by Renraku Red Samurai.

Where does your character live?

Choosing a lifestyle(s) can also provide background. Are you rich enough to live the High Lifestyle and yet you still run the shadows? Why? Where do you live exactly? Do you have a safehouse in the Barrens? Why there? Do you live in a Z-Zone, where each day is an adventure unto itself? How do you get there each day? How do you deal with the gangs and other urban predators? Are you the only troll in an elven district? What's your relationship with your neighbors?

Who are your character's contacts?

While the gamemaster runs them, you can have a hand in creating them. Each contact you choose should fit into your character's background. How did you meet? Is the relationship just business, or do you share mutual interests? Do you meet every Friday at the corner pub? Describe some aspects of their personality as well. Is she a ruthless cop who happens to have a crush on you? Or is he an avid Urban Brawl fan? Level 2 Contacts especially deserve attention, as they should play a significant role in your character's life. Why are you buddies? Were you partners once, or was she your mentor?

Who are your character's enemies?

If you are using the rules for Enemies (p. 68), they too are based on your resources. Using enemies can flesh out the reasons why you shadowrun, how you came up with your gear or any other backstory you wish to create. Their personalities should also be detailed in the same manner as contacts.

How did your character learn magic?

This is a special question that an Awakened character needs to ask themselves. Since magic is individually based and totems "choose" their shamans, it becomes very important to define where or how a character learned about their abilities, and how they were taught how to use them. In the case of shamans, you should define what the totem means to your character and how they fit into the totem's goals and plans.

Even if your character is mundane, you should decide how they feel about magic. Does it spook them out? Are they jealous that they can't cast such wicked fireballs? Do they have misconceptions about how magic works, perhaps even carrying charms and tokens?

PERSONALITY

What are your character's likes and dislikes?

Everyone has likes and dislikes, and nothing makes a better background or roleplaying hook than to establish a few for your character. These can range in intensity from something that is a minor annoyance to something that crushes your character's heart or drives your character to rants and rampages. These can be either serious or funny. Do you hate Aztechnology because they ship BTLs to your city and your father is a chiphead? Or are you such a die-hard Tacoma Timberwolves fan that you'll skip out on shadowruns in order to catch a game?

What is your character's moral code?

A moral code in the shadows? Every character should have a point where they draw the line. Wetwork? Extractions? Does your character prefer using non-lethal technologies, or does she love to whack corp stooges? If your character is amoral, how did they get that way? What dehumanized them?

This question covers other topics of personal morality as well: cyberware, sex, pollution, lying, stealing, free spirits, ghouls and so on. These can run the gamut from questions that arise in daily life (paying taxes) to more esoteric subjects that may never arise (organlegging).

See also the rules for running an amoral campaign on p. 80.

Does your character have goals?

Are you determined to run the shadows until the Humanis Policlub no longer exists? Or just until you can purchase that island in the Lesser Antilles? Possibly all you want is to make sure your kid sister can afford to go to a good school that will help her control her magical powers. Goals help define the character's outlook on life as well as laying groundwork for future stories. Goals may change for characters, depending on events that occur in the game. Perhaps they are even driven to bitter cynicism or difficult soul-searching as they stray from their original plans.

Does your character have personal beliefs?

Are you a radical anarchist? Are you an ultra-conservative who thinks something needs to be done about the Native American Nation "problem?" Do you think the UCAS corporations are better than the Japanacorps? Is Dunkelzahn your hero? Do you believe that magic is the work of a sinister being out to control everyone's mind? What personal beliefs does your character take to heart, and does she affiliate with any religious sects, policlubs or secret societies because of them?

Does your character have personality quirks?

Are you anti-social? Arrogant? Opinionated? Pessimistic? Superstitious? Laid back? Stressed out? Paranoid? Pick a trait or two and invent a story that explains how you got to be that way.

RUNNING THE SHADOWS

Why does your character run the shadows?

This can be as simple as a basic survival instinct or it can be much deeper and much more psychological. The shadows are a prison for some and a land of opportunity for others. Are you out to make a reputation? Are you striking back at the megacorps in the name of the people? Or are you just a sick fragger with a taste for adventure, and maybe a death wish?

How does your character view his/her role as a shadowrunner?

Running the shadows is one thing; liking it may be a completely different thing. Does your character enjoy the thrill of the game or is he always fearful that he will be caught? Are you cocky about your successes, or do you just take it all in stride?

Maybe your character thinks the end justifies the means, or the shadows are a necessity in the flawed society of the Sixth World. Possibly your character hates the shadows and shadowrunners but is stuck in a no-win situation, forced to do whatever is necessary to survive and get back to where they were … back in the "daylight."

POINT-BASED CHARACTER DESIGN SYSTEM

The point-based system provides players with great flexibility when designing characters.

This system rests on a simple premise. In place of the standard priorities—A, B, C, D and E—the gamemaster declares a Building Points allotment. Each player then uses his Building Points to purchase his or her character's Race, Magic, Attributes, Skills and Resources. The Building Points Table, p. 14, lists the costs for the various character components.

Beyond these Building Point costs, characters are designed in exactly the same manner as in the SR3 character creation process (p. 52, SR3). All the limitations to building a character given there still apply. For example, no character may begin with any gear that has an Availability greater than 8, and the cost of skills is still dependant on the linked Attribute Rating (see Assigning Skills, p. 56, SR3).

Using this system, gamemasters still can restrict their players' choices or encourage the creation of certain character types by setting rating limits on characters' Attributes and Skills. By adjusting the starting Building Point amount, gamemasters can control the general power of characters. The point-based system also provides a convenient way to "handicap" players. For example, a gamemaster can make play more challenging for experienced players by reducing their starting Building Points and increasing the Building Points of inexperienced or new players.

We recommend a Building Point allocation of 120. Note that most of the Sample Characters given in SR3 have a Building Point value in the vicinity of 123.

If the gamemaster allows it, characters can also use Build Points to purchase Edges, or receive more Build Points by taking Flaws (see Edges and Flaws, p. 15). We recommend that players should not be allowed to purchase more than 6 Build Points of Edges, nor take more than 6 points of Flaws.

Other rules for creating otaku characters appear in Virtual Realities 2.0 and Renraku Arcology: Shutdown. Rules for ghouls and shapeshifter characters appear on pp. 32 and 34 (respectively) of this book.

Anton and Jenny decide to create two new characters. Anton wants to play a "made man"—either a Mafia wiseguy or a corporate bodyguard. Basically he's interested in the kind of guy who's paid to stand around, look menacing and occasionally beat people up and shoot things. He settles on a former company man who's now working as muscle for an underworld boss. Jenny is looking for a more esoteric character, someone who's dark and creepy and generally shunned, but still useful to a shadowrunner team. She likes magic, but doesn't want to be a spell-slinger. She decides to play a ghoul adept.

Looking at the ghoul rules, she sees that she's supposed to create a normal character, and then make the ghoul transformation modifications when she's done.

Their gamemaster tells them to create the characters using the point-based design system. He gives them 123 Building Points to start with.

RACE

If a player wishes to create a ghoul or otaku character, she must pay the Building Point cost for doing so (10 for ghouls, 30 for otaku) in addition to the Building Point cost for race. For example, a troll otaku would cost 40 Building Points. If a character wishes to play a variant metatype (see p. 37), she must pay 5 Building Points in addition to the cost for the racial type of which the character is a variant. A cyclops character, for example, would cost 15 points (10 for troll + 5 for cyclops).

If desired, gamemasters can vary the Building Point costs for characters of different metahuman races. For example, the cost for humans could be 2, dwarfs 5, orks 7, elves 8 and trolls 11.

Anton decides his character will be a human, as they blend more easily into the background. He spends 0 Building Points on race.

Jenny is looking for a rougher and tougher character, somebody who's had a hard life from the very beginning, so she decides to make her ghoul an ork. She pays 5 points for being an ork, and 10 more for being a ghoul. That takes her Building Point total down to (123 – 15 =) 108.

MAGIC

Decreasing the Building Point cost of magical ability will encourage the creation of magically active characters, and increasing the Building Point cost will discourage players from designing such characters.

Full magicians automatically receive 25 Spell Points at character creation, as in *SR3*. Likewise, aspected magicians receive 35 spell points. Spell Points may be purchased with nuyen during character creation, at the normal cost of 25,000

BUILDING POINTS TABLE

Component	Cost (in Building Points)
Race	
Human	0
Dwarf or Ork	5
Elf or Troll	10
Metavariant	+5 (add to race above)
Ghoul	+10 (add to race above)
Otaku	+30 (add to race above)
Shapeshifter	25
Magic	
Full Magician	30 (25 Spell Points)
Aspected Magician	25 (35 Spell Points)
Adept	25 (Power Points = Magic Rating)
Attributes	1 Attribute Point per 2 Building Points
Skills	
Active Skills	1 Skill Point per 1 Building Point
Resources (in nuyen)	
500	–5
5,000	0
20,000	5
90,000	10
200,000	15
400,000	20
650,000	25
1,000,000	30

nuyen per point, up to a maximum of 50 points total. Players may reduce the number of Spell Points available at character creation in favor of gaining additional Building Points by "selling" them at a ratio of 5 Force Points for every 1 Building Point.

Adepts receive a number of Power Points for purchasing adept powers equal to the character's Magic Rating.

All the standard rules for spending Spell and Power Points apply, per *SR3*.

Note that otaku characters cannot spend any Building Points on Magic.

Anton's character is mundane, so he skips the magic costs. Jenny wants an adept, however, so she spends 25 more Building Points, leaving her (108 – 25 =) 83 points. As a starting adept, she has 6 Power Points to spend on adept powers—though when she transforms into a ghoul, she'll lose one of those Power Points unless she takes a geasa on it (see Magic in the Shadows).

ATTRIBUTES

Every 2 Building Points spent gives the player 1 point to spend on Attributes. All the rules given under *Choosing Attributes* (p. 55, *SR3*) apply. We recommend that starting characters be limited to a maximum of 60 Building Points spent on Attributes during character creation (including Building Points gained from purchasing Flaws).

Anton wants his character to be able to duke it out with the best of them, so he dumps 60 Building Points into Attributes. That gives him 30 points to distribute among them. He maxes out his physical Attributes, giving them each 6, spending 18. Even though he's a thug, he doesn't want to be dense, so he gives himself an Intelligence of 5. His Charisma isn't an important part of his job description, so he gives it 3, leaving 4 for Willpower. He now has (123 – 60 =) 63 Building Points left.

Jenny has to conserve her Building Points, so only puts 40 into Attributes (20 points). She figures Quickness is important for an adept, so gives it 5. Her Strength and

Body will be boosted by her racial modifications, so she only gives them 1 each. With her last 13, she puts 5 into Intelligence and 3 into Charisma, knowing that they'll be reduced. That leaves her 5 for Willpower.

Jenny has 43 Building Points left. Her racial modifications for being an ork are +3 Body, +2 Strength, −1 Charisma, −1 Intelligence. Her ghoul modifiers do not yet apply. After calculating, we get the following Attributes for Anton & Jenny's characters:

	Anton	Jenny
Body	6	4
Quickness	6	5
Strength	6	3
Charisma	3	2
Intelligence	5	4
Willpower	4	5
Essence	6	6
Magic	—	6
Reaction	5	4

SKILLS

Active Skills are bought at the cost 1 Building Point per point, up to the linked Attribute Rating. Each point a skill is given above that rating costs 2 Building Points. A maximum of 60 Building Points (including points gained from Flaws) can be used to purchase Active Skills.

As with *SR3* character creation, Knowledge Skill Points are calculated by multiplying the character's Intelligence x 5. Likewise, each character receives a number of free Language Skill points equal to Intelligence x 1.5. Knowledge and Language Skills cost do not cost Building Points.

All the rules for assigning Skill Points per *Assigning Skills* (p. 56, *SR3*) apply.

Gamemasters may choose to allow characters to buy extra Knowledge Skills with Building Points, using the same 1 for 1 cost as Active Skills.

Otaku characters receive a number of free points equal to their Mental Attributes divided by 3 (rounded up) for distributing among their Channels only. Active Skill Points may be used to increase the Channels as well (their linked Attribute is Willpower); no otaku can start with Channels higher than 6, 5, 4, 3 and 3.

Anton wants to get a lot of cyberware for his character, so he spends 48 of his remaining Building Points on Active Skills (leaving him 15). With his Intelligence of 5, he also has 25 points for Knowledge Skills and 7 points for Language Skills.

He chooses the following Active Skills: Car 5, Computer 4, Cyber-Implant Combat 5, Etiquette 3, Intimidation 5, Negotiation 3, Pistols 6, Stealth 4, Submachine Guns 5, and Unarmed Combat 6. Because Intimidation exceeded its linked Attribute Rating (Charisma of 3), he had to pay 2 extra Building Points for it. For Knowledge Skills he chooses Demolitions Background 4, Italian Cuisine 4, Mafia Business 5, Mafia

Politics 5, Security Procedures 5 and Urban Brawl 2. For languages, he takes English 4 (Read/Write 2) and Italian 3 (Read/Write 1). Looking his skills over, he decides to specialize to Etiquette 2 (Underworld 4).

Jenny decides to splurge and spends all but 5 of her 43 Building Points remaining on skills, giving her 38 Skill Points. With her Intelligence of 4, she also receives 20 Knowledge Skill Points and 6 Language Skill Points.

For Active Skills, Jenny buys Athletics 6, Aura Reading 3, Biotech 4, Etiquette 2, Intimidation 3, Pistols 3, Stealth 5 and Unarmed Combat 6. Because many of these exceed their linked Attribute Ratings, she respectively pays 8, 3, 4, 2, 4, 3, 5 and 9. For Knowledge Skills, she buys Biology 4, Ghoul Haunts 3, Magic Background 4, Organleggers 3, Paranormal Animals 3 and Seattle Sewers at 3. Finally, she takes English 5 (Read/Write 2).

RESOURCES

Once Building Points have been used to determine a character's Resources, players may assign them as described under *Assigning Resources* (p. 60, *SR3*). As usual, characters must buy a lifestyle, and they receive two free Level 1 contacts.

Note that under this system, neither otaku nor shapeshifters may spend any Building Points on Resources; they start with only 5,000 nuyen.

In addition to the standard uses for Spell Points during character creation, gamemasters may allow player characters to use Spell Points in place of Karma Points in order to begin the game as an initiate, to summon and maintain an ally spirit and so on.

Note that shapeshifter characters may not purchase cyberware. Ghoul characters may do so, but they must pay twice the Essence Cost.

Anton has 15 Building Points left, which he spends to get 200,000 nuyen. He'll use this to buy several lifestyles, contacts, cyberware, guns, and other gear.

Jenny has only 5 Building Points remaining, but that's enough to net her character 20,000 nuyen. She also spends this on lifestyles, contacts, body armor and other gear. She also buys her 6 Power Points of adept powers. Now she must make her Willpower roll to determine how well she survives the transformation into becoming a ghoul! (See p. 32 for more details on creating ghoul characters, and to see how Jenny does.)

EDGES AND FLAWS

Edges and Flaws help players create more fully-realized starting characters and give the gamemaster a few good hooks with which to bring new characters into a campaign. Edges and Flaws also enable players to modify and flesh out their characters by providing them with specific advantages (Edges) and disadvantages (Flaws). Edges and Flaws do not represent an "across-the-board" system of altering player characters; each individual player selects specific Edges and Flaws for his or her character, or may decline to use this option at all. Edges and Flaws may be used with either the point-based system repre-

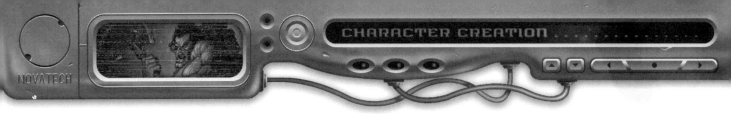

sented in this book (p. 13) or the standard priority system provided in *SR3*.

As with any optional rule, gamemasters have the final say over which Edges and Flaws may be used in their campaigns, and may prohibit the use of this option altogether.

PURCHASING EDGES AND FLAWS

Players purchase Edges and Flaws during character creation. Every Edge and Flaw has a point value—Edges have positive ("plus") values and Flaws have negative ("minus") values. When using the standard priority system, players may select any combination of Edges and Flaws whose combined point values equal zero. For example, a player might select Home Ground (2 points), Color Blind (–1 point), and Combat Monster (–1 point) for his character. A character may take a maximum of five Edges or Flaws (a total of ten) during character creation.

Players can purchase Edges and Flaws in the same manner using the point-based character creation system. Optionally, a gamemaster may allow players to spend or gain Building Points when selecting Edges and Flaws. In this case, a player can spend Building Points to buy Edges or increase the number of Build Points he has available by the point value of any Flaws he takes. For example, a player who takes the Flaw of Blind (–6 points) can add 6 Building Points to his allowance. We recommend allowing no more than 6 Building Points to be gained or spent in this manner.

In the following Edge and Flaw descriptions, a positive value indicates an Edge and a negative value indicates a Flaw. The point values of all Edges and Flaws described in this section also appear in the Edges/Flaws Tables on page 31.

Edges and Flaws During Game Play

If desired, gamemasters may allow their players to add Edges and Flaws to their characters at any time during game play. Because many Edges and Flaws actually represent things that might happen to characters over the course of their lives, however, we recommend that gamemasters require such advantages and disadvantages to be incorporated into existing characters through roleplaying. There should never be additions to skills or Attributes because a character has picked up a Flaw, nor should there need to be a corresponding Edge to counter the Flaw.

LIMITATIONS

In all cases, bonuses from Edges cannot raise Attribute or skill ratings beyond the standard rating limits and maximums for new characters except where noted. In cases where Edges and Flaws modify test target numbers, target numbers can never be reduced below 2.

Unless otherwise noted, Edges and Flaws cannot be combined. For example, a player cannot gain the advantages at character creation that would be allowed by taking both the Pacifist and Total Pacifist Flaws for his or her character.

There are four "educational" Edges and Flaws: University Education, Technical School Education, Illiterate and Uneducated. These represent character extremes rather than

the norm. It is up for players to determine what level of education and formal schooling their character has gone through, based on their background ideas, Knowledge Skills and perhaps the Twenty Questions beginning on p. 10. For most characters, that decision serves as nothing more than plot device; it is not represented by any actual game mechanic. Characters who take one of the four educational Edges or Flaws, however, are representing themselves as extreme cases. For example, someone with the University Education Edge is someone who went through college and miraculously retained vast amounts of the information they were exposed to (not only can they recite the periodic table, but they prefer the Latin translation of Dante's *Inferno*). Likewise, a character with the Illiterate Flaw has suffered exceptionally through their inability ro read.

ELIMINATING FLAWS

With enough effort, individuals can overcome nearly any bad habit or learn to minimize the effects of innate physical or psychological disorders. To reflect this, gamemasters may give their players the option of eliminating their characters' Flaws during the course of game play. If you use this option, make the characters work hard to overcome a Flaw. Just like in real life, eliminating a Flaw should be a difficult and long-term process. For example, in order to eliminate an addiction, the character must endure a painful and lengthy withdrawal process.

Many Flaws can be eliminated or otherwise resolved with sufficiently involved campaign setups and convincing, in-character roleplaying. In addition to any requirements the gamemaster sets for permanently getting rid of a Flaw, the character must pay Good Karma equal to 10 x the Flaw's point value. A character trying to kick Sea Madness, for example, must train themselves to accept lengthy sea travel, and then pay 40 points of Good Karma (10 x 4-point Flaw) to get the monkey off his back for good.

Some Flaws also require medical attention or other radical procedures to eliminate. The gamemaster determines the nuyen cost of these measures, which must be paid by the character in addition to the Karma cost. Players should keep in mind, however, that eliminating one Flaw might just gain the character another: paying Karma and cash for surgery to remove the Night Blindness Flaw might result in an unexpected cortex bomb.

DESIGNING EDGES AND FLAWS

Custom-designed Edges and Flaws provide gamemasters and players with even greater opportunities to give characters distinctive traits. Use the Edges and Flaws described in this section as models when designing your own. In general, no Edge should be worth more than 6 points and no Flaw should be worth more than –6 points. Base the point value of new Edges and Flaws on each one's benefits or drawbacks. For example, an Edge that provides a character with substantial benefits should have a high point value; an Edge that provides only minimal benefits should have a low point value. Finally, all Edges and Flaws must be approved by the gamemaster before players may use them in a game.

Stacy wants to create a character who's a drop-dead gorgeous head-turner—a character who gets noticed right away and uses her looks to get her way. The gamemaster, Bryan, likes the idea and suggests a new Edge to reflect the character's use of her stunning looks.

He calls the new Edge "Good Looking and Knows It." He decides that the Edge provides a –2 target modifier on all Social and Etiquette Tests made when dealing with members of the opposite sex (–1 target modifier when dealing with members of the same sex). Furthermore, members of the opposite sex greet the character with Friendly attitudes when they first meet her (see the Social Modifiers Table, p. 94, SR3). Bryan decides that these benefits are worth 2 points.

Stacy feels that the benefits are not worth the 2 points the Edge will cost. She says that the Edge provides a benefit only during initial contacts between her character and others. Her argument convinces Bryan, who reduces Good Looking and Knows It to a 1-point Edge.

Bryan then decides that the flip side of good looks—bad looks—could make an interesting Flaw. He christens the new 1-point Flaw "Ugly and Doesn't Care." The effects of Ugly and Doesn't Care are simply the reverse of Good Looking's benefits. A character with the Flaw receives a +2 target modifier on all Social and Etiquette Tests when dealing with members of the opposite sex (+1 target modifier when dealing with members of the same sex). New acquaintances display Suspicious attitudes when first meeting the character (see the Social Modifiers Table, p. 94, SR3).

ATTRIBUTE EDGES

Bonus Attribute Point
Value: 2

A player can gain 1 bonus Attribute Point for his or her character. The bonus Attribute Point can be added to any Mental or Physical Attribute.

A bonus Attribute Point can be used to raise the character's starting Attribute above the Racial Modified Limit (see *Exceptional Attribute* below and *Improving Attributes* on p. 244 of *SR3*). Only one Attribute per character may be increased in this manner, and only one bonus point can be applied to any single Attribute.

Exceptional Attribute
Value: 2

A player can increase the Racial Modified Limit for one of the character's Attributes by 1.

This increase also affects the character's Attribute Maximum for that Attribute only. (Attribute Maximum is equal to the Racial Modified Limit x 1.5, round up). For example, if the Racial Modified Limit of a human character's Body is raised to 7, then the Body's Attribute Maximum Rating would be 11.

Player characters can take Exceptional Attribute only once per Attribute. This cannot be used to raise Essence, Reaction or Magic.

SKILL EDGES AND FLAWS

Aptitude/Incompetence
Value: 4/–2

Aptitude or Incompetence reflect expertise or ineptitude in a particular skill.

A character with Aptitude for a skill gains a –1 target modifier to all tests made with the skill. A character with Incompetence receives a +1 target modifier to all tests made with the skill.

Characters can have Aptitude or Incompetence only in skills that they can use. The character cannot use Aptitude or Incompetence when defaulting to that skill.

Characters may take Aptitude or Incompetence only once for any single skill. Gamemasters may also wish to limit characters to one Aptitude, but should allow player characters to be incompetent in as many areas as the player wants. It is strongly recommended that the gamemaster consider carefully before allowing any player character to take an Aptitude in any Combat, Magical, or Computer skill, as these can easily disrupt the balance of a game.

If possible, gamemasters should try to highlight characters' areas of Aptitude and Incompetence at least once per game session.

Computer Illiterate
Value: –3

A character with the Computer Illiterate flaw has extreme difficulty working with computers and other electronic devices. Such characters have trouble performing such simple tasks as using an unfamiliar telecom, sending e-mail or programming a trideo recorder.

During game play, the character receives a +1 modifier to all tests that involve a computer or other electronic device in any way, shape or form (for example, a mage with this Flaw would suffer this modifier when attempting to read another mage's electronic hermetic library). Additionally, the gamemaster may require the character to make Success Tests (Target Number 4) to complete tasks that most people in 2061 take for granted (this can be used to add dramatic tension or comic relief to a game).

Even techno-junkies such as riggers and deckers may have this Flaw, because simsense technology, icon-oriented Matrix programming and the boom of reality filters and sculpted systems have greatly reduced the level of technical know-how needed to rig or deck.

Home Ground
Value: 2

Home Ground provides a character with a –1 target modifier for all Active Skill Tests made within the character's home turf. Any Knowledge Skills using the Home Ground Edge apply a –2 target number modifier.

The character's home turf is a particular location with which the character is intimately familiar. The location must be either a small area—no larger than a single building—or an environment that is encountered infrequently during the campaign. For example, in a Seattle-based campaign, the desert would be an infrequently encountered environment and could be considered home ground for a displaced desert nomad character. The desert would not be a suitable home ground in a campaign based in the magic-soaked Mojave, however. Gamemasters must approve all home grounds in their campaigns.

For a decker character, a home ground might be a particular computer system—a Matrix Host the decker knows extremely well, for example. In this case, the character would receive the –1 target modifier for all tests made while in that system. Favorite data havens, particularly the Denver Nexus, also make suitable home grounds for decker characters. Many corporate deckers have the Home Ground Edge in their corporate systems.

All home grounds must be fixed locations—characters cannot move them around. If a character's home ground is destroyed, the character loses his Home Ground Edge.

PHYSICAL EDGES AND FLAWS

Physical Edges and Flaws stem from a character's physical body and capabilities. Assume that the physical Flaws presented below cannot be corrected with cybertechnology or existing medical technology.

Adrenaline Surge
Value: 2

Adrenaline Surge enables a character to react more quickly than normal during combat situations. A player character with this Edge may use it any time in combat.

When employing Adrenaline Surge, the character uses the Rule of Six for Initiative (p. 100, SR3) but receives a +1 target modifier on Combat Tests and Perception Tests made in combat situations. Once a character uses Adrenaline Surge, he must use it for the remainder of the combat or until the danger has passed.

The Adrenaline Surge Edge applies only to physical actions in the physical world. The Edge has no effect on the actions of a character who is jacked into a rigged system or into the Matrix. Additionally, the Edge has no effect on a character who is driving a rigged vehicle using a datajack link.

Characters whose Reaction or Initiative is already enhanced by cyberware, bioware or magic (including shapeshifters and adepts) may not purchase Adrenaline Surge.

Allergy
Value: –2 to –5

A character with the Allergy Flaw is allergic to a substance or condition. Determining the value of this Flaw requires two steps. First, determine whether the substance or condition is Uncommon (–1) or Common (–2). Then determine the severity of the symptoms: Mild (–1), Moderate (–2), or Severe (–3). Add together the appropriate point values for the condition and the severity to find the final Flaw value. For example, the value of an Uncommon Moderate Allergy is –3 points.

The Allergy Table on p. 19 gives descriptions of conditions and severity.

Bio-Rejection
Value: –5 (–2 for magically active characters)

The immune system of a character with Bio-Rejection is especially sensitive to foreign tissue and material, and the bodies of such characters reject all cyberware implants. Any organ or limb replacements must be cloned from the character's own cells.

For magically active characters (magicians and adepts), Bio-Rejection costs only –2 points. Shaman characters whose totems carry cyberware Essence penalties (such as Eagle or Unicorn) cannot take the Flaw of Bio-Rejection. Characters cannot take both Bio-Rejection and Sensitive System.

Blind
Value: –6 (–2 for magically active characters)

A character with the Blind Flaw receives a +6 target modifier for all visual-based tests. Cyber-replacement eyes cannot correct the Blind Flaw.

Magically active characters with the Blind Flaw may still use astral perception as a form of sight. Such characters receive a +2 target modifier for visual tests based solely in the physical world. However, the Blind Flaw costs only –2 points for such characters. Characters with the Blind Flaw cannot take Color Blind or Night Blindness.

Individual gamemasters and players must determine if this Flaw affects the actions of specific characters jacked into rigs or the Matrix. Simsense works by directly stimulating the vision and hearing centers in the occipital lobe of the brain, so if this Flaw is caused by a nerve defect, it may not affect a character who is rigging or decking. However, if the Flaw is caused by a brain disorder, it can make rigging and decking impossible.

If the Blind Flaw does not affect a character's rigging or Matrix actions, the Blind Flaw is worth –2. If the Flaw does affect a character's riggingor Matrix actions, it is worth the full value.

Borrowed Time
Value: –6

A character with the Borrowed Time Flaw may die at any time. The character might have a fatal illness, be infected with a slow-acting poison or have a deadly implant such as a cortex bomb. In any case, the character's life span can be measured in months.

Whenever a character takes the Borrowed Time Flaw, the gamemaster secretly rolls 3D6. The result indicates the number of game months before the character dies. When the character's time is up, he dies—nothing can save him. Give the character a dramatic death scene.

If the player changes his mind and wants his character to survive, the gamemaster may allow the player to exchange Borrowed Time for another Flaw(s) worth –6 points. This option should not be made available when the player chooses the Flaw, however, because knowing that Borrowed Time need not be fatal effectively negates any drama created by the character's knowledge of his impending death. The gamemaster can make his decision if and when the player makes the request.

Color Blind
Value: –1

A character with the Color Blind Flaw sees the world in black, white and shades of gray. The character receives a +4 target modifier for any tests in which distinguishing between colors is important, such as sifting through the tangle of colored wires in a bomb to find the one that will disarm it.

Note that Color Blind results from a neural dysfunction and cannot be cured with cyber-replacement eyes. Characters cannot take both Blind and Color Blind.

Deaf
Value: –3

A character with the Deaf Flaw cannot hear. The character cannot make Hearing Tests, and receives a +4 target modifier for any tests in which hearing is a factor (such as Surprise Tests).

The Hearing Flaw cannot be cured with cyberware. Individual

ALLERGY TABLE

Condition	Value	Description
Uncommon	–1 point	The substance or condition is rare. Silver and gold are examples of Uncommon substances.
Common	–2 points	The substance or condition is common. Plastic, sunlight and pollutants are examples of Common substances.

Severity	Value	Description
Mild	–1 point	Symptoms are discomforting and distracting. Apply a +1 target modifier to all tests made while a character experiences the symptoms.
Moderate	–2 points	Contact with the substance produces intense pain. Add 2 to the Power of weapons made from this substance when they are used against a character with a Moderate Allergy.
Severe	–3 points	The character receives a Light wound for every minute he touches or remains exposed to the substance. Add 2 to the Power of weapons made from this substance when they are used against a character with a Severe Allergy.

gamemasters and players must determine if this Flaw affects the actions of specific characters jacked into rigs or the Matrix. Simsense works by directly stimulating the vision and hearing centers in the occipital lobe of the brain, so if this Flaw is caused by a nerve defect, it may not affect a character who is rigging or decking. However, if the Flaw is caused by a brain disorder, it can make riggingor decking impossible.

If the Deaf Flaw does not affect a character's rigging or Matrix actions, the Deaf Flaw is worth –1. If the Flaw does affect a character's rigging or decking actions, it is worth the full value.

Double Jointed
Value: 1

A Double Jointed character has unusually flexible joints and can bend and contort his or her body into extreme positions. The character receives a –1 target modifier for Athletics (Escape Artist) Tests. At the gamemaster's discretion, the character can squeeze into small, cramped spaces through which less limber characters cannot pass.

High Pain Tolerance
Value: 2 per box

High Pain Tolerance enables a character to resist the effects of damage to a limited degree. For every two points, the character can resist the effects of one box of physical or mental damage, starting at Light and moving up.

In all other respects, High Pain Tolerance uses the same rules as the adept power Pain Resistance (see p. 170, SR3).

Infirm
Value: –1 to –5

The Infirm Flaw represents a character's deteriorating physical fitness. Infirm characters need not be old or ill—they may simply be individuals who neglect their physical well-being, such as "couch potato" deckers or magicians.

The Infirm Flaw may range from –1 to –5 points. For every Infirm point, reduce the Attribute Maximum of the character's Physical Attributes by 1. If the character's Attribute Maximums fall below the Racial Modified Limit then this new number acts as both the Attribute Maximum and the Racial Modified Limit.

Lightning Reflexes
Value: 2, 4 or 6

For every 2 points spent on Lightning Reflexes, a character receives a +1 bonus to his Reaction Rating. Players cannot purchase more than 6 points of Lightning Reflexes (+3 Reaction bonus). This bonus is used only in Surprise Test situations and is not compatible with the Combat Sense adept power (see p. 169, SR3)

Because they are only used in surprise situations, the extra dice are not used when rolling Initiative, but they are cumulative with any Reaction bonuses from cyberware, biotech or magic in Surprise Tests.

Gamemasters should carefully monitor the use of Lightning Reflexes in their games to prevent the creation of characters with superhuman Reaction Ratings.

Low Pain Tolerance
Value: –4

Characters with Low Pain Tolerance are particularly sensitive to pain. When calculating Wound-related target modifiers for such characters, increase their Wounds by 1 level.

Natural Immunity
Value: 1 or 3

Characters with Natural Immunity (1) have an innate or developed immunity to a single *natural* disease or toxin. The disease or toxin in question cannot affect the character. However, this level of Natural Immunity provides no protection against man-made toxins and biowarfare agents.

Natural Immunity (3) allows a character to take one type of drug or poison, including man-made toxins and biowarfare toxins, without ill effects.

In both cases, the players and gamemaster must agree on the drug or poison to which the character has natural immunity, and it must be something with which the player character would plausibly come into contact. The character can take one dose of the drug or poison every (30 - Body) ÷ 2 hours with no ill effects. If the character ingests more than a single dose in the time allotted, he or she takes normal damage from the poison but begins to recover after (30 - Body) ÷ 2 hours (if the character lives that long).

Night Blindness
Value: –2 (–1 for riggers or deckers)

Night Blindness makes a character effectively blind at night or in darkness. In Full Darkness or Minimal Light conditions (see p. 232, SR3), the character receives an additional +2 target modifier for visual-based tests cumulative with the standard darkness modifiers. Characters cannot take both Blind and Night Blindness.

This Flaw does not apply when rigging because rigged vehicle sensors have image-intensifying capabilities and automatically adjust the brightness level of simsense visual stimuli to match the brain's visual capability. It also has no real impact in the Matrix. Riggers and deckers purchase this Flaw at –1.

Night Vision
Value: 2 (1 for riggers or deckers)

Night Vision provides human characters with improved night vision. This means human characters with this Edge have the metahuman ability of low-light vision (see Perception Modifiers on p. 232, SR3.)

This Edge does not apply when rigging because rigged vehicle sensors have image-intensifying capabilities and automatically adjust the brightness level of simsense visual stimuli to match the brain's visual capability. It also has no real impact in the Matrix. Riggers and deckers purchase this Edge at 1.

Paraplegic
Value: –3

Paraplegic characters are paralyzed from the waist down. Such characters can perform physical tasks that do not require the use of their legs and can move around via wheelchair, but the Paraplegic Flaw reduces their Combat Pools by half (round down). The Paraplegic Flaw has no effect on a character's abilities within the Matrix or in astral space, so full Hacking and Astral Combat Pools can be used.

Characters with the Paraplegic Flaw can and often do become highly effective deckers, magicians and riggers.

The Paraplegic Flaw cannot be treated with cyberware. Characters cannot take both Paraplegic and Quadriplegic.

Quadriplegic
Value: –6

Quadriplegic characters are paralyzed from the neck down and cannot perform physical tasks of any kind. The Quadriplegic Flaw does not affect a character's Attributes or use of Mental Skills. Use the character's Physical Attributes for calculating abilities such as Reaction per standard rules. If desired, a character with the Quadriplegic Flaw may take the Infirm Flaw as well.

Characters with the Quadriplegic Flaw require permanent Hospitalized lifestyles and the attention of hired medical attendants or programmed robot drones to perform physical tasks for them. The Quadriplegic Flaw cannot be treated or cured with cybertechnology or magic. Characters cannot take both Quadriplegic and Paraplegic.

The Quadriplegic Flaw has no effect on a character's abilities within the Matrix or in astral space, so full Hacking and Astral Combat Pools can be used.

Quick Healer
Value: 2

A character with the Quick Healer Edge recovers from damage more quickly than other characters. Reduce the target numbers for the character's Healing Tests by 2 after applying all other modifiers. The target number cannot be reduced to less than 2.

Resistance to Pathogens
Value: 1

A character with Resistance to Pathogens has a vigorous immune system that fights off diseases and infections. The character gains 1 additional Body die when resisting the effects of disease.

Resistance to Toxins
Value: 1

A character with Resistance to Toxins can fight off toxins and drugs more easily than other characters. The character gains 1 additional Body die when resisting the effects of drugs and toxins.

Sensitive System
Value: –3 (–2 for magically active characters)

A character with the Sensitive System Flaw has immuno-suppressive problems with implants. However, these effects are less severe than those of the Bio-Rejection Flaw. The character must double all Essence losses caused by cyberware implants.

If a character with this Flaw is magically active, Sensitive System costs only –2 points. The penalties are the same as for a non-magical character, and the player must also deduct any Essence loss due to this Flaw from the character's Magic Rating. Characters cannot take both Bio-Rejection and Sensitive System.

Toughness
Value: 3

Characters with the Toughness Edge shrug off damage more easily than others. Such characters gain 1 additional Body die for Damage Resistance Tests only. (This bonus die is cumulative with natural dermal armor, so a troll with Toughness is *really* tough.)

Water Sprite
Value: 1 (per ability improvement)

A character with this Edge takes to water like a fish. The abilities granted to such a character are listed below.

Ability	Improvement per Edge Point
Holding Breath Underwater	+20 seconds (see *Drowning*, p. 47, for base seconds)
Swimming	
Distance Increase	Character gains +0.1 when multiplying his Swimming Rate; see *Swimming*, p. 47.
Fatigue	Character gains +1 to the rate of Fatigue (normally Body ÷ 2); see *Swimming*.
Treading Water	
Fatigue	Character gains +1 minute to determine the time between Swimming Tests (normally Strength in minutes); see *Treading Water*, p. 48.
Taking Damage	The character gains –1 to the target number for the Damage Resistance Test; see *Treading Water*.
Floating	
Success	Character gains a –1 modifier to all Buoyancy and Treading Water Tests except for tests made to resist Damage; see *Floating*, p. 48.
Length of time	Character gains +1 Body for determining the length of time the character can float; see *Floating*.

Weak Immune System
Value: –1

A character with the Weak Immune System Flaw is more susceptible to infection by disease than his or her Body Attribute suggests. Reduce the character's Body dice by 1 during tests made to resist diseases (the Body dice cannot drop below 1 on Resistance Tests). Weak Immune System is triggered by the immuno-suppression treatments used in cybernetic and bio-genetic procedures—consequently, it most often afflicts characters who have undergone considerable cyberware modifications.

Will to Live
Value: 1 to 3

For each point spent on Will to Live, a character gains 1 additional Damage Overflow Box. These additional boxes only allow the character to take additional damage before dying. They do not raise the threshold at which the character becomes unconscious or incapacitated, nor do they affect target modifiers based on the character's injuries.

MENTAL EDGES AND FLAWS
Amnesia
Value: –2 to –5

A character with Amnesia has lost some or all of his memory. (Such memory loss can be caused by neurological damage, magic, drugs or brainwashing.) The severity of the character's Amnesia is determined by the selected point value of the Flaw (between –2 and –5). A character with –2 Amnesia cannot recall who he is or anything about his past, but he retains the use of his skills and abilities. A character with –5 Amnesia has no memory of his past, including the skills and abilities he has learned. Gamemasters should create character sheets for characters with –5 point Amnesia, so that the player character does not know his character's abilities, Attributes, and so on until he acts.

Bravery
Value: 1

Characters with the Bravery Edge are not as easily frightened as most people. The character receives a –1 target modifier on tests made to resist fear and intimidation, including Fear caused by spells and critter powers.

College Education
Value: 1

A character with the College Education Edge has not only attended college but has gotten more out of it than a normal student and knows a substantial amount about a diverse group of academic subjects. This character reduces the defaulting modifiers for Academic Knowledge Skill Tests only to +1 to a skill, + 2 to a specialization and +3 to the Attribute. This Edge can be combined with Technical School Education.

Combat Monster
Value: –1

A character with the Combat Monster Flaw becomes irrationally vicious in combat situations. It takes the character at least 3 Combat Turns to break away from a fight. The character can make a Willpower (6) Test to shorten this time—each suc-

cess reduces the period by 1 Turn, to a minimum of 1 Turn. Otherwise, the character can break away from a fight sooner only if he kills or disables all his opponents. Characters cannot take both Combat Monster and Combat Paralysis.

Combat Paralysis
Value: –4

A character with Combat Paralysis tends to "freeze up" in combat situations. On the character's first Initiative roll during any combat, assume the result is the minimum the character can roll with his Initiative dice. This applies to all forms of combat—physical, astral or cybercombat. The character also receives a +2 target modifier on Surprise Tests. Characters cannot take both Combat Paralysis and Combat Monster.

Common Sense
Value: 2

A character with Common Sense has an unusually sharp sense of practicality. Any time such a character is about to do something the gamemaster deems foolish, the gamemaster must warn the player. A remark such as, "You might want to reconsider that," would be appropriate.

Compulsive
Value: Variable

Compulsive characters possess some compulsive behavior over which they have little or no control. The value of this Flaw depends on how dangerous and troublesome the behavior is for the character. For example, a character who is compulsively organized isn't going to suffer much more than the occasional annoyance of his teammates; his Compulsive Flaw will be worth no more than –1 point. By contrast, a decker who compulsively breaks into high-level corporate host systems would receive –3 points for his Flaw.

Flashbacks
Value: –4

The Flashbacks Flaw causes a character to experience vivid memory-based sensory hallucinations, known as flashbacks. These flashbacks are always triggered by specific stimuli. For example, a character who was tortured by the Universal Brotherhood might experience flashbacks of the torture whenever he or she sees an insect.

Any time a character with Flashbacks encounters a potential flashback trigger, he or she must make a Willpower (6) Test. If the test fails, a flashback occurs and incapacitates the character for 1D6 minutes. The character cannot take any useful action during that time.

Characters with the Flashback Flaw should confer with their gamemasters to devise an appropriate flashback trigger before beginning play. The trigger condition can be a particular sight, smell, sound, taste, idea and so on. The condition should be something that the character will encounter a few times during a game. If the trigger is too common, the character may end up experiencing flashbacks all the time. If it is too rare, the character may never experience any.

Impulsive
Value: –2

An Impulsive character tends to jump into dangerous situations without thinking about the possible consequences. When confronted with a dangerous situation, the character must make a successful Willpower (6) Test to avoid blindly jumping into the thick of things.

Illiterate
Value: –3

An Illiterate character cannot read (any character who grew up on the streets or in an isolated rural area may never have learned). During character creation they only receive Intelligence x 3 Knowledge Skills. Such characters cannot have any Academic Knowledge Skills. They also do not receive any free starting Read/Write Skill for any languages that they may have. These characters must rely on other characters to translate written information for them.

Illiterate characters can use computer programs that rely on icons rather than written commands and instructions; however, such characters receive a +4 target modifier to all computer-related tests and cannot have a Computer Skill higher than 1.

Characters may not take both the Illiterate Flaw and any other Education Edge. A character may improve his skills normally per the rules given on p. 245 of *SR3*, but he must always use an instructor and cannot learn them on his own. A character can learn to read, but he must find an instructor to teach him and pay a Karma cost of 5 for the first point in the Read/Write Skill.

Oblivious
Value: –2

An Oblivious character often fails to notice things (this Flaw may result from a short attention span or some other perceptual problem). Such characters receive a +1 target modifier on all Perception Tests, including Astral Perception Tests. The Flaw does not affect combat modifiers for vision or range.

Pacifist
Value: –2

A Pacifist character is unusually principled for the Sixth World. He cannot take the life of another person except in self-defense, and even then he kills as humanely as possible. Such characters cannot participate in premeditated murders or assassinations and are compelled to dissuade their fellow shadowrunners from killing unnecessarily. Some individuals respect the restraint of Pacifist shadowrunners, while others consider them useless wimps. Characters cannot take both Pacifist and Total Pacifist.

Perceptive
Value: 3

Perceptive characters are likely to notice small details and clues that others may miss. Characters with this Edge receive a –1 target modifier on all Perception Tests, including Astral Perception Tests. However, the Perceptive Edge has no effect on detection spells or the use of sensors via a neural interface. The Perceptive Edge does not affect vision modifiers in combat.

Perfect Time
Value: 1

A character with Perfect Time has a split-second sense of timing that enables him or her to always know the current time, to the minute. Prolonged periods of isolation, unconsciousness or the application of mind-benders such as drugs or chips can throw off the character's sense of time, but the character quickly recovers his or her Perfect Time when such conditions are removed.

Phobia
Value: –2 to –5

A character with a Phobia suffers from deep-seated fear activated by a specific triggering condition. Determining the value of this Flaw requires two steps. First, determine whether the condition is Uncommon (–1) or Common (–2). Then deter-

PHOBIA TABLE

Condition	Value	Description
Uncommon	–1 point	The triggering condition is relatively rare; for example, specific sounds or smells.
Common	–2 points	The triggering condition is commonly encountered. Examples of such triggers include sunlight, magic, the outdoors and crowds.

Severity	Value	Description
Mild	–1 point	The character experiences enough fright to distract him from the task at hand. Apply a +1 target modifier to all tests made while the character experiences the reaction.
Moderate	–2 points	The character's reaction is seriously distracting. Apply a +2 target modifier to all tests made while the character experiences the reaction. Additionally, the character tries to avoid the triggering condition. Directly confronting the condition requires a successful Willpower (4) Test.
Severe	–3 points	The character collapses in terror or runs away any time he encounters the triggering condition, unless he makes a successful Willpower (6) Test. If the test succeeds, the character may act while experiencing the reaction, but he suffers a +2 target modifier to all tests.

mine the severity of the symptoms: Mild (–1), Moderate (–2) or Severe (–3). Add together the appropriate point values for the condition and the severity to get the final Flaw value. For example, the value of a Common Moderate Phobia is –4 points. The table on p. 23 gives descriptions of conditions and severity.

Note that Common Severe Phobias (a grave fear of going outside, for example) can seriously impede a character's actions.

Photographic Memory
Value: 3

A character with the Photographic Memory Edge never forgets anything he or she has experienced. The character can perfectly recall faces, dates, numbers or anything else he or she has seen or heard. If the player forgets something that his or her character knows, the gamemaster must provide the correct information.

Photographic Memory is especially useful for decker characters because it enables them to remember complex security codes and other, equally useful information without having to write it down.

Sea Legs
Value: –2

A character gets Sea Legs when he or she has been on land for 24 hours straight without setting foot on a boat. At the 24-hour mark, the character must make a Willpower (4) Test and achieve at least 2 successes; otherwise, the test fails.

If the test fails, the character looks for ways to get back to his or her (or any) ship or boat, even if it means dropping whatever he or she is doing at the time. Target numbers for all tests increase by +1 for each failure on the Willpower (4) Test, except for subsequent Sea Legs Tests.

Regardless of the outcome of the initial Sea Legs Test, the character must make another one every time the character's Intelligence in hours has passed. If the previous test was successful, the next test has a +1 target-number modifier. If the previous test failed, the next one has a +2 target-number modifier. The gamemaster must keep track of how many failures the player has rolled.

The tests end as soon as the character spends time on the water in hours equal to the number of failures rolled. If the character rolls more than 24 failures before spending time on water, the 25th failure means the character must spend 2 days on the water (24 hours, plus another day for the 25th failure) in order to stop making the Sea Legs Tests; the 26th failure requires the character to spend 3 days on the water, and so on.

Sea Legs can manifest in whatever way the player wishes: the shakes, stuttering, forgetting things, general malaise, extreme boredom, a queasy feeling, cramps and other physical pains and so on.

This flaw should only be used by characters who spend time on the water such as pirates or smugglers. Runners who never even see the water should not be allowed to take this Flaw.

Sea Madness
Value: –4

A character with this Flaw gets Sea Madness whenever he or she spends 24 hours or more at sea with no sight of land. At the 24-hour mark the character must make a Willpower (4) Test and achieve at least 2 successes; otherwise, the test fails.

If the test fails, the character slowly begins to go mad. He or she will look for ways to get back to land, even if it means jeopardizing the mission or trying to take over the boat. The character remains well aware of his or her surroundings but begins to fear that others will dump him overboard or leave him out at sea. As the madness worsens, the character will sabotage his own companions and in extreme cases even try to kill them. The character's only goal is to get to land where he will be safe, and he will do anything to achieve it.

Regardless of the outcome of the initial Sea Madness Test, the character must make another one every time his or her Intelligence in hours has passed. If the previous test was successful, the next test has a +1 target-number modifier. If the previous test failed, the next one has a +2 modifier. The gamemaster must keep track of how many failures the player has rolled.

The character continues to make tests as long as land is not visible to him by his or her natural or cyber-enhanced vision. The character will not believe electronic equipment or another character who tells him that land is near. After the character sees land, the madness passes in a number of hours equal to the number of failures rolled. If the character rolls more than 24 failures before seeing land, the 25th failure means the madness does not pass for 2 days (24 hours, plus another day for the 25th failure); the 26th failure means the madness will not pass for 3 days and so on.

This flaw should only be used by characters who spend time on the water such as pirates or smugglers. Runners who never even see the water should not be allowed to take this Flaw.

Sense of Direction
Value: 1

A character with the Sense of Direction Edge never gets lost. The character always knows where true north lies, and can always retrace his or her path. However, Sense of Direction doesn't help a character orient himself if he has been transported somewhere while unconscious or if he is unable to see or otherwise sense his surroundings.

Sensitive Neural Structure
Value: –2 or –4

Characters with a Sensitive Neural Structure have an especially delicate nervous system and are more vulnerable to neural damage from BTLs, black IC, rigger dump shock and other damaging forms of simsense. Whenever a character with this Flaw must resist these types of damage, reduce the character's effective Willpower Rating by 1 for a –2 Flaw, and by 2 for a –4 Flaw. Willpower may not be reduced below 1 this way.

Simsense Vertigo
Value: –2 (–4 for riggers or deckers)

Characters who suffer from Simsense Vertigo experience feelings of disorientation when they use cyberdecks, vehicle control rigs, entertainment simrigs, smartlinks, display links or any other simsense technology. Such characters receive an additional +1 modifier to all target numbers and a –1 modifier to Initiative when operating any simsense-related device.

Spike Resistance
Value: 2 or 4

Characters with the Spike Resistance Edge have increased resistance to high simsense spikes and harmful forms of ASIST, such as black IC or rigger dump shock. When such characters resist these types of simsense-related damage, increase the character's effective Willpower by 1 for every 2 points of Spike Resistance the character possesses. This Edge can only be taken by riggers or deckers.

Technical School Education
Value: 1

A character with the Technical School Education Edge has not only attended a tech school but has gotten more out of it than a normal student and knows a substantial amount about a diverse group of technical subjects. This character reduces the defaulting modifiers for any Background Knowledge Skill Test only to +1 to a skill, + 2 to a specialization and +3 to the Attribute. This Edge can be combined with the College Education Edge.

Total Pacifist
Value: –5

A character with the Total Pacifist Flaw cannot kill any living creature that possesses more intelligence than an insect (this includes insect spirits, which are reasonably intelligent), regardless of the provocation. If the character does so, he suffers from intense regret and depression for 2D6 weeks. During this time, the character refuses to do anything other than eat, sleep and go about his daily routine.

Understandably, the Total Pacifist Flaw is rare among shadowrunners. However, a few shamans of the more pacifistic and healing-oriented totems, such as Snake, exhibit this tendency. Characters cannot take both Total Pacifist and Pacifist.

Uneducated
Value: –2

An Uneducated character possesses only a rudimentary knowledge of reading, writing and arithmetic. During character creation they only receive Intelligence x 3 free points in Knowledge Skills. Such characters cannot begin play with Academic or Background Knowledge Skills. They may also only know one language.

Characters may not take both the Uneducated Flaw and any other Education Edge. A character may improve their skills normally per the rules on p. 245 of *SR3*, but they must always use an instructor and cannot learn them on their own. The first time a new Academic or Background Knowledge Skill is learned, the cost is doubled.

Vindictive
Value: –2

Vindictive characters are especially vengeful and go out of their way to correct any slight against them, no matter how small. The retribution varies according to the slight. A simple insult might call for a coldly delivered threat or punch in the face, while an injury almost always calls for the death or maiming of the offending individual.

Vindictive characters carry grudges until they avenge the perceived wrong they have suffered. They can be loyal and capable comrades, but cross them once and you are on their hit lists forever.

SOCIAL EDGES AND FLAWS
Animal Empathy
Value: 2

A character with the Animal Empathy Edge has an instinctive feel for handling animals of all kinds. The character receives a –1 target modifier for all tests that involve influencing or controlling an animal (including riding). Additionally, the character becomes reluctant to harm animals. Animal Empathy does not affect a character's interactions with sentient creatures such as dragons.

Bad Reputation
Value: –1 to –4

A character with the Bad Reputation Flaw has a dark stain on his or her reputation. Whether or not the stain is deserved, it makes everyone react negatively to the character. The character receives a +1 target modifier on all Social Skill Tests. Increase the modifier by 1 for each point of Bad Reputation the character takes, up to a maximum of 4. For example, a character who takes –4 points of Bad Reputation receives a +4 target modifier.

Blandness
Value: 2

The Blandness Edge enables a character to blend into any crowd. Anyone who attempts to describe the character cannot come up with anything more precise than "he was kinda average."

Any individual who attempts to track or physically locate the character receives a +1 target modifier on all tests made during such attempts. The target modifier does not apply to magical or Matrix searches.

Braggart
Value: –1

While bragging is as much a part of shadowrunning and piracy as the sprawl and the sea, this Flaw means the character doesn't know when to quit. The character with this Flaw will claim that things he or she did were better, tougher and just that much cooler than anything anyone else has done. The character will also falsely claim to have done things if doing so means he can one-up another pirate, crew or team.

The character must roll at least 2 successes on an Intelligence (6) Test to back down from a story or boast.

Connected
Value: 3 or 5

At character creation, the player chooses one contact and one type of merchandise. This contact can buy or sell that contraband at a price that always benefits the player character. The 3-point Edge allows for a one-way transaction (for example, the contact will always buy or always sell weapons for the best possible price). The 5-point Edge allows for a two-way transaction (the contact will always buy *and* sell for the best possible price). Gamemasters should figure the buying price at Street Value and the selling price with no Street Index markup. This Edge can be used by regular shadowrun teams as well as gangs, smugglers or pirates.

Dark Secret
Value: –2

A character with the Dark Secret Flaw has some terrible secret whose revelation could have dreadful consequences. Such a character may have committed a horrible crime, may be the missing heir of a murdered crime family, or may have worked for an organization such as the Universal Brotherhood or the Black Lodge, just to name a few possibilities. Every two or three game sessions, the gamemaster must orchestrate an event that threatens to expose the secret and forces the character to work to conceal it.

If a character's dark secret is exposed, the Flaw may be replaced with a corresponding level of Bad Reputation at the gamemaster's discretion. Alternatively, the character may attempt to redeem himself.

Day Job
Value: –1 to –3

A character with the Day Job Flaw holds down a "real" job besides shadowrunning. A character's day job burdens him or her with responsibilities and time requirements, but it may provide certain advantages as well. A day job can offer a convenient way to launder money, a "cover" persona that can come in handy if law-enforcement people investigate the character, a network of non-shadow contacts, and a little extra cash.

DAY JOB TABLE

Value	Monthly Salary	Min. Hours Per Week
–1 point	1,000¥	10 hours
–2 points	2,500¥	20 hours
–3 points	5,000¥+	40 hours

If desired, gamemasters may allow player characters to take up to –3 points of Day Job. The following guidelines provide suggested monthly salaries for day jobs. Feel free to adjust these figures and restrict the characters' spending or choice of jobs.

Dependent
Value: Variable

A character with the Dependent Flaw has a loved one who depends on him or her for support and aid from time to time. Dependents may include children, parents, a spouse, a sibling or an old friend. Meeting the needs of a dependent should take up a fair amount of the character's time, as well as some of the character's money. The gamemaster should set the point value of the Flaw according to the needs of the dependent and the demands those needs place on the character.

Distinctive Style
Value: –1

A character with Distinctive Style has a flair for the dramatic in dress, behavior and speech, and simply can't stand not being recognized for his or her work. Understandably, this makes the character dangerously memorable at times.

A character who takes this Flaw must choose some way to display his or her style. For example, a character might cultivate a distinctive appearance by sporting a fluorescent green mohawk and a Soviet army jacket at all times. Whatever type of flair a character selects, it must enable other individuals to easily remember the character.

Any individual who attempts to track or physically locate the character receives a –1 target modifier on all tests made during such attempts. The target modifier does not apply to magical or Matrix searches.

Elf Poser
Value: –1

Elf Posers are human characters who want to be elves. This desire prompts them to associate with elves as much as possible, talk like elves, and alter their appearances so that they resemble elves.

Characters who undergo cosmetic surgery to get "elf ears" and "elf eyes" may successfully pass as elves and avoid any negative Social Skill modifiers. However, if an elf discovers the character's secret, the elf treats him or her with contempt and Hostility (see the Social Modifiers Table, p. 94, *SR3*).

Note that only human characters may take the Elf Poser Flaw.

Extra Contact
Value: 1

By spending 1 point, a character can receive 1 additional Level 1 contact during character creation.

Extra Enemy
Value: –1

By spending –1 point, a character can receive 1 additional enemy during character creation (see *Enemies,* p. 68).

Friendly Face
Value: 1

A character with the Friendly Face Edge can easily fit in with new situations, new groups, new cities and new jobs. Whenever he or she tries to fit into a new environment—infiltrating a group or trying to meet contacts in a new city—the character gains an additional −1 to any Social Skill Tests (see the Social Modifiers Table, p. 94, *SR3*).

Friends Abroad
Value: 3

A character with Friends Abroad has a knack for making friends everywhere he or she goes. The character starts the game with an extra contact who must reside in a foreign land. (Because the default setting for *Shadowrun* is Seattle, the extra contact must be from outside UCAS territory, unless the game is based in another country.) Alternatively, gamemasters may allow extra contacts to reside in any major city other than the home city of the campaign. The character must make an effort to maintain this contact—this may be as simple as sending e-mail messages. The character must indicate how he or she plans to maintain the contact when he or she takes the Edge, and the gamemaster must approve the method. If the character fails to appropriately maintain the contact, he or she loses the contact permanently.

Additionally, the character can make new contacts in any foreign land he or she visits. To do so, the player chooses the individual contact (most likely someone his or her character worked with) and, as above, describes for the gamemaster how the character will cultivate that contact. The character must communicate with the foreign contact frequently for one year, then occasionally after that per the *Contact Upkeep* rules, p. 60.

Friends in High Places
Value: 2

Characters with the Friends in High Places Edge have important, influential (Level 2) contacts—such as megacorporate VPs or government officials. From time to time, such contacts can provide considerable help to a character—much more than a regular contact can provide. These contacts will not risk their own positions to help a character, but will do anything short of that. A character who abuses his or her high-ranking contact's trust can quickly lose this Edge, however.

At the gamemaster's discretion, a character can have an even higher-placed contact, such as a megacorporate CEO. However, such individuals rarely have anything to do with lowly shadowrunners. Friendships with such immensely powerful individuals often carry substantial risks as well as benefits.

Human-Looking
Value: 1

A metahuman character with the Human-Looking Edge can "pass" for human in most circumstances. Human non-player characters respond with Neutral attitudes toward such characters when making Social Skill Tests (p. 92, *SR3*). Additionally, human non-player characters do not roll on the Racism Table (p. 92, *SR3*) when interacting with a Human-Looking character, unless they are in close proximity to the character.

Only elves, dwarfs, and orks can take the Human-Looking Edge. Metahuman-variant characters (see *Metahuman Variants*, p. 37) cannot take this Edge.

Hung Out to Dry
Value: −4

For a reason chosen by the gamemaster, the character's contacts suddenly dry up—no one will talk to him or her. The character can try to find out what happened, or simply get on with his or her life. Resolve the effects of this Flaw with roleplaying.

If desired, the resolution of this Flaw can become the subject of an entire campaign. Such a story line can provide an opportunity for the character to redeem his or her reputation among the character's contacts, or further antagonize them until they become Enemies (see p. 68) and the character ends up with a permanent Bad Reputation Flaw (p. 25).

Good Reputation
Value: 1 to 2

Deservedly or not, the character with this Edge enjoys a Good Reputation that makes others trust and respect him or her. For each point spent on Good Reputation, the character receives a −1 target modifier for Social Skill Tests.

Liar
Value: −2

This character lies, and sounds insincere even when he's telling the truth. Every time a character with this Flaw addresses someone, the gamemaster rolls 1D6. On a result of 1, the person or contact being addressed assumes that the character is lying. On any other result, the addressee will believe the character.

The next time the character meets the person who "caught him lying" (that is, the person to whom he was talking when he rolled the 1), the person refuses to believe the character on a result of 1 or 2. The chance of being "caught lying" increases by 1 for every encounter with this person thereafter; the next time they meet, the character is assumed to be lying on a result of 1–3, and so on.

Once the character gets "caught lying" on a result of 1–6, the person will no longer deal with the character. If the person in question is a contact, the character loses that contact permanently. The gamemaster determines if this former contact becomes an Enemy of the character or if the character receives the Hung Out To Dry Flaw, above. No amount of contact upkeep can remove the stigma of lying.

Uncouth
Value: −2

An Uncouth character has no social graces. Such characters suffer a +2 target modifier on Social Skill Tests (including Negotiation and Etiquette Tests).

This Flaw is common among street muscle-types, and many professional shadowrunners consider it the mark of an amateur.

MAGICAL EDGES AND FLAWS

Unless otherwise stated, any character can take a Magical Edge or Flaw.

Astral Chameleon/Astral Impressions
Value: +2/–2

These Edges and Flaws reflect how well an Awakened character's astral signature sticks out on the astral plane. The Astral Chameleon Edge means that a character's astral signature blends into the background of astral space more quickly; treat each astral signature left by the character as if its Force was 1 less. In addition, the character's astral signature is harder to read and recognize; add +2 to attempts by other characters to assense the signature.

The astral signature of a character with the Astral Impressions Flaw sticks out like a sore thumb on the astral plane. All signatures left by the character last as if their Force were 1 higher; subtract –2 from attempts to read the character's astral signature.

Only Awakened characters may take this Edge/Flaw.

Focused Concentration
Value: 2

A magician character with Focused Concentration has a naturally sharp concentration and is less easily distracted when sustaining spells. The character receives only a +1 target modifier when sustaining spells. Additionally, the character can simultaneously sustain a number of spells equal to his or her Intelligence Rating +1. Focused Concentration does not allow the magician to perform any Exclusive Actions while sustaining spells, nor does it allow a magician to sustain an Exclusive spell (p. 160, SR3) while performing another magical activity.

Only Awakened Characters may take this Edge.

Magic Resistance
Value: 1 to 4

For each point spent on Magic Resistance, a character with this Edge receives 1 additional die for Spell Resistance Tests. However, the character cannot be magically active, and the Magical Resistance Edge works against even beneficial spells such as Heal.

Awakened characters (even those with very minor abilities) *cannot* take this edge. A magically resistant character cannot "lower" his magical resistance: it affects all spells and magical effects, good or bad. A character with Magic Resistance is *never* a willing subject for spells with the "requires a voluntary subject" modifier. Such spells automatically fail when used on magic resistant characters.

Poor Link
Value 2

Any ritual sorcery directed against the character receives a +2 target modifier for the Link Test portion of the ritual. Note that this Edge might work against a character in some circumstances, such as when friendly magicians want to use ritual sorcery to locate or aid the character.

Spirit Affinity/Spirit Bane
Value: 2/–2

Character with the Spirit Affinity Edge have a natural affinity with one particular kind of nature spirit. Such spirits tend to find the character interesting, and will be drawn to her. They will be more inclined to do favors for the character (if she is a shaman), or may even occasionally do small favors unasked. In certain situations, they may be reluctant to attack the character (they will likely use a non-lethal power).

On the other hand, a character with the Spirit Bane Edge is actively disliked by a certain kind of nature spirit. These spirits will be likely to harass the character when he is in their Domain, and may be reluctant to do favors for the character or his friends. If ordered to attack a party that includes the character, they will target him first, and attempt to destroy him.

In either case, spirits will most likely reappear in the same form and actually "remember" the character from previous conjurings.

MATRIX EDGES & FLAWS

Note that other Edges and Flaws may apply to the Matrix as well. For example, a character with a phobia of spiders is still going to freak out when an arachnid icon attacks him. Unless otherwise noted, any character may take these Edges and Flaws.

Codeslinger/Codeblock
Value: 2/–1

A codeslinger is particularly adept at performing a particular system operation. She may choose one type of system operation (see p. 215, SR3) during character creation; whenever she performs that specific system operation, she receives an extra die for the System Test.

Characters with codeblock always have trouble with a particular system operation. They lose one die whenever making any test required by that operation.

Codeslinger may only be taken once. Only characters capable of decking may take the Codeblock Flaw.

Cracker/Choker
Value: 4/–2

A character with the Cracker Edge is exceptionally skilled at performing a particular System Test. She may choose one type of test (Access Tests, Control Tests, and so on—see p. 209, SR3) during character creation; whenever she performs a system operation that requires that System Test, she receives an extra die for the test.

Characters with the Choker Flaw always have difficulty with a particular System Test. Whenever they perform a system operation that requires that particular test, they "choke" and lose one die on making the test.

A character may not have both the Cracker and Codeslinger Edges. Cracker can only be taken once. Otaku cannot have the Cracker Edge. Only characters capable of decking may take the Choker Flaw.

Jack Itch
Value: –1

This character has a psychosomatic condition known as "jack itch." Almost every time the character uses their datajack(s) or chipjack(s) or even external smartgun links, they begin to feel a subtle itch … which is impossible to scratch.

Over time, jack itch becomes more and more unbearable, until the character is forced to jack out.

In game terms, a character with jack itch can only stay jacked in for Willpower minutes before they begin to itch. The itch is uncomfortable, and adds +1 to a character's target numbers. For every number of minutes equal to Willpower that the character continues to jack, they receive an additional +1 modifier to all tests. When the modifiers reaches +8, the character goes into a frenzy and jacks out screaming. Once a character has unjacked, the ghost itch remains for some time; reduce the modifier by 1 every (10 - Willpower) minutes.

Natural Hardening
Value: 4

Something about this character's neural structure makes him resistant to neural feedback. This Edge gives the character 1 point of natural Hardening, which has exactly the same effect as (and is cumulative with) a cyberdeck's Hardening.

Scorched
Value: –1

A character with this Flaw had a grievous encounter with psychotropic Black IC (p. 49, *Virtual Realities 2.0*) sometime in their past, suffering near-permanent effects. The exact type of IC and lasting effects are determined by the gamemaster. Characters with this Flaw do not get to make Willpower Tests to ignore the effects of the psychotropic conditioning.

MISCELLANEOUS EDGES AND FLAWS

Bad Karma
Value: –5

A character with the Bad Karma Flaw lives under the weight of some black mark on his soul. This bad karma may result from a past transgression or simply the bad luck of being born under the wrong star. A character with the Bad Karma Flaw must earn double the amount of Karma to increase their Karma Pool.

Cranial Bomb
Value: –6

Someone has planted a cranial bomb in the character's head (see p. 298, *SR3*, for bomb variants). The gamemaster decides who planted it and what that person or group wants. The player need not pay for the bomb with the character's starting Resource points—the bomb's a freebie.

If the character manages to disarm the bomb, the gamemaster may elect to replace it with Extra Enemies, Bad Reputation, Amnesia, a Phobia, or any other Flaw(s) worth an equal number of points.

Cursed Karma
Value: –6

This character is cursed to have his own luck turn against him. Whenever this character uses a point of Karma Pool, he must roll 1D6. On a result of 1, the Karma Point is spent but it

has the exact opposite effect intended. For example, if the player hoped to gain an additional die by spending Karma, he would instead lose a die.

Daredevil
Value: 3

This character is blessed with outrageous luck. Each game session, this character is given 1 extra Karma Pool Point which can only be used in a situation where the character is taking a heroically risky action (such as swinging on a rope to rescue someone from a burning building). Once used, that Karma Pool Point is gone for the session. This Karma point can never be "burned."

Gremlins
Value: –1, –2, –3 or –4

Any equipment touched by a character with the Gremlins Flaw immediately displays an odd tendency to malfunction. Any time such a character handles a piece of equipment, roll 2D6. On a result of 2, the equipment breaks down. The severity of the failure depends on the value of the Flaw.

On a 1-point Flaw, affected equipment operates with a +1 or –1 modifier, whichever works against the character. The modifiers apply to both Success Tests and effect-value ratings (such as a weapon's Power, a sensor's Flux Rating, a cyberdeck's MPCP and so on). To make such equipment work, the character must expend a Simple Action to bang the device against a hard surface. The equipment will function normally during the character's next Combat Phase.

On a 2-point Flaw, affected equipment simply does not work. Again, a sharp jolt (and a Simple Action expended by the character) will bring the unit back on-line in the character's next Combat Turn.

On a 3-point Flaw, the equipment suffers a major malfunction and operates with a +2 or –2 modifier (again, whichever is detrimental to the character). The modifier applies to Success Tests and effect-value ratings. Such equipment must be repaired before it will work again. To find the cost of such repairs, multiply the equipment's cost by .2 and add the result to the repairman's labor charges, if applicable.

On a 4-point Flaw, the equipment breaks down and ceases to work. Only a major overhaul (and some raised eyebrows from the local repairman) will get the unit functioning again. To find the cost of this repair, multiply the equipment's cost by .5. Add labor charges to the result, if applicable.

If a character with the Gremlins Flaw is driving a vehicle, one of the vehicle's major subsystems (steering, brakes, sensors and so on) or special modifications or features (customized engines, vehicle weapons, special accessories and the like) may be affected. The gamemaster can roll for each separate item or simply roll once and choose the system that goes down.

The Gremlins Flaw has no effect on cyberware or magical equipment such as ritual materials, foci and fetishes. However, the Flaw may affect hermetic libraries on electronic media, resulting in lost files, unrecoverable memory errors, short circuits or even an electrical fire.

Pirate Family
Value: 3 (see text)

This Edge can only be taken by players who want to play characters born and raised to the pirate life. The character has extended family in multiple ports who will come out of the woodwork to aid or annoy (as families tend to do) the character in various places around the world. These "relatives" do not count as contacts; instead, they are considered Friends of Friends and can hook the characters into and out of situations in ports and cities utterly unfamiliar to the characters. These "relatives" go beyond blood kin to include anyone who had any contact whatsoever with the family in the past: blood pacts between pirate crews, contacts held by a family member, family friends, mentors and other elders (and, of course, the families of all these assorted people).

In a creative gamemaster's hand, this Edge can become more of a curse. If gamemasters prefer to use Pirate Family to annoy rather than help characters, they can make this Edge a Flaw or reduce its initial Edge Cost to 1. Examples of negative uses of this Edge include an extremely disreputable or cutthroat family member who left many dead in his wake and whose actions cause problems for the character in ports around the world; having to deal with a family member's unpaid debts; or the character finding out that he or she is betrothed to someone in an arranged marriage made when the character was a baby.

Hunted
Value: –2, –4 or –6

The character's Enemies (see p. 68) aggressively hunt down the character. If the Enemy is killed, a new one takes its place, with a starting rank equal to that of the previous Enemy when he, she or it died. The life of the Hunted never gets easier, only harder.

2 point Flaw: A Rank 3 Enemy; or add 1 point to an existing Enemy.

4 point Flaw: A Rank 4 Enemy; or add 2 points to an existing Enemy.

6 point Flaw: A Rank 5 or 6 Enemy (subject to gamemaster's approval); or add 3 points to an existing Enemy.

Mysterious Cyberware
Value: –3

The character has a mysterious piece of cyberware in his body of which he is unaware. The gamemaster chooses the cyberware, and the character does not become aware of its existence until the gamemaster chooses to reveal it—perhaps by having it kick in at an inconvenient time or show up on a detector when the character tries to travel or pass unnoticed into a corporate environment.

As soon as the character discovers and eliminates or otherwise neutralizes the cyberware, the gamemaster can replace the Flaw with Extra Enemies, Bad Reputation, Amnesia, a Phobia, or any other Flaw(s) worth an equal number of points.

Police Record
Value: –6

A character with the Police Record Flaw has fought the law and lost. The character's resulting police record has a number of effects.

First, the character may only have street level contacts (corp types don't hang with ex-jailbirds). Second, most corporate security departments will have a record of the character's face, prints and cyberware, plus a description of his or her modus operandi. Third, Lone Star has copies of the character's records, names, numbers and so on. Lone Star patrolmen recognize the character and harass him or her on sight. Fourth, the character has a criminal SIN, and has to call his or her parole

EDGES TABLE

EDGES	POINT VALUE
Attributes	
Bonus Attribute Point	2
Exceptional Attribute	2
Skills	
Aptitude	4
Home Ground	2
Physical	
Adrenaline Surge	2
Double Jointed	1
High Pain Tolerance	2 per box
Lightning Reflexes	2, 4 or 6
Natural Immunity	1 or 3
Night Vision	2 (1 for riggers or deckers)
Quick Healer	2
Resistance to Pathogens	1
Resistance to Toxins	1
Toughness	3
Water Sprite	1 (per ability improvement)
Will to Live	1 to 3

Mental	
Bravery	1
College Education	1
Common Sense	2
Perceptive	3
Perfect Time	1
Photographic Memory	3
Sense of Direction	1
Spike Resistance	2 or 4
Technical School Education	1
Social	
Animal Empathy	2
Blandness	2
Connected	3 or 5
Extra Contact	1
Friendly Face	1
Friends Abroad	3
Friends in High Places	2
Good Looking and Knows It	1 (example edge, p. 17)
Human-Looking	1
Good Reputation	1 to 2

Magical	
Astral Chameleon	2
Focused Concentration	2
Magic Resistance	1 to 4
Poor Link	2
Spirit Affinity	2
Matrix	
Codeslinger	2
Cracker	4
Natural Hardening	4
Miscellaneous	
Daredevil	3
Pirate Family	3 (see text, may be a Flaw)
Vehicle Empathy	2

FLAWS TABLE

FLAWS	POINT VALUE
Skills	
Computer Illiterate	–3
Incompetence	–2
Physical	
Allergy	–2 to –5
Bio-Rejection	–5 (–2 for magically active characters)
Blind	–6 (–2 for magically active characters)
Borrowed Time	–6
Color Blind	–1
Deaf	–3
Infirm	–1 to –5
Low Pain Tolerance	–4
Night Blindness	–2 (–1 for riggers or deckers)
Paraplegic	–3
Quadriplegic	–6
Sensitive System	–3 (–2 for magically active characters)
Weak Immune System	–1

Mental	
Amnesia	–2 to –5
Combat Monster	–1
Combat Paralysis	–4
Compulsive	Variable
Flashbacks	–4
Impulsive	–2
Illiterate	–3
Oblivious	–2
Pacifist	–2
Phobia	–2 to –5
Sea Legs	–2
Sea Madness	–4
Sensitive Neural Structure	–2 or –4
Simsense Vertigo	–2 (–4 for riggers or deckers)
Total Pacifist	–5
Uneducated	–2
Vindictive	–2
Social	
Bad Reputation	–1 to –4
Braggart	–1
Dark Secret	–2
Day Job	–1 to –3
Dependent	Variable

Distinctive Style	–1
Elf Poser	–1
Extra Enemy	–1
Hung Out to Dry	–4
Liar	–2
Ugly and Doesn't Care	–1 (example flaw, p. 17)
Uncouth	–2
Magical	
Astral Impressions	–2
Spirit Bane	–2
Matrix	
Codeblock	–1
Choker	–2
Jack Itch	–1
Scorched	–1
Miscellaneous	
Bad Karma	–5
Cranial Bomb	–6
Cursed Karma	–6
Gremlins	–1, –2, –3 or –4
Hunted	–2, –4 or –6
Mysterious Cyberware	–3
Police Record	–6

officer every two days and check in with him once a week. The parole officer knows where the character lives, knows his or her usual contacts, and can legally break down the character's door any time he wants.

If the character's record is expunged or the character successfully ditches his or her past life, the gamemaster may replace the Police Record Flaw with Hung Out to Dry, Bad Reputation, Extra Enemies or another Flaw(s) of equal point value.

Vehicle Empathy
Value: 2

Characters with this Edge seem to understand vehicles better than most people and can coax improved performance from vehicles simply by being in physical contact with them. Whenever such a character is in physical contact with a vehicle (either through manual controls or jacked into the vehicle), reduce the Handling of the vehicle by 1.

NEW CHARACTER TYPES

Practically since the introduction of *Shadowrun* to the gaming world, players have requested rules for playing shapeshifter characters—Awakened animals with the magical ability to assume human form (p. 42, *Critters*). Players have also asked for rules on creating characters with alternate metatypes or even characters infected with the Human-Metahuman Vampiric Virus (HMHVV). The following rules allow players and gamemasters to create ghoul and shapeshifter characters and provide guidelines and examples for creating additional metatypes. These are optional rules, and gamemasters have the final say on whether or not to include these new character types in their games.

GHOULS

Of all the humanoid creatures that inhabit the Awakened world, ghouls have probably suffered the most. In recent years, the ghouls' position in society has begun to improve. Increasing (but still small) numbers of ghouls have managed to live in peace with other people, and there are occasional rumors of ghouls with cybereyes and plastic surgery passing themselves off as normal metahumans. Special Order 162, passed by the Illinois legislature in 2053, even granted ghouls legal protection and set up the Cabrini Refuge in Chicago. The act was repealed in 2054 after intense pressure from its opponents, leaving the ghouls on their own once more, but it remained an important step in the slow recognition that ghouls could no longer be dismissed as mere monsters. Ghouls moved a step closer to acceptance in mainstream society when the diaries of Tamir Grey, an influential ghoul spokesperson trapped in the Chicago

Containment Zone, were smuggled out and published in 2057. The firsthand account of the sufferings and nobility of the relief worker who had become a ghoul sparked public sympathy for his plight.

When Ares released copious amounts of Strain-III Beta bacteria into the CZ, the bacteria hit the dual-natured ghouls just as hard as it did the insect spirits. Few survived, and the ill-fated ghouls of the Cabrini Refuge became martyrs for the newly founded Ghoul Liberation League and the Metahuman Rights and Empowerment Coalitions. However, these ghoul-rights movements have not gained much momentum in the public eye. Exceptional individuals like Tamir Grey aside, the vast majority of ghouls are indeed mindless monsters that prey on those incapable of defending themselves. They are liable to snatch children for a midnight snack, and would just as soon eat you as talk to you. This image of the ghoul is most familiar to the average denizen of the *Shadowrun* world.

The source of most people's hatred for ghouls comes from their preference for eating human corpses. They must consume approximately 1 percent of their body weight in metahuman flesh per week in order to maintain their health and get needed nutrition, but the bulk of a ghoul's diet may be any other kind of raw flesh. Ghouls find cooked meat indigestible; it can make them ill, just as raw meat does many metahumans. The generous bequest in Dunkelzahn's will to the first company that develops synthetic flesh for ghouls (see p. 31, *Portfolio of a Dragon*) has sparked ongoing research into this area, but so far these efforts have not gone beyond a few small corporations. (Dunkelzahn's award is a pittance to any megacorp, but a huge draw for smaller companies.) Scientists have not yet managed to isolate the exact chemicals present in metahuman flesh that ghouls need to survive; a popular theory maintains that the ghouls' need for metahuman flesh has something to do with its metaphysical aura.

Metahumans who became ghouls were first thought to have goblinized, in a manner much like genetic expression into orks and trolls. Subsequent investigation, however, showed that ghouls were created by the Krieger strain of the Human-Metahuman Vampiric Virus (HMHVV), a communicable disease. This revelation has fueled the crusade against ghouls as people began to fear that they might become ghouls themselves. Unconfirmed reports exist of some ghouls reproducing by infecting other metahumans, similar to the way vampires pass along their condition. However, the vast majority of ghouls are born that way. As with any disease, it may not be passed to one's offspring; however, most children of ghouls are born infected.

Almost all ghouls who remain functional members of society hide their condition through a combination of perfumes (their dietary preferences give ghouls a foul body odor), plastic surgery (to alleviate their hereditary skin condition) and cybereyes (to hide their telltale milky-white, pupilless eyes). All ghouls suffer from a degree of physical blindness. However, their dual nature allows them to see perfectly well on the astral plane. Ghouls cannot see colors or fine details in non-living objects, which keeps them from making effective use of most technological devices. Many of the more socially adapted ghouls use cybereyes to overcome this problem, provided they can find a street doc willing to implant cyberware in a ghoul.

Ghouls are described on p. 30 of the *Critters Sourcebook*.

Ghouls as Player Characters

With the ghoul community growing and with sympathy for their plight increasing, a ghoul can be a workable player character if the gamemaster chooses to allow it. Characters can be allowed to begin the game as a ghoul, but it may be better for them to become infected during the course of play. The following rules give the gamemaster a way to handle such situations.

If a character becomes infected with Krieger Strain HMHVV during gameplay, follow the rules for infection below.

Players who wish to begin the game as a ghoul character first create a character as normal; they assign Attributes, skills, resources, and even Spell Points or Power Points if their character type alloows for them. Characters who begin play as ghouls must be built with the Building Point system, not the Priority system. They must pay the 10 Building Point cost for starting as a ghoul, in addition to the cost for whatever race they choose. Once they are finished with the character, they also follow the rules for infection below, beginning with the third stage of infection. They make a Willpower (6) Test and compare the number of successes to the Third Stage Infection Table; apply the results directly

KRIEGER STRAIN INFECTION TABLE

Successes	Result
0	Infected
1	Permanent effect (gamemaster's discretion)
2	Sickness
3	No effect

THIRD STAGE INFECTION TABLE

Successes	Effect
0	−2 to Intelligence and Charisma. Inability to deal well with metahumans. Mentally, not much more than an animal.
1	−1 to Intelligence and Charisma. Some semblance of personality left.
2	−1 Charisma. Personality left mostly intact.
3	Standard functional ghoul. Almost complete retention of personality and intellect.
4+	+1 Willpower. Better than normal (almost).

to the character's Attributes, along with the modifiers given on the Ghoul Characteristics Table, p. 34. Because they are starting as a ghoul character, they roll an additional 2 dice for the Willpower Test.

Note that ghoul characters may have cyberware installed in the same manner as any other character, but at twice the Essence Cost. Ghoul characters who begin with such gear are assumed to have obtained it after their transformation.

Ghouls may be of any metahuman race.

Once created (or infected), ghoul characters may continue to advance Attributes and skills in the same manner as any other character.

Infection

Player characters and non-player characters alike can become infected with the Krieger Strain of HMHVV. It is transmitted through bodily fluids, and is most commonly contracted through a bite or scratch inflicted by a carrier of the disease. A character exposed to the virus must make an unaugmented Body Test against the Essence of the carrier of the disease. The results appear on the Krieger Strain Infection Table.

A character who rolls 2 successes escapes infection, but will feel weak, dizzy and ill for ten days or so. One success means that the character feels sick and also suffers some permanent ill effects from his brush with HMHVV: some degree of blindness, skin discoloration and so on. However, the character does not actually become a ghoul. No successes means that the character has been infected, and it is only a matter of time until he suffers all the symptoms of the disease in their worst form. Even if a character rolls 3 successes and fights off the disease without any ill effects, he or she may still become a carrier (possibly without knowing it!).

The disease takes approximately ninety days to run its course, going through three stages of roughly equal duration. No outward signs appear during the first stage, but the virus can be treated if it is detected. During the second stage, outward symptoms of ghoul nature gradually develop: they may include fading eyesight, a craving for raw meat, inability to keep down real food and general discomfort. In the third stage the victim begins deteriorating mentally, as his mind struggles to adapt to the changes in his body, and he also develops the characteristics of a dual-natured being. Some people fare better than others at this point. To reflect this, a character in the

GHOUL CHARACTERISTICS TABLE

+2 Body, +1 Strength, –1 Charisma, –1 Intelligence, –1 Essence, –1 Magic Rating
+1 Running Multiplier
Mild Allergy (sunlight) Flaw (see p. 18)
Enhanced Hearing and Smell (–2 modifier to Perception Test target numbers based on these senses)
Blind Flaw (see p. 19)
Sensitive System Flaw (see p. 21)
Dietary Requirement (raw flesh)
Dual-natured being (see p. 260, *SR3*)
Immunity to VITAS plague

third stage of infection should make a Willpower (6) Test. The Third Stage Infection Table, p. 33, describes the effects of the illness based on the number of successes rolled. Attribute modifiers are cumulative with the common ghoul characteristics in the Ghoul Characteristics Table. Karma may NOT be used for this test.

If a character's Charisma or Intelligence are reduced to zero, they become an insane, mindless beast and are considered NPCs. Alternately, gamemasters may allow such characters to subtract 2 points from another Attribute instead of reducing an Attribute below 1. A character whose Essence is reduced to zero or less dies unpleasantly.

An Awakened character who becomes a ghoul retains his magical abilities and spells, though he is unlikely to be able to use them unless he rolls some successes on the Willpower (6) Test. However, because the character's Magic Rating is reduced by 1, his abilities may be curtailed. Adepts who become ghouls lose a full Power Point's worth of adept powers. If the gamemaster permits, Awakened characters may counteract the Magic Rating loss with geasa, as described in *Magic in the Shadows*.

If a cybered character turns into a ghoul, there is a chance that the cyberware will not survive the transformation. Bioware is automatically lost, completely absorbed into the new ghoul's system—the character no longer receives any bonus or penalty effect from it, as if it was never installed. Any cyberware the character has that is purely "structural"—it merely exists as a modification and does not interact with the body's biological systems—is unaffected by the transformation; this includes 'ware such as bone lacing, dermal plating, fingertip/tooth compartments, flare compensation and so forth. Headware memory would also be unaffected, though its various in/output devices would be. Any other cyberware would be broken by the transformation, and would require cyber repair or surgery to fix.

Note that a character who transforms into a ghoul modifies their Racial Modified Limits (and thus their Attribute Maximums) by the amounts listed on the Ghoul Characteristics Table. The modifiers from the Third Stage Infection Table do not affect the character's Racial Modified Limits.

Jenny has finished up her ork adept character, and is now ready to undergo her character's ghoul transformation. She has a Willpower of 5, and because she's starting as a ghoul she gets 2 additional dice. She rolls and gets a 1, 1, 2, 2, 4, 4 and 6. Against her target number of 6, that's one success. Looking at the table, she sees that her character loses an additional –1 Intelligence and Charisma in additional to the basic ghoul modifications. Because her Charisma can't be reduced below 1, she must lose 2 points from another Attribute; she chooses Willpower.

Re-adjusting her Attributes, her ork ghoul adept now has Body 6, Quickness 5, Strength 4, Charisma 1, Intelligence 2, Willpower 3, Essence 5, Magic 5 and Reaction 3. Her new Racial Modified Limits are Body 11, Quickness 6, Strength 9, Charisma 4, Intelligence 4, and Willpower 6.

SHAPESHIFTER CHARACTERS

Shapeshifters are Awakened animals who have the ability to assume human form. In general, though some shapeshifters mingle with metahuman society and even work as shadowrunners, most shapeshifters prefer to live in wilderness areas, apart from civilization.

This section provides rules for creating shapeshifter player characters. Gamemasters should consult these rules carefully before allowing shapeshifter characters into their game, as they are potentially powerful and unbalancing. As always, these rules can and should be modified to fit your individual campaign and style of play.

The rules below give details for the seven shapeshifter species described in *Critters* (pp. 42–43): Bear, Eagle, Fox, Leopard, Seal, Tiger and Wolf. All of these species are suitable for shapeshifter player characters.

Shapeshifter player characters enjoy three innate advantages over other characters: the ability to shift between animal and human forms, a dual nature and superior regenerative powers. They are also hampered by three disadvantages: their bestial natures, silver allergies and the inability to receive cyberware implants. In addition, the character creation rules restrict the amount of points available for Attributes, Knowledge Skills and Resources during character creation.

Creating Shapeshifter Characters

We recommend using the Point-based Design system for creating shapeshifter characters.

If you are using the Priority System to create a shapeshifter character, you must assign Priority C to Race and Priority A to Resources (unless you choose to be a Full Magician, in which case Priority B must be assigned to Resources). All other Priorities are assigned normally. Regardless of the assigned

Resource Priority, shapeshifters begin the game with only 5,000 nuyen. This reflects the fact that shapeshifters are animal in origin and have less access to gear and funds.

Shapeshifters have two sets of Physical Attributes (Body, Quickness and Strength): one for their animal form, another for their human form. The Mental Attributes (Charisma, Intelligence and Willpower) are always the same, no matter what form the shapeshifter is in. Essence and Magic are likewise always the same. Reaction is determined normally, based on the Attributes for that form.

During character creation, points must be assigned separately to human form physical Attributes and animal form physical Attributes. Once assigned, the respective racial Attribute modifiers are applied, as listed on the Shapeshifter Racial Modifiers Table, p. 36. This means that shapeshifters generally begin the game with lower base Attributes than other characters, but their racial modifiers and abilities make up for the difference.

When assigning skills, use the character's human form Attributes when determining the linked Attribute Rating for skill costs. In addition, shapeshifters begin the game with only Intelligence x 3 free points of Knowledge Skills, and receive only their Intelligence in points for Language Skills. These reductions represent the character's lack of exposure to basic metahuman society and education.

All shapeshifters have an Essence of 8. Magician or adept shapeshifters begin with a Magic Rating of 6.

Because of their bestial nature, shapeshifter player characters do not receive the standard free contacts during character creation. Instead, they must purchase any starting contacts with their allocated Resource Points. However, few metahumans entirely trust a shapeshifter.

During gameplay, the shapeshifter character can raise their Attributes by spending Karma, in the same manner as other characters. However, animal form physical Attributes must be advanced separately from human form physical Attributes. (In effect, shapeshifter characters have an extra three physical Attributes; four if you count Reaction.) The Shapeshifter Attribute Limit Table lists, p. 37, can be used for determining Karma costs for raising Attributes, per normal rules (p. 244, *SR3*). Optionally, gamemasters can base the Karma cost for raising animal form physical Attributes on the human physical Attributes Racial Modified Limits and Maximums; this helps to restrict characters from developing super-powerful shapeshifters.

Note that adept powers that affect physical Attribute Ratings only apply to the character's human form Attributes.

Bestial Nature

Though shapeshifters can assume human form, they are animals at heart. Consequently, powerful animal instincts and emotions drive all shapeshifter characters. Even those who have learned to speak metahuman languages and have assimilated into civilized culture remain beasts at their core, and occasionally act in ways that may horrify even the most hardened shadowrunner.

Understandably, most governments—including the UCAS, CAS and California administrations—do not grant shapeshifters metahuman status. These governments consider shapeshifters no more than wild animals. The NAN government accords more rights to shapeshifters, but does not recognize them as full citizens because of their inability to adhere to metahuman rules and social mores. In nearly all cases, government authorities do not hesitate to destroy criminal shapeshifters as they would a rabid dog.

Animal/Human Form

The ability to shift between animal and human forms is the primary advantage and distinguishing characteristic of shapeshifters. As noted in the preceding section, shapeshifters receive various physical Attribute bonuses in both animal and human forms.

To switch between forms, a shapeshifter must spend a Complex Action. The transformation from human to animal does not include any of the shapeshifter's equipment or clothing; clothing will be ripped and equipment may be damaged during the transformation if the character does not remove it first.

When in animal form, a shapeshifter resembles a larger, more distinguished member of its species; only its astral presence distinguishes it from a mundane—if unusual—animal. A shapeshifter in animal form can communicate with other members of its species, but cannot speak or use Social Skills other than Intimidation. Shapeshifter magicians in animal form can cast spells and summon spirits, but cannot use Centering Skills or fulfill geasa that their beast-forms cannot perform. In animal form a shapechanger cannot use his or her adept powers; they are only usable in human form.

A shapeshifter in human form possesses all the characteristics of a normal human. Typically, a few of a shapeshifter's features vaguely resemble the equivalent features of its animal form: seal shapeshifters often have webbed toes and fingers, and tiger shapeshifters usually retain cat-like eyes. Other than these exceptions, the shapeshifter appears human.

The Shapeshifter Racial Modifiers Table gives the applicable modifiers for shapeshifters in their various forms.

Dual Nature

Shapeshifters are dual beings—they exist on the physical and astral planes simultaneously. Consequently, they can use astral perception at any time as a Simple Action. They also suffer all the disadvantages of having a dual nature: because they cannot shut off their astral presence, shapeshifters are vulnerable to detection and attack on the astral, and magical barriers such as wards block their movement.

A shapeshifter's astral form always appears as an idealized image of its animal form, regardless of the shapeshifter's current form. This means that a shapeshifter in human form can be identified by astral perception unless he is an initiate capable of Masking.

Because they are dual-natured, shapeshifters use their physical Attributes and Combat Pool when engaged in astral combat (unless they are astrally projecting).

Shapeshifter full magicians can only use astral projection when in human form. Their statistics while astrally projecting are equal to their human Mental Attributes, as normal.

Regeneration

Shapeshifter characters regenerate in roughly the same manner as shapeshifter critters (see the rules on p. 13, *Critters*).

Regeneration makes shapeshifters virtually immune to death from injury, unless they suffer massive amounts of damage or damage to the brain or spinal cord.

Whenever a shapeshifter takes Deadly physical damage in one shot, or its cumulative damage reaches Deadly on the condition monitor, roll 1D6. On a result of 1, the shapeshifter does not regenerate, and may die if they do not receive medical care per standard rules. If the damage results from massive tissue injury (burns, trauma and such), the shapeshifter fails to regenerate on a result of 1 or 2. For any other result, the character suffers the standard damage penalties for the Combat Turn in which the damage was inflicted, but the damage vanishes at the beginning of the next Combat Turn.

Weapon foci can permanently slay shapeshifter characters. If a shapeshifter takes Deadly damage from a weapon focus, or damage from a weapon focus pushes the creature into the Deadly range on the condition monitor, the shapeshifter must make an Essence Test with a target number equal to twice the Force of the focus. If the shapeshifter achieves no successes on this test, the character automatically dies. Even 1 success allows the shapeshifter to make a Regeneration Test as above.

A shapeshifter magician who survives Deadly damage must still check for magic loss per standard rules. Additionally, shapeshifter magicians regenerate the Physical damage caused by spellcasting Drain at a rate of 1 Damage box per minute. If a shapeshifter takes Deadly Physical damage from

SHAPESHIFTER RACIAL MODIFIERS TABLE

Species	Modifier
Bear	—
Human Form	+2 Body, +1 Strength, x4 Running Multiplier
Animal Form	+4 Body, +1 Quickness, +4 Strength, +1 Reaction, Dermal Armor 1, +1 Reach, +1 Power (+1 Damage Level) Unarmed Attack, x4 Running Multiplier
Eagle	
Mental	+1 Charisma, +1 Intelligence
Human	+1 Quickness, x4 Running Multiplier
Animal	+2 Quickness, +2 Strength, +1 Reaction, +1D6 Initiative (flying only), +1 Power (+1 Damage Level) Unarmed Attack, x5 Flying Multiplier
Fox	
Mental	+2 Charisma, +1 Intelligence, +1 Willpower
Human	x4 Running Multiplier
Animal	+1 Quickness, +1 Reaction, +1D6 Initiative, x5 Running Multiplier
Leopard	
Mental	+1 Charisma
Human	+1 Body, +1 Strength, x4 Running Multiplier
Animal	+2 Body, +1 Quickness, +2 Strength, +1 Reaction, +2D6 Initiative, +1 Power (+1 Damage Level) Unarmed Attack, x5 Running Multiplier
Seal	
Mental	+1 Charisma
Human	+1 Body, +1 Strength, x4 Running Multiplier
Animal	+2 Body, +1 Quickness, +1 Strength, +1 Reaction, +1D6 Initiative (swimming only), x4 Swimming Multiplier
Tiger	
Human	+1 Body, +1 Quickness, +1 Strength, x4 Running Multiplier
Animal	+3 Body, +2 Quickness, +3 Strength, +1 Reaction, +2D6 Initiative, +1 Reach, +1 Power (+1 Damage Level) Unarmed Attack, x5 Running Multiplier
Wolf	
Mental	+1 Charisma
Human	+1 Body, +1 Strength, x4 Running Multiplier
Animal	+2 Body, +1 Quickness, +1 Strength, +1 Reaction, +1D6 Initiative, +1 Power Unarmed Attack, x5 Running Multiplier

SHAPESHIFTER ATTRIBUTE LIMIT TABLE
Racial-Modified Limits (Attribute Maximum)

	Bear	Eagle	Fox	Leopard	Seal	Tiger	Wolf
Body (A)	11 (17)	6 (9)	6 (9)	7 (11)	8 (12)	10 (15)	7 (11)
Body (H)	8 (12)	6 (9)	6 (9)	7 (11)	7 (11)	7 (11)	7 (11)
Quickness (A)	6 (9)	8 (12)	7 (11)	6 (9)	6 (9)	7 (11)	6 (9)
Quickness (H)	6 (9)	7 (11)	6 (9)	6 (9)	6 (9)	7 (11)	6 (9)
Strength (A)	11 (17)	8 (12)	6 (9)	7 (11)	6 (9)	10 (15)	6 (9)
Strength (H)	7 (11)	6 (9)	6 (9)	7 (11)	7 (11)	7 (11)	7 (11)
Charisma	6 (9)	7 (11)	8 (12)	7 (11)	7 (11)	6 (9)	7 (11)
Intelligence	6 (9)	7 (11)	7 (11)	6 (9)	6 (9)	6 (9)	6 (9)
Willpower	6 (9)	6 (9)	7 (11)	6 (9)	6 (9)	6 (9)	6 (9)
A = animal form H = human form							

Drain, the player character rolls 1D6; the character does not regenerate on a result of 1 or 2.

Note that Karma cannot be used on the Regeneration Test, unless the gamemaster allows the Hand of God rule (p. 248, *SR3*).

Shapeshifters can regenerate in both human and animal form.

Note that these rules do not apply to damage from silver weapons (see *Silver Allergy/Vulnerability,* below).

Silver Allergy/Vulnerability

Every shapeshifter has both a Severe Allergy and Vulnerability to silver (see p. 18 of this book, or p. 15 of *Critters*). The mere touch of the metal causes a shapeshifter pain and burn-like welts. To withstand the urge to retreat from contact with silver, a shapeshifter must make a successful Willpower (6) Test. Weapons made from silver or coated with it receive a +2 Power bonus and +1 Wound Level bonus against shapeshifters. They would also automatically cause an additional Light Wound upon contact. For example, a 4L knife made of silver would do 6M damage to a shapeshifter, plus cause an additional automatic Light Wound.

Shapeshifters only suffer the effects of wounds caused by silver until the beginning of the next Combat Turn, as with other damage (see *Regeneration,* p. 36). However, if a shapeshifter takes Deadly damage from a silver weapon or accumulates Deadly damage from a combination of silver and non-silver weapons, roll 1D6; on a result of 1 or 2 the character fails to regenerate and dies immediately.

Cyberware Rejection

Shapeshifters cannot willingly accept any type of cyberware implants. Their regenerative powers make the surgery next to impossible; even when it has been successful, the cyberware is usually purged from the body in a particularly messy—and painful—fashion soon after.

Particularly sadistic rumor-mongers occasionally suggest that un-named governments have found a way to restrict criminal shapeshifters to their human forms by implanting cyberware into their human bodies in especially damaging ways.

METAHUMAN VARIANTS

Nearly all metahumans possess the basic qualities described in *SR3*, but members of metahuman-variant subgroups may also possess unique characteristics. The following entries describe a few metahuman-variant subgroups. Players and gamemasters can use these descriptions as guidelines for different types of metahuman characters.

Because they possess such unique physical characteristics, even other metahumans consider the metahuman variants described in this book to be, well, freaks. Gamemasters must be sure to constantly bombard metahuman variant characters with social awkwardness and backlash. These characters receive a Hostile reaction (p. 94, *SR3*) in all initial social contacts with other metahumans. Players and gamemasters also must find creative ways for these characters to manage everyday life—just where does a giant sleep, how does he hold a fork, how does he travel—heck, he can't even fit through most doors!

Metahuman Albinism

The condition of albinism continues to exist in the world of *Shadowrun,* and all races manifest albino members. The typical manifestations of an albino remain essentially the same: a deficiency in skin and hair pigmentation, usually appearing as white hair or skin, and eyes showing a pink or blue iris with a bright red pupil. In *Shadowrun,* albinos' skin, eyes, and hair can also take on a silvery hue, they are often noticeably thinner and taller than average for their race, and they suffer a Mild allergy to sunlight. There is no character creation priority change for albinism, though an albino character must have at least one of the following Flaws (see p. 15–30) without gaining the value of the Flaw in Building Points or in an equal Edge: Bio-rejection, Color Blind, Low Pain Tolerance, Night Blindness or Sensitive System. The player can take more than one of the above Flaws for an albino character. Each additional Flaw beyond the required one provides the standard number of Building Points or can be balanced with an Edge. Albino characters have responded positively to the increase in mana and gain +1 to Willpower in addition to any other Willpower increase they receive at character creation (this also raises their Racial Modified Limit for Willpower by 1).

Cyclops (Troll)

Greek and Mediterranean trolls, known as cyclops, are often larger and more heavily muscled than other trolls. They lack most of the dermal bone deposits common among trolls, but are most easily distinguished by the fact that they have only a single eye located in the middle of their foreheads. All cyclops either have only one horn or, in rare instances, no horns.

Cyclops have the following racial modifications: +5 Body, −1 Quickness, +6 Strength, −2 Intelligence, −2 Charisma. They receive +1 Reach like other trolls, but they do not have Dermal Armor or thermographic vision. Cyclops also receive a +2 target modifier for ranged attacks because they lack depth perception.

Koborokuru (Dwarf)

Japanese dwarfs, called *koborokuru*, are slightly smaller than their Western counterparts and possess extensive body hair. Like other metahumans, koborokuru are not looked upon kindly in Japanese society. In fact, Japanese anti-metahuman prejudice has saddled koborokuru with an undeserved reputation as rude and primitive individuals. Like gnomes, koborokuru prefer rural and wilderness areas over urban enviroments.

Koborokuru receive the standard dwarf racial modifications, except that their Quickness running multiplier is 3. They also recieve both the 1 point and 3 point Natural Immunity Edge (p. 20) with no corresponding Flaw. They must choose the natural and the man-made toxin at character creation.

Fomori (Troll)

Fomori are Irish/Celtic trolls. They lack dermal bone deposits, and are generally considered comparatively attractive by other races. Like many metahumans of Celtic descent, fomori possess a higher-than-average propensity for magical ability.

Fomori receive the following racial modifications: +4 Body, –1 Quickness, +3 Strength, –2 Intelligence. They receive +1 Reach and thermographic vision like other trolls, but have no dermal armor.

Menehune (Dwarf)

The *menehune*, or Children of the Land, are named for the original "little people" of Hawai'i. Menehune are shorter than most dwarfs and possess luxuriant body hair, thick muscles, large noses, bushy eyebrows and stringy hair. According to local legends, the menehune's ancestors came from the lost continent of Mu, or Atlantis, but modern biologists and anthropologists place little stock in such fables.

Menehune receive the following racial modifications: +2 Body, +1 Strength, +1 Willpower. They also possess thermographic vision and the standard dwarf resistance to diseases and toxins.

Hobgoblin (Ork)

The hobgoblins of the Middle East are smaller and slighter than most ork variants. Hobgoblins' greenish skin tones, sharp teeth and dark, beady eyes give them a fierce appearance, which has contributed to general anti-metahuman prejudice in the Middle East, especially among Fundamentalist sects. Hobgoblins are also distinguished by their vicious tempers and strong sense of personal honor, which demands that hobgoblins avenge any slight or disrespect directed toward them.

Hobgoblins have the following racial modifications: +2 Body, +2 Strength, –1 Charisma. They also have low-light vision.

Giants (Troll)

Nordic trolls, or giants, are fairer and taller than other trolls. The average giant stands 3.5 meters tall, and most lack horns and the dermal bone deposits common to their race. For as-yet-unknown reasons, giants seem to have a greater-than-average tendency toward genetic reversions—one out of every four female infants born to giant mothers is human (*homo sapiens sapiens*).

Giants possess the following racial modifications: +5 Body, −1 Quickness, +5 Strength, −2 Intelligence, −2 Charisma. They receive +1 Reach and thermographic vision, but have no dermal armor.

Gnomes (Dwarf)

Members of the gnome subgroup inhabit Central Europe and Asia Minor. Gnomes are distinguished from other dwarfs by longer noses and a shorter, more childlike physique. Gnomes tend to favor rural environments over urban settings. Most cling to the behaviors traditionally attributed to their race by mythology and seem unnerved by modern technology. All known magical gnomes are shamans.

Gnomes have the following racial modifications: +1 Body, +1 Strength, +2 Willpower. They also have thermographic vision, but lack the dwarf resistance to disease and toxins.

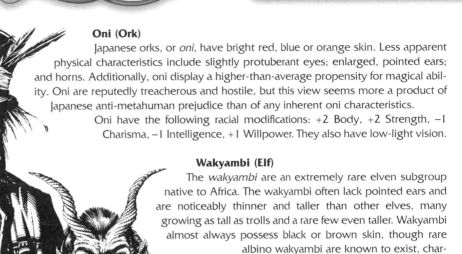

Oni (Ork)

Japanese orks, or *oni*, have bright red, blue or orange skin. Less apparent physical characteristics include slightly protuberant eyes; enlarged, pointed ears; and horns. Additionally, oni display a higher-than-average propensity for magical ability. Oni are reputedly treacherous and hostile, but this view seems more a product of Japanese anti-metahuman prejudice than of any inherent oni characteristics.

Oni have the following racial modifications: +2 Body, +2 Strength, −1 Charisma, −1 Intelligence, +1 Willpower. They also have low-light vision.

Wakyambi (Elf)

The *wakyambi* are an extremely rare elven subgroup native to Africa. The wakyambi often lack pointed ears and are noticeably thinner and taller than other elves, many growing as tall as trolls and a rare few even taller. Wakyambi almost always possess black or brown skin, though rare albino wakyambi are known to exist, characterized by white skin, no body hair and red eyes. All known albino wakyambi shun the modern world and live deep within the jungles of the African heartland.

Numerous African legends refer to a group known as the Heaven People that has given many gifts to humans over the millennia, for their own mysterious reasons. Those legends describe the Heaven People as closely resembling the wakyambi. Seeking to gain the prestige, reverence and other benefits accorded to the wakyambi, some non-wakyambi African elves claim to be members of the Heaven People—but no true wakyambi ever makes such a claim.

The wakyambi have the following racial modifications: +2 Charisma, +1 Willpower. They also have low-light vision.

Ogre (Ork)

Members of the European ogre subgroup are shorter and stockier than most orks. They possess smoother skin and less body and head hair than other orks, as well as pronounced jaw lines.

Ogres receive the following racial modifications: +3 Body, +2 Strength, −1 Intelligence. They lack low-light vision.

Minotaurs (Troll)

Minotaurs are an unusual Mediterranean mutation of the troll metatype, distinguished by pronounced snouts in place of noses, wide-set eyes, long horns and extensive body hair. They possess the following racial modifications: +4 Body, −1 Quickness, +3 Strength, −1 Intelligence, −1 Charisma. They have the standard troll thermographic vision, +1 Reach, and dermal armor.

Satyr (Ork)

Members of the Mediterranean satyr subgroup often possess relatively small physical builds, furry lower bodies, cloven hooves and small, curly horns. Popular myth to the contrary, satyrs are not all musicians or "party animals." Nearly all satyrs possess magical abilities and follow the way of the shaman. Most follow the totem of Bacchus (see *Magic in the Shadows*), which resembles the Greek god of the same name.

Though metahuman satyrs are often confused with wild satyrs (p. 41, *Critters*), members of the ork-satyr subgroup are fully sentient metahumans. Satyrs have the following racial modifications: +3 Body, +2 Strength, −1 Quickness (due to their hooves), −1 Intelligence, −1 Charisma, +1 to Willpower and x4 Running multiplier. They also have low-light vision.

The Night Ones (Elf)

A mostly European metavariant of elves, known by their own choice as the Night Ones, possesses the distinguishing physical characteristic of fine fur covering their bodies. This layer of fur is indistinguishable from skin at a distance, but the fact that the fur ranges in color from black to violet to blue, with some rare examples of green and very deep orange, makes this metavariant quickly apparent at close range. The Night Ones' hair and eyes are usually a tint of their skin color, though a few rare Night Ones have silver hair and eyes.

Because the most common colors of fur are the dark shades, the general public almost immediately dubbed these elves the Dark Elves. Despite popular urban myth, however, the Night Ones are not a cult or an "evil" elven subgroup. Found mainly in Europe, an increasing number of Night Ones have been appearing in the Tir nations. Night Ones have a mild allergy to sunlight and so prefer to live and work at night, but otherwise they resemble other elves.

The Night Ones receive the following racial modifications: +2 Quickness, +2 Charisma. They also have a Mild allergy to sunlight (see p. 18).

Dryads (Elf)

Dryads are an all-female metavariant of elves characterized by an average height of just more than 1 meter and hair color that appears to change with the seasons of the areas in which they live (for example, brown or white in winter months, bright green in the summer and various oranges, reds and yellows in the autumn months). All dryads have dark brown eyes with no visible pupils.

No matter where they are born, all dryads migrate to forested or wooded areas as soon as they are capable of traveling on their own—the further away from the urban sprawl, the better. The longer they live in these isolated areas, the more feral they become, in a voluntary separation from society that includes speaking a language only other dryads understand. While scientific studies cannot pinpoint any specific medical reason for it, dryads exhibit a Mild allergy to urban areas, displaying all the physical and mental strains common to any allergy sufferer whenever they travel away from their home. All known dryads are shamans who follow a variation of the Great Mother totem (see *Magic in the Shadows*). The dryads call their totem Father Tree, but the game stats are the same.

Dryads receive the following racial modifications: –1 Body, +1 Quickness, –1 Strength, +3 Charisma. They also have a Mild allergy to urban areas (see p. 18) and a limited version of the Edge Animal Empathy (this Edge does not need to be balanced by a Flaw; see p. 25). For dryads, the Animal Empathy Edge only affects birds and small tree-living animals such as squirrels and chipmunks.

SKILLS AND TRAINING

I n *Shadowrun*, a character's various skills largely define his or her overall abilities. Consequently, the use and improvement of skills is one of the most important aspects of character development in *Shadowrun*. This section presents material designed to fine-tune and expand the basic skill system to provide more satisfying play.

The section includes rules for using Athletics Skill and optional training rules that enable players to improve their characters' skills and Attributes during the course of play.

USING ATHLETICS

The following rules apply to resolving Athletics Tests, specifically for running, jumping, climbing and swimming. In all instances, Damage Modifiers apply (see p. 126, *SR3*).

CLIMBING

Characters normally perform assisted or unassisted climbing. In unassisted climbing, the character climbs using only his or her own ability. Assisted climbing involves the use of climbing equipment.

Make the Climbing Test (a Complex Action) against a target number that reflects the difficulty of the obstacle being climbed. The gamemaster determines the base target number by how easy the surface is to climb (craggy, sheer and so on), modified by the height of the obstacle and the current environmental conditions (see the Climbing Table, p. 46).

Unassisted, characters can normally climb upward a number of meters each Combat Phase equal to (Quickness + Strength) ÷ 8 (round down). For each Climbing Test success, add 1 meter. Climbing down is easier: characters can move down a number of meters equal to twice the average of their Quickness and Strength, plus 1 for each success.

Assisted climbing makes the upward climb slower, but allows the character to overcome the conditions listed in the Climbing Table. Assisted climbing requires the use of climbing gear (see p. 293, *SR3*). When using climbing gear, modify the base target number for the Climbing Test by −10, making a Climbing Test once every three minutes to reflect the time it takes to safely position the climbing gear on the surface being climbed.

CLIMBING TABLE

Condition	Target Number
Easily climbable surface (i.e., chain-link fence)	3
Broken surface (i.e., debris, tree, loose stone wall)	5
Flat surface (i.e., brick wall, side of old building)	8
Sheer surface (i.e., metal wall, seamless stone)	14

Height:	Modifier
less than 2 meters	No modifier
2–4 meters	+2
4+ meters	+4
Obstacle is slippery or wet	+2
Obstacle is greased, gel-treated and so on	+4

Assisted climbing downward, known as rappelling, is a lot faster than climbing up. With the proper equipment, rappelling allows characters to make a controlled descent at close to free-fall speeds, slow the descent and land safely. A rappelling character falls at a rate of 20 meters per Simple Action expended. Only one of the two Simple Actions available in a Combat Phase can be expended in this manner. For example, a character can rappel and shoot in the same Combat Phase; however, he or she must add a +4 modifier to both the Firearms Test and the Climbing Test.

Rappelling characters increase the number of meters descended during that same Combat Phase by 1 for each success from a Climbing (4) Test. When the character reaches the bottom (or his destination), he must make another Climbing (4) Test. On an unsuccessful test, the character falls 4 meters and takes appropriate damage. See *Falling*, below.

If the Rule of One applies during any Climbing Test, the character plummets to the ground. Benevolent gamemasters may allow the character to make a Quickness (6) Test to grab something and prevent the fall.

Falling

When a character falls, use the Falling Damage Table to determine the Damage level. The Power of the fall is equal to half the number of meters fallen. Subtract half (round down) of the character's Impact Armor Rating from the Power of the fall. Characters may also make an Athletics Test against a target number equal to the full distance fallen (in meters). Each success from this test also reduces the Power of the fall by 1.

FALLING DAMAGE TABLE

Distance Fallen (in meters)	Damage Level
1–2	Light (L)
3–6	Moderate (M)
7–20	Serious (S)
21+	Deadly (D)

A falling character has a "Falling Action" once per Initiative Pass. At that time, the character is considered to have fallen a number of meters equal to 40 times the number of Initiative Passes (including the current one) spent in rapid descent. A falling character has an Initiative of 30 for every turn until the character lands.

ESCAPE ARTIST

This Athletics Skill specialization allows the user to escape from restraints and confinement, such as ropes, handcuffs and other bindings, through contortion and manual dexterity. The difficulty for an Athletics (Escape Artist) Test is based on the complexity of the restraints. Use the Escape Artist table as a guideline for determining target numbers.

The base time to escape is 5 times the target number in minutes, divided by the number of successes. A failure means that the character cannot break free. The character can try again after the base time has expired. For example, if a character tried to break free of handcuffs and failed, he cannot try again for 30 minutes (5 x 6 = 30).

ESCAPE ARTIST TABLE

Restraint	Target Number
Ropes	4
Handcuffs	6
Straitjacket	8
Containment Manacles	10

Adepts with the Pain Resistance power gain an additional advantage in using this skill, because they can safely dislocate joints and twist them in otherwise painful contortions. The ability to resist each Wound level subtracts 1 from the target number of the test. This means that an adept who can resist up to Moderate damage (3 levels of Pain Resistance) may subtract 2 from the target number, an adept able to resist Severe damage can subtract 3, and so on. Any pain resistance used to counter penalties from injuries that the adept may have does not count toward this bonus.

Toshi is captured and worked over by some corporate goons, then put in handcuffs and locked up. Toshi has Athletics 3 (Escape Artist 5) and 4 levels of Pain Resistance. He has also taken Moderate Stun damage. His target number to escape from the handcuffs would normally be 8 (6, plus the damage modifier). His pain resistance negates the effect of the damage, bringing the Target Number to 6, with one level left over. Because he can resist an additional Light level of damage, Toshi subtracts one from his target number, making it 5. He rolls 1 success on his Escape Artist Test and works his way out of the cuffs. Now he begins planning how to get out of the cell to pay back the corp goons ... .

JUMPING

Characters may make two kinds of jumps: a running jump and a standing jump. If a character is jumping vertically, treat it as a standing jump.

For running jumps, use the distance the character wishes to jump (in meters) as the target number for an Athletics Test. Apply any appropriate modifiers. Only one success is needed to achieve the jump. The maximum distance for a running horizontal jump is equal to the character's Quickness in meters.

For standing horizontal jumps and vertical jumps, make an Athletics Test against a target number equal to twice the distance in meters the character wishes to jump. A single success indicates a successful jump. The maximum distance for these jumps is equal to the character's Quickness divided by 3 in meters.

If a character is attempting to jump as far as he or she can, make an Open Test using Athletics and divide the high roll result by 2 (for a running jump) or 3 (for a standing jump). That number is the distance the character has managed to jump in meters (round down). The maximum distance for these jumps is equal to the character's Quickness in meters.

Characters attempting to jump without Athletics Skill may default to Quickness instead of Body, at the standard +4 modifier. A failed jump or a jump down may result in a fall (see *Falling*, p. 46).

LIFTING/THROWING

A character can lift from the ground weight equal to 25 kilograms per point of his or her Strength without making a test. A character with augmented strength makes a Strength Test against a target number equal to the weight of the object being lifted, divided by 10 (round up). For each success, the character can lift an additional 10 percent (round down). A character can lift over his head weight equal to 12 kilograms per point of Strength by making a standard Strength Test.

Once a character lifts an object over his head, he can throw that object a number of meters equal to his Strength, minus the object's weight divided by 50 (round down). The character can attempt to increase the distance thrown by making a Strength Test against a target number equal to the weight of the object being lifted, divided by 10 (round up). For every 2 successes, the object flies an additional meter.

RUNNING

Characters with Athletics Skill and/or the Running specialization may attempt to increase the distance they can run by spending a Complex Action and making an Athletics (4) Test. Each success increases the character's effective Quickness by 1 point for that Combat Phase. The gamemaster may apply modifiers for various types of terrain (slippery, rocky, and so on) and other conditions. Normal Movement rules apply (see *Movement*, p. 108, *SR3*).

Fatigue

No one can run forever. After a period of sprinting, even the most conditioned athlete begins to slow down. The Fatigue rule simulates this phenomenon.

Under the Fatigue rule, a character can sprint for a number of turns equal to half his or her Body (rounding up) before he or she begins to lose steam. If the character continues to run beyond this base period, he or she begins taking Fatigue damage. The base damage is 4L (Stun), and can be staged down with an Athletics Test or an Athletics (Running) Test. (If a character is not sprinting, but is merely running or jogging, the gamemaster may increase the base period.)

Each time the character repeats the Skill Test (successfully or not), he or she can run for an additional number of turns equal to half his or her Body, suffering Fatigue damage at the end of each base period. The character may attempt to stage down the Fatigue damage using an Athletics Test or an Athletics (Running) Test, but the Power of the Fatigue damage doubles for each subsequent test. For example, if a character has Body 4, he may sprint for 2 turns. After that, he must take 4L damage or make a successful Athletics Test or Athletics (Running) Test to stage down the damage. He can then sprint for another 2 turns, then must take 8L damage or make a successful Athletics Test or Athletics (Running) Test to stage it down.

Eventually, the runner will take enough Stun damage to convince him to stop running, or he will reach Deadly on the Stun Condition Monitor and will collapse from exhaustion. A character who collapses from exhaustion is not unconscious—he is simply unable to continue any sort of strenuous activity.

Generally, Fatigue damage has the same game effects as Stun damage. However, Fatigue damage reflects exhaustion and aching muscles more than actual injury, and so it does not contribute to a character falling unconscious due to other Stun damage or to a character's death from accumulated damage. Characters may heal Fatigue damage as if it were standard Stun damage.

SWIMMING

Using Athletics Skill or the Swimming specialization to swim requires a Complex Action. Characters swim at one-fifth their normal Running rate (use the same rules to determine swimming speed and distance as for running, except divide all resulting distances by 5). Similar to running, characters make an Athletics Test or Swimming Test against a Target Number 4. Each success increases the character's effective Quickness for swimming by 1 point for that Combat Phase. A character wearing swimming fins swims at half the normal walking or running rate.

Swimming characters suffer from fatigue in the same manner as running characters.

Holding One's Breath

A typical character can hold his or her breath for 45 seconds (15 Combat Turns). A character who wants to hold his breath longer makes an Athletics (4) Test. Each success increases the length of time the character can hold his breath by 20 percent (round down), or 3 Combat Turns. After that point, the character takes 1 box of Stun damage in each phase of the

Combat Turn in which he has an action. This damage cannot be resisted. Once all the Stun boxes are filled, the character passes out, and the lungs attempt to fill with air again. The character will continue to take Physical damage at the same rate as he took Stun damage until dead.

Treading Water

Treading water requires a character to make periodic Treading Water Tests against a Base Target Number 2, modified by applicable conditions listed on the Treading Water Modifications Table.

Each character must make a Treading Water Test when he or she initially falls into water, and once every (Strength) minutes afterward. A swimmer treading water gets tired, using his Body to resist Light Stun damage at a Power equal to the cumulative number of tests. As long as the character is in the water, these tests add up, even if the character spends time floating.

A character who is treading water using a survival float makes tests and resists damage every 15 minutes, regardless of the character's Strength. In the case of rough seas, the gamemaster may reduce this time.

If a character fails a Treading Water Test, he or she begins to drown but can try to resume treading water or swimming after making a Body (8) Test to resist Light Stun damage. If this test is successful, the character can attempt to swim, tread water or float again. However, he continues to suffer from whatever fatigue and damage he took previously.

If the character fails the test and takes damage, he or she begins to use up his or her last 45 seconds of air. The character cannot attempt to tread water, float or swim until he or she makes a successful Damage Resistance Test or someone rescues the character.

Floating

Floating depends partly on natural buoyancy. In general, excluding cyberware or bioware from consideration, elves tend to be buoyant in water and can float on their own without external support (such as a life jacket). Orks and trolls have little buoyancy and usually sink without some form of external support. Dwarfs and humans may be buoyant or not, depending on their physical condition (highly muscular folks will tend to sink; fat people will float).

To float, a character makes a Body (4) Test using the appropriate modifiers from the Treading Water Modifications Table. If the test is successful, the character can float for (Body x successes) Combat Turns. If the test is unsuccessful, the character must tread water or swim, or else he begins to drown.

OPTIONAL TRAINING RULES

Technically, player characters can simply purchase skill and Attribute improvements with Good Karma points (see p. 244, SR3). However, gamemasters can more accurately simulate the time and dedication needed to improve a skill by requiring player characters to spend time training when they want to improve skills or Attributes.

SKILL TRAINING TIME

Under the training rules, the time a character must spend to improve a skill depends on the type of skill being learned, as shown on the Skill Improvement Table (p. 49).

The training time requirements apply to skill specializations as well. Every specialization must be improved separately.

Characters can reduce the base training time by making a Skill Test using the skill they are improving (this test represents how quickly the character comprehends new topics and relates them to his existing ability in the skill). The base target number is equal to the new skill rating being trained for plus 2. If the character has used the skill often in game play, especially in stressful situations, the gamemaster can apply a –1 target modifier to the Skill Test. (Gamemasters may adjust this modifier to suit the character and game situation, if desired.) Characters may also reduce their training time by enlisting the aid of a live or virtual instructor (see Training with an Instructor, p. 49).

Characters may also default to another skill or Attribute for the above test, per standard rules.

TREADING WATER MODIFICATIONS TABLE

Character has:	Target Number
Cyberlimbs or torso	+1 per part replaced
Aluminum/Titanium bone lacing	+2
Waterlogged clothing	+1
Dead weight (clothes and armor)	+1 per 2 kilos
Metatype	
Seal shapeshifters	–2
Elves	–1
Dwarfs and humans	0
Orks and trolls	+1
Physical Condition	
Obese	–2
Physically fit	0
Out of shape	+1
Highly developed muscles or exceptionally low body fat	+1
Supported by a mildly buoyant object (plank of wood)	–1
Supported by a very buoyant object (life jacket)	–2
Wounded	Damage Modifiers apply
Rough seas (crashing waves)	+2 to +4

To calculate the final training time, divide the base time by the number of successes achieved on the Skill Test. If the character achieves no successes, multiply the base training time by 1.5 and round up.

Generally, training time must be uninterrupted—otherwise, the required time period increases. If the character fails to train for a number of days equal to his or her Intelligence Rating plus the new skill rating, he must allow for extra training time. The extra time equals the number of days remaining in the required training time, multiplied by 2. This extra training time reflects how long the character must spend "getting back up to speed." Characters may incur extra training time an unlimited number of times.

Sasser wants to raise her Medicine Knowledge Skill from 2 to 3, which will cost her 3 Karma Points. That means a required training time of 45 days (required Karma Points 3 x 15 for Knowledge Skills). That seems like a long time, so Sasser decides to make a Medicine Test to reduce the required time. The Target Number is 5 (new skill rating + 2). Sasser rarely uses her Medicine Skill, so the gamemaster declines to reduce the target number with a modifier.

The test yields 2 successes, which produces a final training time of 23 days (base training time of 45 days ÷ 2, rounded up). So, after training for 23 days, Sasser can spend 3 Good Karma Points to raise her Medicine Rating to 3.

After training for 18 days, however, Sasser needs to go on a run. The run goes poorly, and Sasser doesn't make it back to Seattle until 14 days have passed. That's a problem. Sasser has Intelligence 5, and the new Skill Rating is 3—so any time she misses 8 or more days of training for the improvement, she must add extra training time. She had only 5 days left in the original training time when she stopped, so she must now train for 10 days to improve the skill (remaining days x 2 = extra training time).

LEARNING A NEW SKILL

Though the *Shadowrun* rules have always allowed player characters to learn new skills during the course of the game (post-character creation), *Shadowrun, Third Edition* only offers a very basic outline for doing this (see pp. 245–46, *SR3*). Characters can learn new skills through self-directed study (the do-it-yourself method), or by training with a live or virtual instructor. Generally, characters can use the do-it-yourself method to learn only skills related to those the character already possesses. At their discretion, however, individual gamemasters

may drop this restriction, limit it to certain specific skills, or even expand the restriction.

Do-It-Yourself Method

The do-it-yourself me-thod enables characters to learn new skills without the aid of an instructor. This method often makes learning more difficult, and even dangerous at times (especially when learning skills such as Demolitions, Biotech or Vectored Thrust Piloting, to name a few). In addition to these common-sense examples, the gamemaster may otherwise restrict the choice of skills that a character can learn on his own.

To determine the final training time required to learn the new skill, divide the base training time by the number of successes from the test. If the test yields no successes, multiply the base training time by 1.5 to calculate the final training time. At the end of the training period, the character possesses the new skill. (Characters who interrupt their training may incur extra training time, as noted in *Skill Training Time,* above).

Characters always learn new skills at Skill Rating 1.

Training with An Instructor

Instructors can aid characters in two ways. First, they may enable characters to learn new skills they cannot learn on their own. Second, they can help reduce the training time required to improve an existing skill or learn a new one.

Any qualified character can serve as an instructor. The student character can try to convince a friend to teach him or her a skill, enlist the aid of a contact, or seek out a professional instructor. Friends and contacts may accept favors in return for instruction, but professional instructors usually demand nuyen for their services (see *Instructor Fees,* p. 50).

An instructor must possess two basic qualifications. First, the instructor must know the skill the student wishes to learn at a rating of 3 or higher. If the student wants to improve a skill, the instructor must have a skill rating that equals or exceeds the rating the student wishes to achieve. Second, the instructor should possess the Instruction Skill (see pages 87 and 95, *SR3*). An individual without the Instruction Skill can attempt to teach a skill, but the person must default to Charisma to do so.

Teaching

When teaching a new skill or helping a character improve an existing skill rating, an instructor makes an Instruction (4) Test. If the instructor does not possess the Instruction Skill, he or she makes a Charisma (8) Test (as if defaulting from Instruction). For every 2 successes the test generates, add 1 to the student's Skill Test success total, for purposes of reducing the student's required training time.

If the Instruction Test or Skill Test generates no successes, the instructor simply cannot teach the student. To simulate this failure in the game universe, the student must compensate the instructor for his or her

SKILL IMPROVEMENT TABLE

Skill Type	Base Training Time Required to Improve Skill (in days*)
Active Skills	Required Karma Points spent x 7
Knowledge or Language Skills	Required Karma Points spent x 15

*See *Training Days,* page 50, for an explanation of training days.

efforts by forfeiting one day's worth of pay to the instructor, and must also add 1.5 days to his training time for the skill—this represents the character's disappointment at failing with one instructor and the need to shift gears to find another teacher, not to mention the nuyen spent on the first instructor. The gamemaster can use any number of reasons to explain the failure in roleplaying terms—the instructor and student may have philosophical differences, the instructor's methods may clash with the material, or the two characters may distrust one another or simply be incompatible.

Characters who are learning a new skill with the aid of an instructor also receive a –1 target modifier on their Skill Tests for learning new skills.

An instructor must train with the student for the student's entire training time. If the instructor leaves before the student has completed the training, double the remaining training time. This increase represents the greater difficulty of learning on one's own.

Instructor Fees

Instructor fees present a convenient way for gamemasters to curb characters that may threaten game balance by accumulating massive skill sets. The Suggested Instructor Fees Table provides suggested daily instructor fees, but gamemasters should modify fees as they see fit. After all, better instructors will command higher fees than mediocre instructors, and instruction in rare or highly prized skills will cost more than instruction in common skills.

Scarecrow wants to improve his Edged Weapons Skill Rating from 3 to 4. Edged Weapons is an Active Skill (linked to his Strength 5), so the increase costs 6 Karma Points. That means the base training time is 42 days (6 x 7 = 42). Scarecrow makes an Edged Weapons (6) Test to reduce the time and achieves 2 successes. That brings the training time down to 21 days (42 ÷ 2).

However, Scarecrow has arranged for Oak, a fellow runner, to teach him swordplay. (Oak has Edged Weapons 6, so he's qualified to teach Scarecrow at Edged Weapons 4.) Oak achieves 2 successes on his Instruction Test, so Scarecrow adds an extra success to his Edged Weapons Test result. That brings the training time down to 14 days (42 ÷ 3).

Scarecrow is pretty happy—and so is Oak as he calculates his fee. (Oak's not that good of a friend. And besides, the streets are the streets—if you have something of value, you need to cash in on it.) Professional instructors with Instruction 4 usually charge about 100 nuyen per day, so Oak figures his services are worth 1,400 nuyen. (Teaching Edged Weapons 4 doesn't take any advanced knowledge or special expertise.)

Oak knows Scarecrow doesn't have that kind of cred, so he makes Scarecrow a deal. In lieu of the fee, Scarecrow agrees to introduce Oak to

Scarecrow's contact, the one with all the cool advanced weaponry. Oak figures a contact like that is worth a thousand or so nuyen—plus, Scarecrow has agreed to buy him dinner every day this month.

Virtual Instructors

If a character cannot find a live instructor or does not want to use one, he or she can purchase a "virtual instructor" (p. 95, SR3). Virtual instructors may take the form of simsense chips, optical computer disks or trideo tapes.

As with living instructors, every virtual-instructor program has an effective skill rating in the skill it teaches and an Instruction Skill rating. The program cannot make an Instruction Test to reduce the student's base training time, but all other standard instructor rules apply. Perhaps the most important advantage a virtual instructor offers is that a character can purchase a chip with a very high skill rating and then use that same program when training for multiple advanced ratings in a single skill.

TRAINING DAYS

A standard training-time "day" is 4 hours. Thus, a training time of 30 days equals 120 hours of study.

A character who is particularly eager to learn or improve a skill can train for more than 4 hours a day, though no metahuman can train 24 hours a day. A character's daily training limit equals half of his or her Willpower (rounded up) + 4.

Characters can train beyond their daily training limit, but such training may prove ineffective. A character who wants to train in this manner must declare how many hours beyond his limit he intends to train. To determine how many of these hours will pay off, the character makes a Willpower (10) Test. The result is the number of extra hours of effective practice the

SUGGESTED INSTRUCTOR FEES TABLE

Instruction Skill Rating	Daily Fee (in nuyen)
1	40
2	50
3	75
4	100
5	200
6	400
7+	+100 per skill level over 6

Fee Modifiers

Skill at Rating 2 or 3	–25¥ per day
Skill at Rating 4 or 5	No modifier
Skill at Rating 6 or 7	+25¥ per day
Skill at Rating 8 or higher	+50¥ per day
Specialization	+50% of total fee
Instruction provided in a classroom setting	–50% of total fee
More than 4 hours of instruction per day	+50% of daily fee

character can put in beyond his or her daily training limit. No matter what the test result, the character may not exceed his declared extra practice time.

To determine the number of days the character will need to complete his training at the new pace, simply divide the total number of hours in the training time by the character's total daily training period.

Remember Scarecrow? He needed 14 days to improve his Edged Weapons Skill (that comes out to 56 hours). Scarecrow is impatient, however, and he has lots of time on his hands. Consequently, he decides to spend 10 hours a day training. He has Willpower 6, so his maximum daily training limit is 7 hours ([6 ÷ 2] + 4).

To determine how many of the extra 3 hours will be effective, Scarecrow makes a Willpower (10) Test. The test yields 1 success. That means each day's training session will yield 8 hours of effective training (even though Scarecrow slogs away for 10 hours).

However, the extended daily training sessions reduce Scarecrow's training time to 7 days (56 ÷ 8).

IMPROVING ATTRIBUTES

If desired, gamemasters may allow player characters to improve their Attributes in the same manner they improve skills. (For roleplaying purposes, the player character will need to devise some way to "work out" using the Attribute. For example, a character might lift weights for several hours each day to improve his or her Strength. In all cases, the gamemaster determines if a proposed training regimen is appropriate.)

The base training time to improve an Attribute is the same as the base training time for an Active Skill (7 days times the number of Karma Points required for the improvement). See p. 244, SR3, for Karma costs of Attribute increases. To reduce the training time, a player character can make an Attribute (6) Test, using the Attribute he or she is improving.

Generally, player characters can raise their Attributes without the help of instructors. However, gamemasters may require that characters use an instructor if they want to raise an Attribute beyond its Racial Modified Limit. Gamemasters may also require that characters use instructors when increasing their Willpower, Intelligence or Charisma Ratings.

Instructor rules and fees for Attribute training are generally the same as for skill training. However, the instructor skill qualifications do not apply. Instead, the instructor must possess an Instruction Skill Rating that exceeds the Attribute Rating the student wants to achieve. (The instructor's ability to motivate the student is much more important than his own skill during Attribute training.)

Golden Eyes wants to raise her Charisma Rating from 6 to 7. The increase costs 21 Karma Points, which gives her a base training time of 147 days (7 × 21= 147). Golden Eyes is human, so her Racial Modified Limit for Charisma is Rating 6. Because she's going above the limit, the gamemaster insists that she train with an instructor.

After a little asking around, Golden Eyes finds Mizz Manners, a troll who "can take a ghoul and make it Miss Universe." Mizz Manners puts Golden Eyes on a regimen of hard-core socializing. Golden Eyes spends her nights hopping between the hippest gallery openings, the trendiest clubs and the most exclusive parties. During her days, Golden Eye rigorously trains to polish her manners, speech and dress, and reads up on sophisticated conversational topics.

To reduce the length of her training period, Golden Eyes makes a Charisma (6) Test. The test yields 2 successes. Meanwhile, Mizz Manners achieves 2 successes on her Instruction (4) Test. She can contribute 1 success to Golden Eye's Attribute Test success total—which brings it up to 3. That means Golden Eyes' training time drops to 49 days (147 ÷ 3).

HOW TO HIRE A SHADOWRUNNER

For those of you who might think this posting is old hat just because Fuchi fell into the shark pool during the Corp War—think again. Fuchi may no longer be with us, but you can be sure that Mr. Ager and the other "Resource Adjusters" in their employ have merely moved on to greener pastures; namely Shiawase, Renraku and Novatech. And rumor has it that Ager, himself, is now working the Seattle shadows for Novatech. So while most Johnsons may not follow this material to the letter, you can bet your hoop that Johnsons in at least three mega-corps view these guidelines as Standard Operating Procedure.

◉ Captain Chaos
   Transmitted: 7 December 2061 at 06:11:27 (EST)

◉ Just about everyone on this board thinks he or she knows everything there is to know about shadowrunning. You take a job from Mr. Johnson, do your homework, go on the run and get paid when you're finished (assuming you live). You blow your hard-earned nuyen on some nifty toys that extend your lifespan while shortening your opposition's, and as you're buying them through your fixer, you let her know you're available again. She puts out feelers and sets up a meet when she finds something promising. Repeat cycle until further notice.

It's true that shadowrunning tends to follow this pattern. So it's important to recognize the biggest link in this circular chain—the Johnson. Without those shady characters to give runners an income and something to do at 02:38 on a Wednesday night, the cycle stops. Joe Runner, desperate and credless, knocks over a Stuffer Shack for groceries and "rent" money to pay the local gangers. At 02:40 Joe Runner gets capped by the overly nervous clerk with the Mossberg behind the counter, or by a random customer with Shiawase's May 2055 batch of wired flexes who never paid attention to the recall. Joe-boy ends up cremated and dumped into a near-by lake, to become an integral part of the hard rain that eats away layers of paint on our cars and homes.

Okay, maybe I'm going a bit overboard—but clearly, without Mr. Johnsons there is no shadowrunning biz. Like it or not, we depend on these people for our livelihoods. So, as the latest in a long line of public services (for which I rarely get the thanks I deserve), I offer this post—

snagged by my ever-helpful friend JJ—as an example of the kind of drek to expect from the average Johnson.

This e-pamphlet crawled out of the brain of William Ager, veep hopeful to Kenneth Brackhaven (may they both burn in Hell). Before his fifteen seconds of fame, Mr. Ager worked for Fuchi America's New York office as Head Resources Adjuster (read: "professional Johnson"). My personal experience has given me every reason to see this inspiring piece of work as typical of Johnsons in general, even though the details may differ from Johnson to Johnson or corp to corp—so everybody read to the end of the paragraph, 'kay? Stuff like this could save your hoop, or at least get you an extra five percent in advance. And if you ever deal with Mr. Ager, you'll know exactly what to expect.

⊙ Captain Chaos
   Transmitted: 18 September 2057 at 20:33:13 (EST)

⊙ Headzup, folks— I'm only going to post this once. Within three hours of putting this thing online, it had garnered nearly 800 comments. The file expanded to 14,000% of its original size because so many people had so much to add. That made for a fragging BIG post, and we just can't spare the room right now. So I did some judicious editing. All the comments that appeared within the first thirty minutes of posting I've left untouched, as word hadn't spread to every fragging bithead in the world until after an hour or so went by. The rest, I moved to a new SIG under Ager E-Pamphlet: Open Forum. If you want to say anything, say it there. But don't try to edit this file, unless you're dying to experience some bleeding-edge IC that our SS friends like to call "Cascade Ork." You've been warned.

⊙ Captain Chaos
   Transmitted: 19 September 2057 at 02:50:21 (EST)

FUCHI INDUSTRIAL ELECTRONICS E-MAIL SYSTEM v6.011
FUCHI AMERICA BRANCH … "We Love America!"
TO: <<NULL FIELD>>   FROM: William T. Ager
OF: <<NULL FIELD>>   OF: Resource Adjustment Division
SUBJECT: Resources Adjustment Division information
DATE: <<NULL FIELD>>
THOUGHT FOR THE DAY: "Gyo kan o yomu"—*Read between the lines*

Congratulations on your recent achievements for Fuchi America! Because you have exhibited exceptional loyalty to Fuchi America and Fuchi Industrial Electronics, >>RETRIEVE_subject-advance-type: <<|PROMOTION | SEC_LEVEL_RAISE | REFERRAL|? **REFERRAL**>> you are now qualified to use the Resources Adjustment Department, courtesy of >>RETRIEVE_subject-referral-REFERRED-BY: <<NULL FIELD>> : <<**INSERTING DEFAULT**>> your superiors. This e-pamphlet describes the workings of the Resources Adjustment Department (RAD) and will answer any questions you may have about this important department.

IMPORTANT! The RAD falls under Security Level OME49-AA, Subheading 3G. If you divulge the RAD's existence to anyone not cleared for Security Level OME49 or greater,

>>RETRIEVE_subject-standing:<<|AVERAGE | EXCELLENT | SUPERIOR|? **AVERAGE**>> you will be summarily executed, your SIN purged from all company records, and your family deported from and permanently barred entry to all property or properties owned by Fuchi Industrial Electronics and/or any subsidiaries of Fuchi Industrial Electronics.

As part of our mandate to help our clients as far as our budget and department charter permit, we have included a list of "Frequently Asked Questions" about the Resources Adjustment Department. To refer to these questions in the future, and for a detailed description of the RAD's inner workings, connect to: NA/UCAS-NE.fuchi.com/pub/faq/restricted/RAD.doc. Supply your password for access.

⊙ Incidentally, the programmer left a backdoor. Only the drek-hot need apply, but if you can pick your way through the subsystems, you'll find a unidirectional dataline that appears at 01:40:34 for exactly three seconds on the ninth and twenty-fourth of each month. If you dive through it, the line'll dump you into a Green-4 datastore with four more unidirectionals leading into it. The datastore connects to nothing. The data is protected by Tar Baby-8, but the IC will let you pass if you give the password, "Nadja Daviar has luscious gams." Other than the Probe-3 in the node, it should be smooth decking.
⊙ Webster Was A Patsy

⊙ "Luscious gams"? Those corp programmers don't get out much.
⊙ Marabellum@pip.cc.brandeis.edu

⊙ And us non-corp deckers do?>>DISPLAY_big-cheesy-grin
⊙ DarkElf@NA/CAS-SB.watt.seas.virginia.edu

WHY SHOULD I USE THE RAD?
The Resources Adjustment Department exists to provide outside personnel who can perform various specialized services for our clients. Supplemental resources—"shadowrunners," to use the vulgar term—are available through the RAD to accomplish tasks that Fuchi America's official assets cannot perform because of questionable legality, lack of departmental funds, insufficient border clearance to enter other sovereign nations or corporate nation-states, and other such inconveniences. Our goal is to provide you with non-Fuchi personnel who can assist you as needed to help you maximize Fuchi America's profits with a minimum of exposure or personal danger to yourself and other Fuchi employees.

⊙ Minimum risk for Fuchi's pet people, maximum risk for us. How d'ya like them soycakes?
⊙ Koss@NA/UCAS-MW.heartland.org

⊙ What—you got into this business not knowing that maiming or death are the most likely ends to your career? What chip are you slotting, and where can I avoid it?
⊙ Chelle@NA/UCAS-NE.rime.swith.hell.com

WHOM DO I HIRE?

Whenever you need outside help, the RAD makes hiring easy for you! We search our databases for unofficial assets whose track records most closely match your stated needs. The RAD then contacts these assets through intermediaries and informs them of your job offer. Finally, RAD staffers arrange a suitable meeting time and place. Then the RAD steps out of the picture unless directed otherwise. If you feel that attending the meeting in person constitutes an unacceptable risk to your or your department's security, a RAD representative will attend the meeting in your stead.

○ This means that if the actual Johnson is afraid to meet because he thinks somebody'll geek him, they'll send one of their "officially unofficial" slots in lieu of the paranoid J. Or the Johnson thinks he can't show his face because someone is tracking his movements, so he uses the anonymous stooge to do his dirty work while he camps out in his fancy doss. Or the Johnson can't make the meet because he's indulging in a little "late-night account balancing" with his secretary or the tea lady, but he needs the deal to go down RIGHT FRAGGING NOW. Whatever the reason, keep in mind that any J. hiring you may be one of these RAD people. If so, then for fragging sure everything isn't as it seems.

Come to think of it, that's how it works most times (in my experience).
○ Kotick

○ I did some digging to check if this e-pamph was legit, and even in the blackest of Fuchi's black heart there's NO MENTION of the RAD. Maybe Cap's friend JJ is just yankin' his crank or something.
○ Todd@NA/UCAS-NE.rime.swith.god.com

○ Sorry to disappoint you, Todd, but it's a straight-arrow doc. The security clearance on this file is OME49-AA. The prefix OME stands for "Omega," which is the highest-rated security level Fuchi uses (that we know of). Anything with Omega clearance is kept on-site in a closed system. It cannot be transferred to a system that doesn't have Omega status. If anyone attempts to do so, the internal code destroys the file and tries to take down the non-Omega system (your cyberdeck). Omega systems have special circuitry hardwired into all optical chips, datalines, etc. that integrate with all files. So attempting to copy the RAD.doc file to a local system will only result in much fuss and lost nuyen. Don't bother trying.
○ Webster Was A Patsy

○ How much would it cost to outfit my deck with this "Omega" circuitry? If things work out, I may be going on-site in the next month or so.
○ McLeod@NA/UCAS-MW.tmo.com

○ More than you could afford. I ended up "borrowing" a Fuchi-7 from a very surprised secretary after the Omega circuitry slagged my deck. I didn't realize until after the run why the wageslave's out-of-date, off-the-shelf, poor-excuse-for-a-real-cyberdeck could snag the files I wanted when my half-million-in-accessories, home-cooked, state-of-the-fragging-art deck-from-hell literally fried in my hands. At least the nuyen we pulled will more than make up for a replacement.
○ JJ Flash

○ If Omega stuff can only be transferred to other Omega stuff, how'd you get this file onto the board without it crashing Shadowland?
○ Rathceet

○ Simple. I ran the e-pamphlet once on the Fuchi-7 and then typed up the output into a document on my handy Backup System (an ancient machine that's slower than the average tortoise). If you notice, none of Fuchi's usual bells and whistles (and I mean that literally) are turning up in this post; no "FuchiFuchiFuchi for your Computer Needs!" jingle, not even a Full Multimedia Demo of the newest spreadsheet application. I put in some of the graphics because it looked so darn bare without them, but aside from that, it's just a glorified text file.
○ JJ Flash

All non-Fuchi "supplemental resources" employed by the Resources Adjustment Department are designated one of the following: long-term, short-term and expendable.

○ I always knew we were cannon fodder to these slags ... but to see it in cold text like that ... (shudder).
○ Bung

○ Yeah, and I bet you cried when you found out there ain't no Santa Claus neither.
○ Jingo

○ There's NO SANTA CLAUS??!!! Oh, now I'm really depressed.
○ Bung

LONG-TERM SRs have proved their ability to work well for Fuchi America in past assignments or excel in three or more "focus categories" that the RAD looks for in prospective supplemental-resource employees. They are generally dependable, reasonably loyal to Fuchi as a source of steady income, and tend to approach contract negotiations amiably. A long-term supplemental resource may only be used with the approval of this department's Head Resources Adjuster. As a matter of policy, Fuchi personnel who have recently gained access to the Resources Adjustment Department are restricted to working with short-term or expendable supplemental resources until the Head Resources Adjuster deems the client experienced enough in working with SRs to have developed the proper attitude toward them. On occasion, long-term SRs may be assigned indefinitely to a single client.

○ We have our word for these wastes of air—"sell-outs."
○ Yegah@nowhere.com

SHORT-TERM SRs, the most numerous category, have shown a certain indifference to Fuchi America's interests in past assignments (short of an outright breach of contract) or are new to working for Fuchi America. In either case, they are considered possible security breaches and must be watched closely for any sign of disloyalty. A short-term SR who demonstrates willingness to work at a high professional standard for Fuchi America will be evaluated by RAD staffers and may be raised to long-term status. As long-term assignments pay considerably more than short-term assignments, many new short-termers are strongly motivated to perform well on the job.

● Where do I sign up?
● BCP@NA/UCAS-NE.datastorm.com

● Mail Ager at "AgerW@NA/UCAS-NE.fuchi.com" and ask him for a job.
● Sidekick

● Hey, Sidekick, there's something dripping off of your chin … you might want to clean it up. Oh wait, that's just sarcasm.>>DISPLAY_wink-grin
● Yegah@nowhere.com

EXPENDABLE SRs have failed to further Fuchi's goals or have breached their contracts. They are reserved for "black-flagged" assignments, in which Fuchi America's interests are served by the termination of the SRs. Only the Head Resources Adjuster may earmark an SR as expendable.

● Bet your hoop Ager slides metahumans more often than humans into this category.
● Ma Ork from Peoria

● And that he "earmarks" elves most of all.
● Makkanagee

WHAT SHOULD I EXPECT?

Regarding the initial meeting with your designated SRs, the RAD strongly recommends following certain procedures. Most clients will deal with short-term SRs, who are not known for treating potential employers with respect. To compensate for this treatment, the RAD offers the following guidelines for business success:

TREAT THE SRS AS HOSTILE. Even if they appear wholesome (a statistically improbable occurrence), assume that they are willing to kill you for any trivial reason should the opportunity present itself. These people are hardened criminals who commit heinous crimes for nuyen. They are mercenaries, living merely for the next payment, and they will try to squeeze you for all they can get. Remember that every nuyen you pay them is one less nuyen for Fuchi America. They are tools, no more; your job is to get as much work out of them as possible while compensating them as little as possible.

No matter how well they may present themselves, these are not honorable, decent people. As criminals, they have no claim to fair treatment or respect. Treat them like the beasts they are; toss them their dinner from a safe distance and make sure that Fuchi America does not get bitten. If you think of them as being "just like us" even for a moment, you have already failed.

● The Ager paranoia surfaces again. Nice to see some things never change!
● Makkanagee

● Of course, we won't say a word about the honor or decency of the fine folks who hire us "hardened criminals" to "commit heinous crimes for nuyen."
● Miz Liz

● Scareda gettin' their nice clean hands all dirty, thass what.
● Lark

◗ Come on. They're not all this dreadful. I've worked with a Johnson or two who was pretty much on the level, and who didn't look at me like she smelled something bad. This Ager slot is just feeding into a stereotype.
◗ La Marquise

◗ Every stereotype has a grain of truth in it, Marq—that's why they endure. I agree, Ager's a little over-the-top, but the same general attitude is more common than not among Johnsons in my experience. Get as much as you can for as little as you can, and remember the street grunts are expendable. Ager's just being a little more blatantly venomous about it. Given his history, I'm not surprised.
◗ Miz Liz

◗ As to getting a lot for a little, are most of us any different?
◗ StreetWyze

CONCEAL YOUR IDENTITY. If the SRs recognize you or your affiliation, they may attempt to blackmail you at a later date. Such a development would be harmful to you and to Fuchi America. Departmental research indicates that SRs are prone to make snap judgments about clients based on observations they make at the initial meeting. The RAD therefore supplies "plainclothes" for these meetings—generic suits of a conservative cut that cannot be easily identified as contemporary corporate fashion.

If the situation calls for a greater degree of misdirection, RAD staffers can suggest various ensembles and accoutrements that incorporate the hallmarks of other corporations or organizations. Cosmetic changes can also be made at a client's request, including wigs, contact lenses, melanin pills to change skin tone, and so on. Using these, a client may conceal his own identity or temporarily adopt someone else's.

◗ "Hey, Mr. Johnson is really Richard Villiers!" " … And I would have gotten away with it, if it hadn't been for you pesky shadowrunners!"
◗ Reaches-for-the-Stars

◗ Do they got pointy-ear kits an' fake horns, too?
◗ Lark

BEGIN BY OFFERING NO MORE THAN 80 PERCENT OF THE PAYMENT. These people invariably attempt to negotiate higher fees, sometimes even presuming to double your opening bid. If you offer 80 percent or less of the approved payment to begin with, you can "bargain" with them up to the total sum authorized, leaving them convinced that they have "won" without cutting any deeper into Fuchi America's profits than your superiors have deemed acceptable. Beginning your bid below the 80-percent threshold may even allow you to pay the SRs less than the maximum authorized amount. Fuchi America appreciates such efforts to save the corporation nuyen, and is likely to reward the conscientious employee accordingly.

On those occasions when it is not possible to hold the SRs to the approved payment, a certain "overhead" is authorized—

generally 20-25 percent of the approved payment. When bargained down within this overhead, the SRs will believe they are receiving 150 percent of the initial offer, which should be sufficient to satisfy even the greediest of these criminals. DO NOT UNDER ANY CIRCUMSTANCES EXCEED THIS 25 PERCENT OVERHEAD. There are always more SRs than there are assignments available, and Fuchi America's profits must always be the prime consideration. If the asking price of any given group of SRs exceeds the overhead, walk away from the meeting. Notify the RAD, and our staffers will contact another group of SRs ASAP.

◗ Does everybody understand that? If you get greedy, you'll get drek!
◗ Death Angel

HOW CAN I GUARANTEE SUCCESS?

Strictly speaking, you cannot guarantee success. You can, however, maximize the opportunity for success to occur by following the guidelines we've put together and keeping a few facts in mind. First of all, no SR can be fully trusted. Even long-term SRs with excellent track records are not Fuchi employees, and should not be afforded the trust given to members of the Fuchi Community™.

◗ Oh man, I think I'm gonna Yarf™!
◗ Bung

◗ Me too. "Maximize the opportunity for success to occur" <<THROWUP-NOISE WAVE>>
◗ WyrdNyrd

Statistically, 98 percent of all short-term SRs have satisfactorily completed their assignments for our clients. The RAD has achieved this excellent success rate with our Keep An Eye Out surveillance program, founded in 2037 to prevent breaches of contract. (This program should not be confused with the Put An Eye Out campaign, established in 2054 to combat unauthorized trid broadcasts from Fuchi facilities by non-Fuchi employees.) The KAEO program uses sophisticated surveillance gear and techniques to keep track of SR teams, including (but not limited to) the following:

Credsticks with Active On Demand™ locator bugs. When the credstick logs a transaction, the signal activates a trace program that heads for the nearest Fuchi domain. The trace program lets KAEO personnel instantly ascertain the whereabouts of any SR using an AOD credstick.

High-altitude surveillance drones. Most frequently used in conjunction with AOD credsticks, the drones acquire their targets at the initial meeting. The credsticks serve as target beacons for the drones, allowing them to patch into the Global Positioning System and track the movements of the SRs within 1.25 meters.

Watcher spirits. These spirits report any and all unusual activity of an SR directly to RAD mages. If weather permits (and the situation calls for it), RAD mages may also dispatch storm spirits to remind recalcitrant SRs where their interests lie.

◦ Bill Ager—Master of the Euphemism.
◦ WyrdNyrd

Tissue samples for use as material links. Tissue samples are more useful as a psychological than a physical threat; Fuchi America does not have the time, manpower, or inclination to employ full-fledged ritual sorcery to track down every SR who breaks a contract. Extreme cases, however, warrant extreme responses, and Fuchi America will not hesitate to mete out the appropriate punishment when necessary. For most SRs, the simple threat of such punishment suffices to keep them in line.

Observation of the companions and relatives of SRs. If necessary, the RAD will use strong-arm tactics upon these close associates to ensure adequate job performance on the part of the SRs. As a matter of policy, Fuchi prefers not to resort to such measures unless absolutely necessary, as they frequently elicit a counterproductive level of resentment in those SRs subjected to them. In most such cases, the RAD must make arrangements for the SRs' termination at the end of the assignment.

◦ Pre-emptive geeking. About what I'd expect from a megacorp.
◦ Cynik

◦ Yikes. Bugs in the credsticks? GPS tracking? Material fragging LINKS?!? I shoulda stayed in prison.
◦ John Spade

◦ Scary, neh? It gets worse. Think for a moment ... these are the tactics employed by Fuchi. As megacorps go, Fuchi's a bit tamer than Aztechnology or Saeder-Krupp. Kinda makes you wonder how far the others will go to keep us on our best behavior ...
◦ Tomtom

◦ Thanks, Tom. I'm already anticipating the years in therapy it'll take to make the nightmares stop.
◦ Soylent Grin

Once again, congratulations on achieving access to the RAD. Please>>RETRIEVE_subject-standing: <<**DEFAULT**>> do not contact us unless absolutely necessary.

Sincerely,

William T. Ager

William T. Ager

◦ I'd like to emphasize something Tomtom touched on. This screed is a Fuchi America document, shown only to Fuchi employees with Omega-level security clearance. Johnsons from other companies may follow similar precepts, but the spe-

cific procedures described above may only be valid when you're dealing with Omega-level Fuchi employees. In other words, just about anything else may go.
◦ Argent

◦ Assuming you can tell at the meet that they are Omega-level Fuchi employees. The first rule of dealing with Johnsons is, you never know who's really on the other side of the table.
◦ Valmont

◦ And even a Fuchi skag might not be hiring you for Fuchi's best interests. Some of these corpboys are so twisted, they meet themselves coming around corners. So even all the drek about how their RAD works may not apply.
◦ JackPalanceSh@bigger.than.you

◦ How do you figure?
◦ Rathceet

◦ I'll type slowly so you can understand. Fuchi Exec A and Fuchi Exec B are both up for promotion. Fuchi Exec A has slightly better standing, so he looks like the winner. So Fuchi Exec B hires Shadowrunning Team C to break into Fuchi Exec A's doss and "steal" compromising balance sheets that "prove" Fuchi Exec A has been skimming from the company. Fuchi Exec B makes the tradeoff with Team C on the property of a Fuchi subsidiary, and as they're leaving he informs Fuchi Corp Strike Team D that site security's been breached. Fuchi Corp Strike Team D blows the drek out of Shadowrunning Team C, leaving crispy chunks with which to feed Security Paranimal E. Endgame: Fuchi Exec B is a hero for exposing Exec A's perfidy, and for preventing a serious on-site security breach. Exec A gets canned, most likely followed by a bullet to the back of the head. The runners who could crack the whole thing open if they put two and two together are safely fried. Exec B gets his promotion and sits pretty, even though he's cost Fuchi a valuable fellow employee. To make sure his little scheme comes off, of course, he's most likely going to subtly frag up the RAD's SOP whenever it threatens to get in his way. Scan me?
◦ JackPalanceSh@bigger.than.you

◦ Folks with access to the RAD who hire us on their own initiative will most likely end up in deep drek. Which means, so will we.
◦ Johnny Demonic

◦ How so?
◦ IHateC@s.named.striper

◦ Let's just say I'm now "Actively Unemployed" by Fuchi and leave it at that.
◦ Johnny Demonic

CONTACTS AND ENEMIES

Contacts and enemies are non-player characters (NPCs) that gamemasters can use to make *Shadowrun* games richer, more unpredictable and more exciting for players.

The following section offers new contacts rules that gamemasters and players can use to expand the use of contacts in their games, as well as rules for creating and using enemies—NPCs that hold grudges, personal and otherwise, against player characters.

MAXIMIZING CONTACTS

Contacts are often the best, and occasionally the only way a runner can find out just what kind of drek he's gotten into. Furthermore, gamemasters can use contacts to make the *Shadowrun* world a fuller, more colorful place to play. Despite those advantages, many *Shadowrun* groups don't exploit the full potential of contacts. Too many gamemasters don't take the time to flesh out their players' contacts, and too many players never even consider exploring the roleplaying opportunities contacts provide. Character interactions with contacts remain nothing more than Etiquette Tests and the expenditure of a few nuyen.

The best way to do this is to whip out a quick background for the contact, with one or two hooks that will make the character memorable. Start with a brief descriptive catch phrase for the contact, then give him a few Edges or Flaws from the *Character Creation* section (p. 15) and a distinguishing personal look or style that will make the contact a distinct personality. For example, a player decides he wants a talismonger contact. The gamememaster decides he'll make the contact a Welsh dwarf who is a practitioner of Celtic druid beliefs. As a follower of Moon, he stays on the rural edges of the city, but trips to visit him are usually worth it because he's also a collector of secrets, rumors, and arcane lore. To make the contact distinctive, he makes him an albino who prefers to meet only at night under the moon's gaze, illuminating his ghostly pallor. Additionally, he has the Animal Empathy Edge, so that he's usually accompanied by small forest critters, particularly owls. This information gives the gamemaster enough background to roleplay the contact convincingly, and makes him enough of a character that the players will remember him.

CONTACT UPKEEP

Contacts are people too, and characters must treat them as such. Contacts are not simply handy sources of information that can be ignored until the character needs to learn the identity of the new sales VP at the Big Pyramid or the latest scuttlebutt at the local Lone Star station. If a character treats her contact as nothing more than a convenient reference to be consulted like a book, that contact will eventually become disillusioned and uncooperative.

Keeping a contact happy is known as "contact upkeep." Contact upkeep is a two-part process. The first part consists of roleplaying. The gamemaster decides what constitutes adequate contact upkeep in terms of a player's portrayal of his or her character's rapport with, concern for and relationship to a contact. Generally, characters simply need to treat their contacts with the respect they deserve in order to maintain them. Characters need not shower their contacts with gifts or visit them every day of the week. But they should treat the contact to a soykaf every once in a while or slide him a loan when he needs one.

Part two consists of spending the required annual upkeep cost to maintain the contact. Characters can pay a contact's required upkeep cost, as listed on the Contact Upkeep Table, over the course of a game year. Characters can use upkeep nuyen to buy their contacts drinks or dinner, do the occasional favor, or simply give the contact an occasional credstick. Basically, anything that's worth hard nuyen can be considered part of the upkeep payment for a contact. For example, the value of letting your buddy know that he should sell his Ares stock because you expect it to take a major dive now that the corp's hot new drone prototype happens to be sitting in your bedroom closet may be equal to an entire year's upkeep cost. Gamemasters determine the value of such favors, advice, services and so on.

A contact's level drops if a character fails to spend the required upkeep nuyen on him, or if the gamemaster determines that the character has failed to adequately maintain the contact with roleplaying. Gamemasters should feel free to create additional, unique requirements for maintaining contacts in their campaigns.

If a Level 2 or Level 3 contact drops a level, a character can regain the contact's previous level by using the rules in *Improving Contact Levels*.

A gamemaster has at least three options when a character fails to maintain a Level 1 contact, and may use any one or all three options at his discretion. The character may simply never hear from the contact again; in that case, the character cannot use the contact or any of the contact's contacts for information (see *Friends of a Friend*, p. 62). The contact can become the character's enemy (see p. 68). The character may also earn himself the Bad Reputation Flaw (see p. 25).

If a character loses all his or her contacts by failing to fulfill upkeep requirements, the character receives the Flaws Hung Out to Dry and Bad Reputation (pp. 27, 25). Increase by 1 the Priority levels of all the character's enemies as well (see *Enemies*, p. 69).

CONTACT UPKEEP TABLE

Level 1 Contact:	500¥
Level 2 Contact:	3,000¥
Level 3 Contact:	7,000¥

Billy Boy, just your average mercenary looking to make a name for himself, starts the game with 2 contacts. Joe is the bartender down at Droogies, where Billy Boy likes to spend his extra nuyen. Timmons is a Lone Star beat cop, who's actually a Level 2 buddy. (Billy Boy once dated Timmons's sister. Billy Boy and Timmons got along real well, and remained friends even after Billy Boy and the sister broke up.)

Billy Boy spends plenty of time and nuyen at Droogies, and he tips well. Consequently, the gamemaster decides that Billy doesn't have to spend additional nuyen or go out of his way to maintain Joe as a Level 1 contact.

Timmons, however, is a Level 2 contact, so Billy has to make more of an effort to maintain him. Besides taking Timmons out on the town and buying his drinks on a semi-regular basis, Billy tips him off to small-time criminals like the "no-good ganger kids" who harass the elderly and occasionally rob the mom-and-pop diners where Billy Boy gets his cheap eats. When Billy's gamemaster decides these things may not be enough to maintain a Level 2 contact, Billy decides to fix up Timmons with a nice chica he knows down Tacoma way. The gamemaster thinks this is a creative idea and decides that as long as Timmons and the girl continue to see each other, Billy need only spend half the usual upkeep cost buying drinks for Timmons.

IMPROVING CONTACT LEVELS

Usually, characters may only increase a contact's level through roleplaying. For example, if a character "courts" a Level 1 contact, regularly buys them dinner, sees them often, starts off a friendly relationship and takes good care of the contact, then the gamemaster may decide that contact has graduated to a Level 2.

Alternatively, gamemasters may allow characters to improve the level of their contacts by spending Karma. When using this option, the character must spend a number of Karma Points equal to twice the new contact level. For example, a character using Karma to improve a Level 1 contact to a Level 2 contact would have to spend 4 Karma Points. Improving a contact to Level 3 would cost 6 Karma Points. Contacts cannot be improved more than 1 level in this manner.

Gamemasters must approve all contact level improvements, based on the fictional relationship between character and contact. A contact who only occasionally sees a character and who does not have a particularly friendly relationship with that character is not an appropriate choice for a Level 3 contact.

This process works in reverse as well. If a character has significantly ignored or treated a contact without respect for long enough, that contact will likely go down one level. Level 1 contacts that are not maintained will no longer be usable as contacts, and may even disappear or become an enemy. If a character loses all of her contacts by failing to maintain good relationships, she will receive a blotch on her street reputation and find few people who are willing to talk or deal with her. At the very least, she will be facing target number modifiers to any Interaction Tests she engages in.

FRIENDS OF A FRIEND

Because contacts have lives of their own, they have contacts of their own as well. These secondary contacts, one step removed from the characters, are known as Friends of a Friend (FOFs). Thus, Billy Boy from the preceding example not only has access to any help Joe and Timmons can give him, he also has access to the people that Joe and Timmons know. These people are Billy's FOFs.

FOFs provide more options to characters, more color and background to games, and more realism. For example, Joe the bartender wouldn't realistically have a stockpile of Ares' finest weapons organized next to the synth-alcohol on the shelf. However, he could very plausibly know a guy who has a warehouse full of such goodies.

Generally, every character contact starts the game with a Level 1, a Level 2 and a Level 3 contact. Fixers and Mr. Johnson contacts are exceptions to this rule—because of the line of work they pursue, these contacts know two other contacts at each level.

FRIEND OF A FRIEND MODIFERS TABLE

FOF Level	Target Number Modifier	Cost/Time Multiplier	Wrong Party Target Modifier
1	+6	3	–2
2	+4	2	–1
3	+2	(see text)	0
Each FOF after the first	+2	(see text)	–2
"Asking around"	—	—	–3

Gamemasters may adjust these numbers to fit their campaigns (see *Special Contacts*, p. 64), though giving non-fixer and non-Johnson primary contacts more than three secondary contacts might make it too easy for player characters to acquire both equipment and information. On the other hand, allowing primary contacts to know a greater variety of secondary contacts can provide a needed jump-start to a campaign that may have gotten bogged down or reached a dead end. Additionally, because FOFs come from "outside" the characters' sphere of knowledge, gamemasters can use FOFs to generate adventures outside the expected parameters of a campaign.

USING FOFS

To acquire information, equipment or other help from FOFs, characters must make the appropriate tests. Any bonus dice a character receives for making tests in interactions with his contact apply when the character interacts with the contact's FOFs as well. Test target modifiers appear in the Friend of a Friend Modifiers Table. These modifiers represent a FOF's willingness to help a character—a FOF who's a mere acquaintance of a character's contact won't be as ready to help a relative stranger as will a contact's good friend.

Like all contacts, FOFs expect a little nuyen in exchange for their help. To calculate the fee a FOF expects, first determine the basic contact fee (see p. 254, *SR3*), then multiply the basic fee by the appropriate cost/time multiplier from the Friend of a Friend Modifiers Table. Gamemasters may choose to increase the cost modifier if the character has to go through multiple FOFs to get what he wants. At the gamemaster's discretion, a Level 3 FOF may reduce or even waive his fee as a favor to the contact.

The cost/time multiplier is also used to calculate the time a character must wait for a FOF to deliver information or goods (see *Waiting for the Goods*, p. 63). The Wrong Party modifiers are used when making Wrong Party Tests (see *The Walls Have Ears*, p. 63).

Billy Boy's had a run of good luck lately and has some nuyen in his pocket, so he decides to pick up a less-than-legal Ares Alpha combat gun (Availability 8) with the optional grenade launcher. Billy starts out by making a standard Etiquette (8) Test for Joe the bartender. The test generates only 1 success, so Joe gives Billy an odd look and says he "might know someone." (The gamemaster has decided that Joe's three secondary contacts are a Mafia foot soldier (Level 1), a decker whom Joe's known for years (Level 2), and Joe's brother (Level 3), who's a bouncer at a swanky downtown club.)

Billy approaches Timmons, his Lone Star officer contact. Timmons is a Level 2 contact, so Billy gets an extra die for his Etiquette Test and generates 3 successes. Consequently, Timmons is more than willing to help Billy. He tells Billy he'd be happy to introduce him to any of his own secondary contacts—a Renraku security officer (Level 1), a former Lone Star employee who now operates his own private sec firm (Level 2), and a reformed fixer who happens to have been Timmons's first arrest (Level 3).

Billy decides that Joe's mob foot-soldier friend and Timmons's ex-fixer chum are his best bets.

Billy first approaches Joe, who tells him to come back after midnight and he'll introduce him to Tony the Snake. When Billy returns, Joe directs him to a private booth, where Tony's waiting. At this point, Billy Boy makes his Etiquette Test. The standard base target number receives a +6 modifier because Tony's a Level 1 contact. The test fails, and Tony says he can't help him. Tony says he deals only in olive oil, not guns.

Billy then turns to Timmons's ex-fixer friend, Sexy Sioux. Sioux is a Level 3 contact of Timmons, so Billy makes his Etiquette Test against a Target Number 10. (Billy adds 1 extra die for the test, because Timmons is a Level 2 contact.)

The test generates 2 successes, and Sioux says she knows someone who can help Billy get his new toy. Instead of a cash fee, though, Sioux wants a favor from Billy. She needs some runners to help with a hit on a Humanis Policlub training camp, and she wants Billy to help. Billy Boy accepts the offer—he figures it'll give him a chance to fieldtest his new gun.

If Billy rejects Sioux's offer, he must pay her a fee for her help, which the gamemaster calculates according to the following formula. Sioux's a fixer with Charisma 3 and Intelligence 5. Using the basic contact fee formula, the gamemaster calculates the basic fee at 375 nuyen:

(Contact's Charisma x Intelligence x 50) ÷ number of Etiquette Test successes = basic contact fee
(3 x 5 x 50) ÷ 2 = 375¥

Because Sioux is a Level 3 contact for Timmons, the gamemaster decides what she'll charge Billy Boy. As it turns out, she's willing to help out her friend's friend. Sioux can reasonably be expected to charge Billy Boy any amount from nothing ("Hey—I don't charge nuyen to help my buddy Timmons's friends.") to her usual fee of 375 nuyen ("I like your looks, so I'm giving you my services at cost today."). Billy will have to pay the cost of the gun, regardless of Sioux's fee. If appropriate, Billy can make a standard Negotiation Test to lower Sioux's fee.

WAITING FOR THE GOODS

To calculate the base time a FOF needs to locate information or equipment for a character, the gamemaster uses the item's Availability as normal (see p. 272, SR3) then applies the appropriate cost/time multiplier from the Friend of a Friend Multipliers Table to the result. If the FOF is searching for information or something that has no Availability, roll 2D6 to randomly determine the base waiting period in days, and multiply it by the FOF time multiplier as above.

Characters may reduce the waiting period by spending any number of their Etiquette Test successes or by paying the contact additional money. For each success or for each additional 10 percent of the contact's fee the character chooses to pay, the period is reduced by 1 day.

Note that this waiting period only reflects the time that a FOF needs to track down the requested information and/or goods. The gamemaster should also apply all standard Availability rules.

Billy Boy now knows his new Ares Alpha combat gun is on the way, and he wants to know how long he'll have to wait. The gun's standard Availability is 48 hours. Because Sioux's a Level 3 FOF, the gamemaster determines her cost/time multiplier. He decides to give Billy a double-or-nothing deal.

Sioux tells Billy Boy she can have the gun for him in a few hours if he agrees to hit the Humanis camp. If he refuses to help with the hit, Sioux says she'll need four days to locate and obtain the Ares Alpha.

Billy can't help with the Humanis hit, but he doesn't want to wait four days for his gun, either. He decides to slip Sioux some extra nuyen to speed things along. Ten percent of Sioux's 375-nuyen fee is 38 nuyen; Billy decides he can afford to pay some extra nuyen if it means getting his new toy faster, and so he pays Sioux an extra 152 nuyen (38¥ x 4) and cuts four days from the waiting period.

THE WALLS HAVE EARS

Any time a character discusses biz with a contact—whether a personal buddy or a go-ganger who agrees to meet the character at the docks in the middle of a rainstorm at 4 a.m.—other parties may hear about the character's interest in information, equipment or any other commodity potentially worth nuyen. These other people, appropriately designated "wrong parties," can be any individuals, groups or organizations that might feel threatened by the character's inquiries, have an interest in grabbing a piece of the character's action, or simply dislike the character enough to mess with his or her plans.

To reflect the chances of wrong parties learning of a character's inquiries, the gamemaster makes a Wrong Party Test every time a character uses a contact or FOF. The number of dice for the test equals the number of individuals involved in the inquiry. For example, if a character talks biz to one contact, the gamemaster uses 2D6 for the test. If the inquiry is made by an eight-man team speaking to a contact who must enlist the help of another contact, the gamemaster uses 10D6. (The more people involved in an inquiry, the greater the chance that someone, somewhere, will slip up.)

The base target number for the Wrong Party Test is 6, but gamemasters may increase it for especially careful or paranoid characters, or decrease it for particularly careless characters.

If a Wrong Party Test generates successes, the gamemaster determines the consequences, based on the suggestions provided in the Wrong Party Table and also based on the campaign, the nature of the character's inquiries and the nature of the wrong party. For example, Ares is accustomed to runners trying to steal its latest weapons prototypes, so it might not act until a line of inquiry generates 10 or more Wrong Party Test successes. On the other hand, even 2 or 3 successes might prompt a paranoid paramilitary policlub group to go code red. All successes are cumulative—add together the successes of all Wrong Party Tests made during a single line of inquiry.

When characters use FOFs, apply the appropriate Wrong Party modifier from the Friend of a Friend Modifiers Table (note that these are negative modifiers—they reduce the target number, making it more likely that word will leak out). The number of dice for the test equals the number of individuals involved in the inquiry—all characters, FOFs, and the contacts who introduced the characters and FOFs.

If a character asks a contact to "ask around" about a particular subject (see p. 254, SR3), add the appropriate modifier from the Friend of a Friend Modifiers Table.

If several successes are generated during first-stage inquiries, a gamemaster may decide that the wrong party begins a disinformation operation that sends the characters wrong or planted information via their contacts and FOFs.

The Ares Alpha combat gun is a new, highly illegal weapon. In fact, only Ares possesses the gun. Even the manufacturer's corporate and military clients are waiting for it.

Consequently, Billy Boy's attempts to obtain a combat gun are potentially a sensitive matter, so the gamemaster makes Wrong Party Tests to determine if Ares notices and takes action.

Billy's first level of inquiries consists of his meetings with Joe the bartender and Timmons the cop. For each of these meetings, the gamemaster uses 2D6 to make a Wrong Party (6) Test. The test for the meet with Joe generates no successes. The test for Timmons yields 1 success. Billy's not the first runner to try to acquire a secret Ares weapon, and he probably won't be the last. Consequently, Ares doesn't even note his inquiry.

Billy's second level of inquiries consists of his meetings with Tony the Snake and Sexy Sioux. For the meeting with Tony, the gamemaster rolls 3D6 (1 die for Billy, 1 for Tony and 1 for Joe the bartender). Tony is a Level 2 FOF, so the base Target Number 6 receives a –2 Wrong Party Modifier, as noted on the Friend of a Friend Modifiers Table.

For the meeting with Sioux, the gamemaster again uses 3D6 (1 die for Billy, 1 for Sioux and 1 for Timmons the cop). The test receives no wrong party modifier (Sioux is a Level 3 FOF), so the Target Number is 6.

The test for the meet with Tony generates 1 success; the test for the meet with Sioux also generates 1. That produces a total of 3 successes for both levels of inquiry. That's still a relatively low level of successes, and Ares is a big corporation, so the gamemaster decides that Ares still takes no notice of Billy Boy's inquiries.

SPECIAL CONTACTS

Special contacts provide characters with access to greater resources than standard contacts. Special contacts fall into four categories: members of clubs and organizations, fixers, international contacts and Shadowland.

MEMBERS OF CLUBS AND ORGANIZATIONS

By acquiring a contact who is a member of a club or organization such as the Humanis Policlub, Ork Rights Committee

WRONG PARTY TABLE

Successes	Potential Consequences
1–4	Word has hit the street that you or your team is on a job. Your enemies prick up their ears, hoping to hear something they can use against you. Other runners start watching you, looking for the chance to horn in on your action. Corporate flunkies at all levels talk to their contacts, trying to pinpoint your target.
5–8	Somebody used the wrong words to the wrong people, and now the street knows what you're up to. Your competition, your enemies and every potential target has a theory about your biz, but no one knows the particulars of the assignment. If you work fast, you can keep ahead of the game.
9–12	It was inevitable—only under the rarest circumstances can you plan, execute, and get paid for a job without some outside party somehow jeopardizing the run. Your competition is workin' the other side of the street; your enemies now know enough to figure out how to screw it up for you in the most dramatic way; your target is 99 percent confident that you're coming for them. Fortunately, you're professionals—you knew this would happen, and you've got a plan to cover all the bases.
13+	You're running a disinformation campaign of epic proportions, but it seems that the only detail that hasn't hit the streets is the color of underwear you'll be wearing when you pull the job. You know you're now up against the best your target, your enemies and your competition has to offer, and all you can do is trust that Plan B will get you in and out with a minimum of bloodshed. And you already know your next piece of biz—finding the loose lips that complicated your life this way and stapling them shut (assuming you survive the trap/death squad/Matrix warfare/private detective/general harassment campaign that someone is sure to throw at you).

or other metahuman-rights groups, a character can gain FOFs who may be able to provide inside information about the group's activities or members.

Nearly any contact can be a member of a club or organization. Clubs and organizations that espouse causes with broad appeal are especially likely to include a wide range of members. Wide appeal, however, also means that the chances of a contact knowing anyone in the group privy to the real secrets are slim.

To determine the number of group members a character must wade through to get inside information, the gamemaster rolls 2D6 and divides the result by 2 (rounding up). The final result equals the number of people the character must talk to before reaching a knowledgeable FOF. Consider each FOF to be a contact of the previous FOF, and apply all appropriate cost/time multipliers and wrong party modifiers from the Friend of a Friend Modifiers Table.

FIXERS

The fixer (see p. 257, *SR3*) is a combination pawn shop, Hollywood agent, politician, arms dealer, drug smuggler, underworld crime boss, con man, used-car salesman and, in rare cases, normal person, all rolled into one. The fixer knows a wide range of individuals of diverse talents, and he makes his money using these contacts to supply a client with whatever the client needs or wants—for a fee, of course. To reflect this, all fixers possess at least six secondary contacts, usually including another fixer and, occasionally, a Mr. Johnson.

While many fixers maintain their edge by serving as Jacks-of-all-trades, some fixers specialize in a particular field—such as supplying high-tech goods and services, magical goods and services, or corporate connections. A specialist fixer's secondary contacts should reflect his specialty. For example, a magical middleman might know a talismonger, a former wage mage, a magical research specialist at Aztechnology, a member of the Illuminates of the New Dawn, a street shaman and so on. (Gamemasters should determine the fields of specialized fixers based on their campaign needs.) A fence is a fixer who specializes in buying whatever a team has managed to scrounge after the run is over (see *Fencing the Loot*, p. 237, *SR3*).

Basically, fixers earn their livelihoods by "doing favors" for clients. Therefore, most prefer to maintain only "professional" relationships with their runner contacts rather than developing personal ones—it just makes matters far less complicated in the long run. And they almost never provide information or services for free. Typically, fixers demand payment in nuyen or a return favor down the road.

INTERNATIONAL CONTACTS

An employee of a multinational megacorporation, a member of a multinational organized-crime or political group, a soldier formerly stationed overseas—these are just a few examples of individuals who may serve as international contacts.

In addition to receiving information and/or assistance directly from an international contact, a character can solicit help from FOFs gained through that contact. To determine the number of people the character must talk to before reaching a knowledgeable and helpful FOF, the gamemaster rolls 2D6 and divides the result by 2 (rounding up). Consider each FOF to be a contact of the previous FOF, and apply all appropriate cost/time multipliers and wrong party modifiers from the Friend of a Friend Modifiers Table.

Any time contacts meet international FOFs, gamemasters can apply appropriate modifiers from the International Contacts Table to the FOF Etiquette Test.

As always, money opens more doors than anything else in *Shadowrun* (see *Using FOFs,* p. 62). For each additional 10 percent of the total fee the character pays, decrease the target numbers for tests with the contact or FOF by 1 (to a minimum of 2).

Players can also acquire foreign contacts by purchasing the Friends Abroad Edge (p. 27) during character creation.

SHADOWLAND

The organization/information service/clearing-house known as Shadowland may well be a shadowrunner's most useful "contact." In addition to providing a valuable bulletin-board service and a secure, reliable line into the Matrix, Shadowland is host to Hacker House (see *Virtual Realities 2.0*) and serves as a link to numerous "private chat rooms" and other specialty boards. Characters must remember, however, that nothing in Shadowland is private. Unlike metahuman contacts, who may agree to keep a secret and then actually keep their word, once a piece of information appears on Shadowland, it instantly becomes available for public access. A character can hide the plans for a revolutionary new laser technology in Shadowland, but anyone else who finds it can take it. Shadowland is strictly an "all or nothing" proposition.

Any character with Computer 1 or higher may select Shadowland as a contact during character creation. Shadowland is a Level 2 contact, and characters may not improve its contact level. The upkeep cost for Shadowland

INTERNATIONAL CONTACTS TABLE

Contact	Target Number Modifier
Contact is a member of international group	−2
Contact is out of favor with locals	+2
Character has enemies looking for him	+ Rating of each enemy
(penalty waived at the cost of alerting enemies)	
Contact is customs agent/border patrol	−2
Contact is in law enforcement	−1
Main contact is a fixer	−1
Racism of FOF	As appropriate (see p. 92, *SR3*)

Services	
More than 2 weeks to arrange travel	−1
More than 2 months to arrange travel	−2
More than 1 year to arrange travel	−3
Less than 72 hours to arrange travel	+1
Less than 24 hours to arrange travel	+2
Less than 6 hours to arrange travel	+4
Character wants to smuggle:	
Class A paralegal equipment (i.e., sporting rifle)	+1
Class B security equipment (i.e., smart SMG, silencers)	+3
Class C military equipment (i.e., cannons/biowarfare agents)	+5

consists of the time and effort required to learn and maintain the elaborate codes, and the Matrix fees shadowrunners must pay to use this service. As part of their upkeep requirements, characters must also periodically post information to the Shadowland boards and to its databases. Any communication in search of information conducted between a character and another individual on Shadowland may be considered a FOF meeting, regardless of form (e-mail, icon-based interaction and so on).

When dealing with Shadowland as a contact, the character must do the work needed to find information; unlike other contacts, getting information from Shadowland is not a simple matter of asking a question, paying some nuyen and getting an answer. Think of Shadowland as a combination dorm room and massive private library—a somewhat messy room filled with personalized icons scattered about in a random fashion. All the really good stuff is there, but characters have to wade through a bunch of really weird stuff to get to it. The person who created each icon determines the appearance of each file—ranging from the frighteningly realistic Dunkelzahn icon that represents his last will and testament to the "standard" default Matrix icon of a document stolen from Ares.

Characters must know the right codes and pass several ID checks in order to gain access to Shadowland and to the desired information. Like all contacts, Shadowland protects itself with a well-established security screen. Rather than relying on systems created and manufactured by outside sources, however, Shadowland relies on the skills and talents of some of the best living deckers and programmers to manage its security. As a concession to the users' safety, characters are identified only by their street name and decker icons—which do not indicate the location of the character's meat body or the motivation of his data search.

Any information search in Shadowland takes time, depending on how the search is done: 3D6 days to search by line commands from a telecom, 1D6 days to search by tortoise, and 2D6 hours to search using a cyberdeck. This period reflects the time required to go through the millions of datapulses to find what the character is looking for. Gamemasters may reduce or increase the time required depending on the specifics of the search. For example, a search for all available information on Ares head honcho Damien Knight might take several days, while compiling all the information available on a tattooed razorpunk by the name of Zaz may require only a few minutes. When each search is completed, Shadowland compiles the requested data in a folder known as a sourcebook.

Shadowland also allows characters to use their own search knowbots, as long as those programs are approved by and registered with the Shadowland deckers and programmers—a process that usually takes less than an hour. Knowbot searches take 2D6 hours. After completing its initial task, a registered knowbot can remain in the Shadowland matrix and feed its controlling character any new information on the selected topic as soon as the information becomes available.

The main benefit to using Shadowland as opposed to other Matrix-based searches (see *Searching the Matrix*, p. 254, *SR3*) is that Shadowland provides a –2 target number modifier to the Etiquette (Matrix) Test. If desired, gamemasters can increase the difficulty of finding specific information in the Matrix (including Shadowland) by applying an appropriate target number from the Contact Knowledge Table (p. 67) to all Matrix-based tests made to locate data. Gamemasters may also increase the search period for characters using tortoises or line-command searches simply by adding the target number to the number of days required for the search. (This time increase reflects the painstaking effort required to access each and every document potentially related to the topic in question.)

CONTACT KNOWLEDGE

The result of a player character's Etiquette Test indicates how successful he or she was in persuading a contact to reveal information. A failed Etiquette Test simply means that the character hasn't convinced the contact to share information—the Etiquette Test does not necessarily indicate what the contact actually knows.

To determine what a contact knows, the gamemaster makes an Etiquette or Intelligence Test for the contact, whichever is most appropriate to the situation. Base the target number on the type of information the player character wants from the contact and the information's apparent value, as shown on the Contact Knowledge Table. The level of the contact does not affect the target number.

Generally, a single success on the test means the contact knows the requested information (as well as the information for lower target numbers). If the information requested covers a particularly broad spectrum, the gamemaster can adjust the contact's knowledge higher or lower on a sliding scale based on the number of successes the test generates.

If the Etiquette or Knowledge Test fails, the contact simply does not know the requested information—though he or she may still try to be helpful. For example, a contact who doesn't have the answer the character is looking for may deliberately or inadvertently provide incorrect information for any number of reasons: to stay on the character's good side by telling him *something*, to throw the character off the track, because he believes his information is true, as a favor to one of his friends, to save his skin from his own enemies—the list of reasons goes on forever.

> Our friend Billy Boy has dropped in at Droogies to see if Joe the bartender knows what's up with a certain megacorp named Renraku. Billy specifically wants to find out where Renraku is testing its latest cyberdeck prototype and who's in charge of those trials.
>
> The gamemaster decides that this information qualifies as fairly sensitive, and so he decides that Joe will know only part of what's being said on the streets. He then makes an Etiquette (Street) Test against a Target Number 8 to determine Joe's level of knowledge regarding the new deck.
>
> The test generates no successes. Consequently, the only news Joe has heard is that Renraku recently beefed up security at a few of its local warehouses.

CONTACT KNOWLEDGE TABLE

Target Number	Requested Information	Sample Question
2	General information	" Hey, did you hear that the Big D died?"
4	More details	"What are your sources saying about Dunkelzahn's physical remains?"
6	Even more details	"Sheesh! I asked one lousy yak one lousy question about the security on Inauguration night and she couldn't run out on me fast enough. What's the connection?"
8–11	Specific names, places and really cool things	"Nadja Daviar can't be as squeaky clean as she looks. Get me the name of her personal shopper and I'll show you the dirt behind her ears."
12–13	Info not yet on the streets	"'Project Ragnarok' obviously means something to somebody. Will you be the lucky recipient of my certified credstick, or should I go to one of my other contacts?"
14+	Info beyond the realm of the streets	"What does the phrase 'techno-magical elf cabal' bring to mind in reference to our late, lamented president?"

Modifiers	Special Circumstance
–2	The field in question is the contact's specialty
–3	The contact is a fixer or a Mr. Johnson

SPILLING THE BEANS

What a contact knows and what he or she is willing to tell are two very different things. In most *Shadowrun* games, gamemasters and players assume that contacts will reveal any information they know without argument. This section offers rules that more realistically reflect the facts of life: even contacts have good days and bad days, personal crises and expensive habits to support, and on any given day they may give away their secrets for free or decide to keep their information to themselves—or even worse, sell it to the highest bidder.

The simplest way to simulate this type of interaction between character and contact is to modify the target number for the Etiquette Test that a character makes to obtain information. The default Target Number 4 can change, depending on the subject of the character's question. For example, a snitch may be quite ready to spill the beans on a penny-ante local gang, but the same contact might be quite reluctant to answer questions about the local Mafia boss, especially if the Mafioso is particularly powerful in the shadows or if the contact has some sort of professional or personal relationship with the Mafia. In this case, getting information about the Red Stilettos from Mongo the street snitch may require only a successful Etiquette (4) Test. Retrieving any information regarding the local mob from Mongo the Mafia soldier might require a successful Etiquette (12) Test—a much more difficult task, even though the character is asking the same contact both questions.

When making the Etiquette Test to determine the contact's willingness to talk, the gamemaster can follow the standard system and use the number of successes from the test to determine how much information the contact reveals. Alternately, gamemasters can make a Negotiation Success Contest between the character and contact, applying any appropriate target modifiers from the Contact Success Contest Table, p. 68, to the contact's tests. The result determines how much information the contact reveals: the greater the number of successes, the more the contact tells.

If the contact's test generates more successes than the player character's test, the gamemaster may decide that the contact simply refuses to tell the character much of anything, or the contact might spin tall tales or give misleading information.

The modifiers on the Contact Success Contest Table can apply to Opposed Tests or Success Contests made during bargaining or any other type of negotiation.

Billy Boy still wants that information about Renraku, so he visits Timmons the cop. First, the gamemaster makes an Etiquette Test for Timmons to determine if the cop knows anything about the new Renraku deck prototype. The gamemaster sets the Target Number at 8 (Renraku would understandably keep security tight around the project). The test generates 2 successes, and so the gamemaster decides that Timmons knows who's running the prototype testing, and where the testing lab is located. (If pressed, the gamemaster will explain that Timmons knows this info because Renraku hired Lone Star to provide some extra patrols around the lab site and to control after-hours access.)

Being a cop, Timmons is naturally a little reluctant to give Billy such information, because if something happens to Renraku it could affect Lone Star and his job. Because Billy is prying into a sensitive topic and Timmons is close-mouthed, the gamemaster calls for a

CONTACT SUCCESS CONTEST TABLE

Condition/Circumstance	Target Modifier
Character's Essence below 1	–2
Character's Essence below 0 (cybermancy)	negative Essence – 2 (rounded down)*
Contact is suspicious	–2
Desired results of character's planned actions are:	
Beneficial to target	+2
Pleasurable to target	+1
Annoying to target	–1
Harmful to target	–2
Disastrous to target	–3
Character displays racist attitudes	gamemaster's discretion
Level 1 contact	0
Level 2 contact	+1
Level 3 contact	+2
FOF	–1 per level between FOF and primary contact
Contact owes a debt to character	+1
Character owes a debt to contact	–1
Contact is hostile	–3
Contact is an enemy (secret or known)	–4
Mild cultural differences (UCAS to CAS)	–1
Moderate cultural differences (UCAS to NAN)	–2
Dramatic cultural differences (UCAS to Japan)	–3
Extreme cultural differences (UCAS to insect spirit or AI)	–4
Language barrier	–1 per point below 5 in Language Rating
Nuyen paid to contact above normal fee	+1 per 10% increase of fee

Notes: All modifiers are cumulative. Target numbers cannot be reduced below 2.

*In interrogations, a negative Essence may benefit a character. Gamemasters can apply a target modifier equal to the absolute value of the character's negative Essence (simply remove the negative sign) plus 2.

Success Contest pitting each character's Negotiation against the other's Intelligence.

Because Timmons is a Level 2 contact, the gamemaster grants Billy an extra die for his test. He rolls 2 successes.

The gamemaster applies a +1 target modifier to Timmons's test because he is a Level 2 contact to Billy. However, the information is also potentially harmful to the target (Timmons's job), so a –2 target modifier applies as well.

The test for Timmons generates 4 successes, which negate Billy Boy's 2 successes. Consequently, Timmons tells Billy to stay away from Renraku. He says can't believe that Billy would even think about asking Timmons to jeopardize his job by revealing such information. In the end, Billy Boy doesn't get the information he wanted—but he realizes that Timmons is too scared to talk and deduces that Lone Star is somehow involved in the security around the new cyberdeck project.

ENEMIES

All shadowrunners make enemies during the course of their careers. It goes with the territory. Shadowrunners who are doing their jobs are bound to make someone angry at some point. They lie, steal, own more weapons than small armies (and probably killed someone to get them) and regularly foil the plans of evil megacorporate execs, mob bosses, and other assorted heavy hitters. The following Enemies rules reflect this fact of the shadowrunning life.

CREATING ENEMIES

Gamemasters may create personal enemies for all player characters during the character creation process. Enemies may be individuals or organizations, ranging from spurned lovers to disgruntled contacts to the buddies of a dead partner to paramilitary groups and even whole megacorps. Personal enemies can become team enemies and vice versa. And if a character's life proceeds along normal lines for a shadowrunner, he or she will continue to collect enemies like trophies throughout his or her career. Every time a character or team makes a big score, destroys property, steals a researcher's life's work, extracts a wageslave or performs some other action that results in collateral damage to life and livelihood, their name appears on someone's drek list—and what they did will come back to haunt them

ENEMY RATING TABLE

Standard System Resource Priority	Point-Based System Starting Resources	Enemy Rating	Characteristic Points
E	5,000¥	0	0
D	20,000¥	1	4
C	90,000¥	2	6
B	200,000¥	3	8
A	400,000¥	4	11
—	650,000¥	5	14
—	1,000,000¥	6	17

if their target has the opportunity, power, contacts or resources to make them pay for what they did. In short, the very nature of a shadowrunner's existence guarantees that the character will always have an enemy or two or three plotting against him or her, ever alert for the chance to get a little payback.

To create an enemy or enemies for a player character, the gamemaster first determines the character's enemy Rating, according to the Enemy Rating Table. The more powerful and influential a character is, the more trouble he will attract, and so a character's resources provide a convenient basis for the Enemy Rating. Characters with low Resources will have enemies designed using a relatively low Enemy Rating; characters with high Resources will have enemies designed using a relatively high Enemy Rating. The enemies You Deserve table suggests rough guidelines for the type of enemy each Enemy Rating represents.

Gamemasters can allocate an Enemy's Rating as they see fit. For example, a gamemaster can give a character with Resources Priority A a single enemy at an Enemy Rating of 4, two enemies each at Enemy Rating 2, four enemies each at Enemy Rating 1, one Rating 3 enemy and one Rating 1 enemy, and so on. Remember that certain character Flaws increase the number of or ratings for a character's enemies (see *Edges and Flaws*, p. 15.

Though the Enemy Rating Table includes Ratings 5 and 6 enemies, these types of opponents are probably best reserved for over-the-top supervillain games. A high-Rating enemy's efforts to catch or kill a character can easily become the major theme of a campaign—and such campaigns can quickly become tiresome for other players if the gamemaster cannot find a way to keep their characters involved in the game. In most cases, no single character should start a game with a Rating 5 or 6 enemy, though the Hunted Flaw (see p. 30) might justify such a circumstance.

ENEMY CHARACTERISTICS

Every enemy is defined by three characteristics: Power, Motivation and Knowledge. As shown in the Enemy Rating Table, the Enemy Rating determines how many total Characteristic Points the gamemaster may assign to the characteristics. The gamemaster assigns each characteristic a Rating of 0–6, basing the number of points on the type of enemy being created, the

demands of the campaign, the character's actions and the complexity of the gamemaster's (and/or player's) plan for the player character's ultimate fate. (The Characteristic Points can also be thought of as "drek points," because they represent how much drek the enemy can throw at the character.) Depending on how the gamemaster weights the enemy characteristics, that enemy may be a persistent annoyance or a constant threat, or every attack may seem arbitrary—the character simply doesn't see a connection, and trouble from the enemy always comes as a complete surprise. An enemy makes an ideal plot device for sending off a character with the Borrowed Time Flaw (p. 19) in a blaze of glory (and helping out the team in the process).

Power

An enemy's Power rating indicates the resources the enemy can use to harass the character. For example, an enemy with a low Power Rating (1 to 2 points), such as a corporate secretary, can't perform a hit herself. To harass a character, a corporate secretary will have to come up with a low-tech, easy way to hurt a character—like tipping off the cops. An enemy with a moderate Power Rating (3 to 4 points) might be able to geek the character himself, or he'll have the resources to hire assassins to do the job. An enemy with a high Power Rating (5 to 6 points) can mess with a character any way she pleases. She can send an initiatory group full of physad killers after the character, sabotage his contacts, buy off his closest friends, or slowly destroy everything he's ever held dear.

An enemy with a Power level of 0 has little means to hurt a character. However, such enemies can spread nasty rumors very effectively and bide their time.

Motivation

An enemy's Motivation Rating indicates how badly the enemy wants to hurt the character. An enemy with low Motivation (1 to 2 points) might simply want to "teach that punk a lesson" and will settle for smacking the character around or stealing his possessions. An enemy with moderate Motivation (3 to 4 points) will want to beat the character to within a centimeter of his life or "do back what he did to me." An enemy with high Motivation (5 to 6 points) will continent-hop and go into low-Earth orbit to track down the character and exact revenge.

An enemy with Motivation 0 may wait for the character to fall into her lap—which can be arranged, with cruel gamemaster plotting.

Knowledge

An enemy's Knowledge Rating indicates how much the enemy knows about the character's whereabouts. An enemy with low Knowledge (1 to 2 points) has no idea of the character's location. If the character's face appears on a KSAF broad-

THE ENEMIES YOU DESERVE

Enemy Rating	What It Means
0	You're such a good boy. Your mother would be proud.
1	You showed up that ganger in front of his chica.
2	You butted heads with his friends, too.
3	Uh-oh—those gangers just got some new toys from their corp buddies.
4	How flattering—your chummers at Aztechnology hav hired some bounty hunters to deal with you.
5	The boys at Fuchi want their wiz new cyberheart back—and they're not planning to sew you up after they rip it out of your chest.
6	You're dating whose son? Are you aware he was the head of magic-based biowarfare for that corporation you hit last week—you know, the wageslave whose life you ruined?

cast, the enemy might see it and figure out where the character was a month ago. An enemy with moderate Knowledge (3 to 4 points) knows which city the character calls home, but must wait for the character to make the first move in order to pinpoint his or her current location. An enemy with high Knowledge (5 points) might have round-the-clock surveillance on the character, or be an intimate, trusted friend turned sour. An enemy with Knowledge Rating 6 knows exactly where the character is as play begins.

An enemy with Knowledge 0 has feelers out trying to locate the character but the trail is ice cold.

When Kelly created her decker character, St. Jude, she decided that Jude was raised to believe in God and the sanctity of the family, and that her father, a moderately successful businessman, was always right. When he informed his daughter that she was to marry an elderly, ailing rival businessman, Jude's faith in her father's judgment was completely destroyed. Trained as an information specialist (business jargon for "decker") Jude found it easy to steal proprietary data from both her father's and her fiancé's businesses. She then sold that data, bought herself a cyberdeck and took off for Denver.

The gamemaster decides that Jude has 3 enemies—her ex-fiancé, her father and the head of her father's security team, whom she used to get to the information and then hung out to dry.

Kelly set Jude's Resources Priority Level at A during character creation, so that means Jude has an Enemy Rating of 4. The gamemaster divides the Enemy Rating as follows:

Father
Rating 1
  Power: 0
  Motivation: 3
  Knowledge: 1
  Daddy is moderately angry with Jude. He has a rough idea where she might have run, but lacks the power to find her or bring her back.

Ex-Fiancé
Rating 1
  Power: 1
  Motivation: 3
  Knowledge: 0
  Jude's ex-fiancé is moderately miffed at her sudden departure. He has the power and resources to do something about being dumped and ripped off, but doesn't know where to start looking.

Security Head
Rating 2
  Power: 1
  Motivation: 4
  Knowledge: 1
  The security head is really angry at Jude—she made him look like a fool and tarnished his reputation. He has the power to track her down, and he has a rough idea of where she is.

Jude's troubles really begin if her enemies decide to cooperate—and in this situation, they might easily do just that.

USING ENEMIES

Once the gamemaster establishes an Enemy for a character, that enemy can become more and less influential throughout the course of the campaign. The enemy's initial rating may increase or decrease depending on the character's actions, the campaign's story line, events elsewhere in the universe—or, to be honest, gamemaster whim. Used judiciously, an enemy can spice up a campaign, derail a carefully laid plan, launch a shadowrun, add a much-needed or disastrously ill-timed complication (depending on your point of view), or even distract a character by *not* showing up when expected. Gamemasters choose when, how and why an enemy surfaces and may raise or lower the enemy's ratings and Characteristic Points according to the current threat the enemy poses. The gamemaster can also simply adjust the enemy's actions to suit the story's needs, without crunching the numbers.

Managing multiple enemies for multiple characters can become tricky, but if gamemasters can find a way to successfully track all the enemies of a shadowrunning team, the rewards in roleplaying and storytelling will make the effort worthwhile. From adding a touch of gritty realism to an adventure to contriving the most fantastic and humorous coincidences, enemies offer a gamemaster a multitude of useful, enjoyable options in his or her *Shadowrun* game.

As in real life, the potential for mayhem increases exponentially when enemies join forces against a character or team. Though the partnership may fall apart before the enemies accomplish their shared goal, together they represent a greater threat than any enemy individually. Combining the Enemy Ratings of multiple enemies would quickly send their threat level off the charts, and so gamemasters should simply create an operation of appropriate size and menace to let the player characters know that the drek they're standing in has reached new heights.

Circumstances force Jude to make a run into New Orleans, her hometown. While she's there, she's spotted by a friend of the family who informs her father. The gamemaster decides that her father, a Rating 1 enemy, instantly becomes a Rating 2 enemy with appropriate increases to his Motivation, Power and Knowledge Ratings. Similarly, the security head's rating increases to Rating 3. Jude's appearance really rankles her ex-fiancé, however, whose rating jumps to Rating 3.

Jude quickly completes her business in New Orleans and escapes to Seattle before any of her enemies catch up with her. Her father quickly loses interest in punishing his daughter and soon becomes a Rating 0 enemy. Other business demands the attention of her ex-fiancé, who reverts to a Rating 1 enemy. However, the security head picks up her trail while she's in town and grows determined to catch her. He remains a Rating 3 enemy and follows her to Seattle.

Why An Enemy May Want to Kill Your Character

The following list represents only a fraction of the innumerable reasons an enemy may have it in for a character. People turn into enemies for both more and less serious reasons than these, and each of the reasons provided here has many variations. Be creative—imagine the player character's surprise when he discovers that the mysterious force that has been messing with his cred rating for the past two years and causing him no end of headaches and embarrassment is none other than his former accountant, whom the character only left because his sister married a CPA.

- You left her for dead, or something close to it.
- You ruined his career/business/art, and he has nothing left to lose by hunting you down.
- You burned/blackmailed/double-crossed/set her up—was it for your profit or for her own good?
- You're a (INSERT CHARACTER'S METATYPE/ETHNICITY/POLITICAL AFFILIATION/RELIGION HERE), and he's gonna put you in your place.
- She's been competing with you since childhood. Now it's serious.
- His job or sense of honor requires him to hunt you down.

- You and she used to be friends, teammates or lovers. She never forgave you when you left.
- He's just plain mean and petty, and you're a convenient target.
- Stuff as dangerous as what you've gotten hold of can't be allowed to fall into the wrong hands.
- For some reason he thinks you're the baddest mage/samurai/decker/detective on the streets, and he has to knock you off to prove that he's the best.
- You killed someone she cared about—a friend, spouse, lover, teacher or relative—or someone who was useful to them, such as a researcher, informant or contact.
- They want to "make an example" of you.
- They hate what you represent—your cause, your person, whatever.
- You exposed his underhanded dealings to his superiors—or maybe to the law.
- You have something she needs for career advancement.
- You ruined or delayed their master plan with your deliberate or unknowing actions.
- You're on opposite sides of the law—but now it's getting personal.
- She's jealous of what you can do or the way you live.
- You know that nifty deck/cyberarm/focus you got last month? It once belonged to him or someone he cared about.
- You just uncovered their conspiracy, and they have to silence you.
- She just doesn't like shadowrunners.

DEATH AT THE ENEMY'S HAND

The primary purpose of enemies in a *Shadowrun* campaign is to keep the characters on their toes—and nothing keeps a person on his toes more effectively than the constant threat of imminent death. At times, enemies may devote all their time, energy and resources toward getting rid of a character or team or, depending on the other distractions occupying their attention, enemies may limit their efforts toward eliminating a character or team to passive surveillance. Regardless of the enemy's current level of interest in a character or team, the gamemaster can always find ways to remind the character or team that the enemy still exists, still knows where they are and still intends to take care of them as soon as it's convenient. An enemy is always a threat, even if the character or team is not his or her current target.

After all the build-up of an enemy hunting down a character or team throughout a series of adventures or campaigns, with each event bringing the character or team a little closer to death, if the enemy is going to succeed in his goal the final denouement must be dramatic and meaningful. If the gamemaster's group enjoys a realistic style of play, the enemy may kill the character in cold blood and the player may not object to this harsh ending to his character's life. If, however, players are particularly attached to their characters—as well they might be, considering the amount of time and effort required to create and maintain them—the gamemaster should design a big death scene that will satisfy everyone's sense of fair play and serve as a major event in the campaign. A character's death should mean something: his sacrifice could keep the team alive; his death might provide the necessary breakthrough in a case to bring down the bad guy; her heroic action may change the course of someone else's life, and if the character lingers long enough, she might be able to die with the satisfaction of knowing her death accomplished some good; the character might die in the process of killing the enemy (a classic climax to a story)—the possibilities are limited only by the gamemaster's imagination.

Miraculous Escapes

Often, gamemasters and players may be reluctant to let a character die. The player may have spent a lot of time developing the character, the character may play a key role in the gamemaster's campaign plans, the group may simply like the character too much—there are many reasons why a character should escape death.

In these cases, gamemasters can arrange circumstances that foil the enemy's efforts to kill the character. Anyone who's read comic books or seen action films will already know a handful of ways to keep a character alive in the face of obviously superior enemies and daunting odds. For example, characters may survive explosions by sheltering behind or in a convenient vehicle/steel crate/pile of building materials/vault; escape from a sniper by being nursed back to health by a kindly stranger; overcome grievous injury through cyber- or bioware replacements; suddenly manifest magical ability under pressure and walk away from an attack completely unscathed (physically, at least); and so on. Alternatively, the gamemaster can decide that a character's enemies have some fate other than death in store for the character. The following list provides reasons why an enemy might not kill a character when he or she really should.

- They aren't in it for revenge, they want the money they lost. Placate them.
- They don't want you *dead*—they want you to suffer.
- They don't want you dead *yet*—they want you to *suffer* first.
- Killing people is illegal and unjustified. *You're* going to prison.
- They want you dead, but you've got something to hold over them.
- They don't want you dead—they want you to join the Hive.
- They don't want you dead—they want to offer you a suicide mission.
- They'll give you a sporting chance.
- You'll do nicely as an experimental subject—or food for the others.
- They want to humiliate you and force you to do something that violates your code of honor.
- They want the names and addresses of your accomplices and your employer.

- They've left you strapped to the bomb/rear bumper/diving bell from which "no one could possibly escape."
- They want to "expose" you as a corporate informant and let your friends or associates turn on you.
- They won't dirty their hands—but Rocco's on his way, and Rocco never washes anyway.
- They're going to set you up in order to put their plans into motion.
- Your would-be assassin doesn't really trust his bosses anyway, and you've just convinced him that they'll have someone killing him next.
- They weren't really after you in the first place—tell them who they want, quickly.
- You've got powerful friends you never knew about. Of course, they'll expect something in return for saving your hoop … .
- The ritual must take place at a certain time (bwah-ha-ha). You wait in this cell.
- "No really, I'm on your side—INSERT ENEMY'S NAME HERE is on the way! Let's get out of here!"

KILLING ENEMIES

Killing an enemy should be a cathartic and momentous event—a climax of biblical proportions. The death of an enemy should have as much impact in the game as the death of a character, and can happen for as many different reasons. An enemy might also survive a team's efforts to kill him or her for the same reasons that a character escapes death. Killing an enemy, however, does not guarantee that he or she is gone from a character's life. Player characters may learn the hard way that there's more to living a carefree existence than geeking all their enemies.

Usually, attempts to kill bad guys simply make them madder. *Shadowrun* gamemasters can use a wide variety of explanations to justify why an enemy keeps coming back, even after the team thought he or she was dead. Begin with the ever-popular, "Did you see/find the body?" and move on to escapes based on magic, cyberware, or a combination of any number of devices to explain the enemy's continued existence.

If it serves the story for a character or team to actually succeed in killing their enemy, the conflict rarely ends there. Enemies are people too, and they will have friends, relatives, co-workers, hive-mates, mentors, protégés, contacts, bodyguards, employers and any number of other interested parties willing and able to avenge their deaths—and to step into their shoes as a new, improved, unknown enemy.

NEW CONTACTS

Basic contacts appear on p. 257 of *SR3*. The contacts that follow are similar, though they tend to specialize more in their specific fields. These contacts should come in handy as both gamemaster NPCs and actual character contacts.

In the statistics below, Active Skills and Knowledge Skills are noted separately. In some cases, skills are specifically left open to allow you to choose skills to meet your campaign's needs. Language Skills are not given for these contacts. Assume that they can speak, read and write whatever languages the gamemaster deems necessary. Alternately, you can choose Language Skills for them per the character creation rules in *SR3*, p. 59.

Specific gear that we felt was necessary for the contact has been listed. Any other gear can be given to the contact as the gamemaster chooses.

Remember that the information contacts can provide is usually specialized and limited to specific areas of interest. Contacts should not be experts in everything.

CORPORATE CONTACTS

Corporate contacts can offer shadowrunners inside information on corporate doings—everything from the name of the guy running the secret prototype drone trials to what time security personnel change from day to night shift. The type of information available from a corporate contact depends largely on his or her position. For example, a corporate secretary may know about the latest research breakthrough because she frequently types and files the memos; the front-desk security guard probably knows exactly what time Mr. Suit leaves the building for lunch every day; and so on. How much information the contact is willing to spill can depend on several factors: the contact's sense of loyalty to the corp (or lack thereof), what kind of information the runner is after, how much money the runner can offer to supplement the contact's measly salary, even the contact's level of boredom with the "respectable" wage slave's life.

Because a corporate contact is likely to know the most about his or her own employers, runners are very likely asking these people to put their livelihoods on the line every time they come looking for inside information. A corporate contact may be in a position to spill dirt on a rival, but will likely know much less about what the competition is doing than about goings-on in his or her own corporate backyard. Gamemasters and players should keep this in mind when dealing with corporate contacts, and make it worth their while to spill the beans.

Common corporate contacts include secretaries, office ladies, wage slaves, deckers, riggers and security guards. (Some runner teams may acquire corporate contacts a bit higher up the food chain, but high-level executives, top-flight scientists and other VIPs are less likely than the lower echelons to have dealings with "criminal lowlife" shadowrunners.)

GOVERNMENT CONTACTS

Just as corporate contacts do for corporations, government contacts can offer runners inside information on the governments they serve, and also on the doings of law-enforcement agencies attached to them. If you need to back up the latest street rumor about the local mayor's alleged shady dealings, get a parking ticket fixed or find out how far the UCAS FBI's investigation into Dunkelzahn's death has progressed, a gov-

ernment contact is the person to go to. Just what the contact is willing to tell or do for the runner depends on the contact's position, attitude toward the matter in question, and what the runner can offer. A minor city official or crooked alderman may fix a parking ticket or procure an under-the-table magic license if offered a hefty bribe; a government agent who prides himself on being a straight arrow may need to be convinced that his information will save lives or avoid a PR debacle instead. That same government agent, by contrast, may be perfectly willing to spill the beans about his superiors if he believes that his government/agency has fragged him over or is involved in a cover-up.

Government contacts include government agents, various city officials and Metroplex guardsmen.

STREET CONTACTS

A street contact is anyone that a runner might meet on the streets who has access to useful information, goods or services. Street contacts vary widely, from the snitch who eavesdrops on private conversations in every neighborhood saloon to the street doc who runs the free clinic in the Redmond Barrens to the plainclothes cop who sometimes passes on the latest precinct scuttlebutt as a way of paying back his informants in the shadow community. Most street contacts are primarily sources of information, though some may offer services or gear as well; for example, the Paramedic is a potential source of medical supplies such as slap patches and medkits, while the Street Doc offers cheap medical care (including cyberware installation).

What a street contact has to give and his or her motive for giving it varies as much as the contacts themselves. A taxi driver may unwittingly spill useful information during an interminable drive to SeaTac airport in heavy traffic, just because the cabbie feels chatty. A street kid may tell a runner something he needs to know in order to impress the runner and get attention. A snitch generally offers information for cash, and so on.

Street contacts include street docs, snitches, street kids, store owners, taxi drivers, squatters, paramedics and plainclothes cops.

UNDERWORLD CONTACTS

Underworld contacts offer information about and connections to the various organized-crime syndicates for which they work: the Mafia, the Yakuza, the Triads and the Seoulpa Rings. Gang leaders are also considered underworld contacts, because most gangs make their livings through some kind of petty crime. Sources of stolen or illegal items, such as weapons dealers, dock and warehouse workers or even store clerks and stockboys, are a third type of "underworld" contact; these contacts can get their hands on anything from guns and armor to cyberdecks to electronic toys that "fell off the back of a truck."

Most syndicate-connected underworld contacts will be soldier-level or below; not many runners are on easy speaking terms with the local Mafia don or Yakuza oyabun. Soldiers, enforcers, made men and the like are the mob-connected people with whom shadowrunners are likely to interact. These people may know a great deal or very little about their syndicates' activities, and will not easily spill what they do know if they believe that the runners intend to "inconvenience" the big boys with it. (Even a Level 3 contact won't be eager to wear cement shoes for shooting off his mouth to the wrong person.) They may be more than willing to talk about other syndicates, however, provided the leak can't be traced back to them. Lower-echelon underworld contacts spend a lot of time on the streets, and they learn to keep their ears to the ground so that the actions of rival syndicates don't catch them by surprise; a runner's Mafia-soldier buddy may know far more about the plans of the local Yakuza gumi than the Yakuza suspect.

In addition to getting information, player characters interested in working for a syndicate themselves can use their underworld contacts to give them an "in."

Underworld contacts include gang leaders and Mafia, Yakuza, Triad and Seoulpa Ring soldiers.

MEDIA CONTACTS

The world of *Shadowrun* runs on information, and media contacts are in the forefront of it. They dish up the dirt for public consumption, complete with wiz computer graphics to catch the eye and make sure Joe Citizen doesn't head for the kitchen or the bathroom.

With regard to shadowrunners, media contacts are particularly useful if a runner team uncovers a secret that they need to expose (or threaten to expose) to the light of day. Sometimes, going public is the only way to nail the bad guys hard enough to keep them from coming after you. Media contacts also have a wide range of acquaintances in their line of work, and may be able to hook up runners with people who can help them disappear if they need to. More often, media contacts serve as repositories of varied (and usually juicy) information; they're constantly on the prowl for the next ratings-grabbing story, and will gladly trade dirt for dirt if the runners have anything tempting.

Media contacts include reporters and media entrepreneurs/producers.

AMERINDIAN TRIBESPERSON

Uses: Rural contact, can help with tribal customs and contacts, telesma

Places to Meet: Any place outside the sprawl

Similar Contacts and Connections: Any contact living outside the city, usually Native American shadowrunners, smugglers

The tribe member comes in many forms and attitudes, but knowing one opens up a whole new world to you. She is the link with the world outside the sprawl—the world of Amerindians and their culture, a place where most likely a sprawl urchin like yourself wouldn't begin to know how to fit in.

She can offer you tribal secrets, hideouts, smuggling routes and even places of magical power if it will aid her tribe and her people in some way. But don't double-cross her or her tribe; if you do, she will find you and make you pay.

Just because she's a tribesperson doesn't mean she won't be found in the sprawl. She also has business to attend to, whether it's trading in tribal goods or working the shadows. She isn't naive or ignorant—she knows the score and she can pass that information on to you.

Game Statistics

B	Q	S	I	W	C	E	R
4	5	3	4	5	3	6	4

INIT: 4 + 1D6

Combat Pool: 7

Karma Pool/Professional Rating: 3/3

Skills: Athletics 7, Biotech 3 (First Aid 6), Etiquette 3 (Tribal 6), Negotiation 4, Projectile Weapon 4 (Pull-Bow 6), Stealth 5 (Hiding 7), Rifles 4, Unarmed Combat 5

Knowledge Skills: Tribal Lore 6, Paranormal Creatures 4, plus 3 more skills no higher than Rating 5

Gear: Armor clothing (3/0), survival knife

ARMS DEALER

Uses: Weapons and ammo, armor, grenades and explosives, security vehicles

Places to Meet: Back room at downtown bars or nightclubs, any back alley or rundown building, gun shows

Similar Contacts and Connections: Underworld street operative, gang leader, smuggler, military or ex-military contact

Weapons and armor are the arms dealer's business, and since you probably lack a SIN and have a police record, he's a lot easier to deal with than your local Weapons World™ discount gun store. From easily concealable hold-out pistols to SMGs to rocket and grenade launchers, the arms dealer can sell you just about any grade of bang-bang without the need to jump through a bunch of legal hoops. He can also get you that Armani armored jacket you've had your eye on, or the ballistic riot shields used by Lone Star SWAT teams, or a few blocks of plastic explosive for that structure hit some Johnson hired you to do. Arms dealers with military connections can even get their hands on mil-spec gear, weapons and vehicles.

Arms dealers may also have valuable connections: fences and smugglers who sell them stolen guns, Army grunts who swipe the odd case of ammo or explosives from the supply depot, mobsters involved in the illegal gun trade, and regular customers of all kinds. Everyone in the shadows comes to the arms dealer sooner or later, because sooner or later they all need his merchandise. If you can pay him back with a little favor now and then, he may give you a small discount on your next box of APDS ammo, or find that FN-HAR assault rifle you've been meaning to buy. He may also introduce you to his friends, providing you with a whole network of potential new contacts.

Game Statistics

B	Q	S	I	W	C	E	R
3	3	4	7	4	4	5.2	5

INIT: 5 +1D6

Combat Pool: 7

Karma Pool/Professional Rating: 3/3

Active Skills: Computer 3, Electronics 3, Negotiations 6, Pistols 5, Submachine Guns 5, Unarmed Combat 4, plus 6 Build/Repair Skills (Ratings 3 through 6)

Knowledge Skills: Weapon Acquisition 6, plus 5 others (Rating 4)

Gear: Armor clothing (3/0), heavy pistol (your choice) with APDS ammo, several well-armed bodyguards
Cyberware: Datajack, Display Link, Headware Memory (150 MP)

BOUNTY HUNTER

Uses: Information, hard-to-find people or critters, police contacts, connections with arms dealers
Places to Meet: Back rooms of local bars, dark alleys, seedy hotel rooms
Similar Contacts and Connections: Underworld bosses, hit man, terrorist

The bounty hunter makes a living by tracking people, especially those who don't want to be found. If you need to find the hiding place of the missing corp scientist you were hired to kidnap, or learn the daily routine of a corporate bigwig so that you can break into his well-guarded house, the bounty hunter can help you out … if the pay is good enough. The bounty hunter might also be able to tip you off if one of her colleagues has a contract with your name on it. Just don't go to her for information on one of her own targets; in those circumstances, you're the competition and she'll use any means necessary to edge you out.

Given their line of work, bounty hunters also know reputable arms dealers who don't gouge their customers too badly, especially dealers who specialize in mil-spec weapons and equipment. Bounty hunters sometimes go after various paranormal creatures that governments offer rewards for; on some hunts, having the best gear makes all the difference. Bounty hunters are usually familiar with law enforcement and security agencies, and may be able to get info on those who are trying to catch shadowrunners.

Game Statistics

B	Q	S	I	W	C	E	R
6	5	5 (6)	4	4	1	1.3	4 (8)

INIT: 8 + 3D6
Combat Pool: 6
Karma Pool/Professional Rating: 3/4
Active Skills: Car 4, Computer 6, Etiquette 3 (Street 5, Corporate 5, Matrix 5), Rifle 8, Pistols 6, SMG 4, Stealth 4 (Sneaking 6), Unarmed Combat 6
Knowledge Skills: Data Tracing 3, Tracking 3, plus 4 more (Rating 4 or 5)
Cyberware: Cybereyes with Electrical Vision Magnification (Rating 3), Flare Compensation, and Thermographic Vision; Smartlink; Synthetic Cyberarm (Strength Increase 1); Wired Reflexes (Rating 2)

COMPANY MAN

Uses: Sensitive corporate information and biz, higher-level corp contacts
Places to Meet: Back rooms in bars and nightclubs, other places with plenty of privacy
Similar Contacts and Connections: Corporate security guard, corporate suit, corporate wage slave, hit man, shadowrunner

The company man is a troubleshooter—when trouble rears its head, usually in the form of shadowrunners, he shoots it. Dead.

The company man is one of the corporation's special agents and his name doesn't appear in employee records. Whenever the corporation needs illicit work done and doesn't want to dirty its hands with shadowrunners, the company man takes care of it. Some company men are little more than glorified security guards, some are bodyguards, some are specially trained hit men.

In the course of his duties, the company man often spends time in the halls of corporate power, privy to the secrets high-level executives spill in his presence while playing golf with each other or meeting in a guarded location. He also may know where the corp's valuable research scientists go slumming for drinks and what their security detail is like. But since he is more loyal to the corp that pays his (generous) salary than to you, if you're going to get anything out of him, you'd best make it worth his while.

Game Statistics

B	Q	S	I	W	C	E	R
6	5	6	4	5	2	2.3	4 (8)

INIT: 8 + 3D6
Combat Pool: 7
Karma Pool/Professional Rating: 3/3
Active Skills: Electronics 4, Etiquette 4 (Corporate 7), Pistols 7, Stealth 5, Unarmed Combat 6, plus 1 Vehicle Skill at Rating 5
Knowledge Skills: Corporate Politics 5, plus 4 more at Rating 4
Cyberware: Skillwires (Alphaware, Rating 5), Smartlink, Wired Reflexes (Alphaware, Rating 2)

CORPORATE WAGE SLAVE

Uses: Information on the corporations, other corporate connections
Places to Meet: Favorite lunch spots, slightly upscale bars and clubs, corporate shopping malls, trendy hangouts like art galleries and museums, the ballpark or urban brawl games
Similar Contacts and Connections: Corporate suit, corporate secretary, corporate decker, rigger or security guard

The corporate wage slave is the drone in the hive of the megacorporation. She does the work, 40-plus hours a week. She's not an expert on the big picture of megacorporate intrigue, but depending on her specific job, she may be able to spill all kinds of useful info picked up around the office water cooler. The corp decker might know high-level system passwords. The security guard knows exactly what security measures are in force at various corp facilities. The secretary types or files memos dealing with all kinds of corp projects. The wage mage might be able to tell you about experimental spells and magical breakthroughs. The corp suit knows of management decisions, business dealings and new projects.

Of course, what the wage salve is willing to tell depends on her reason for talking. She may have been unfairly passed over for a promotion and be eager to hit back at the higher-ups; she may hate working for The Man, and deal with it by fragging the corp over in little ways; she may be a recent arrival from another corp, all too willing to spill the secrets of her former employer in order to advance the fortunes of her current one; or she may be a shadowrunner wannabe who sees dishing the dirt to "criminal" shadowrunners as an entertaining walk on the wild side. She may also simply be looking to supplement her measly salary with cred from your pocket.

Game Statistics

B	Q	S	I	W	C	E	R
2	2	2	3	3	3	6	2

INIT: 2 + 1D6
Combat Pool: 4
Karma Pool/Professional Rating: 1/1
Active Skills: Computer 3, Etiquette 2 (Corporate 3), plus any skill required by their job at a rating no higher than 4.
Knowledge Skills: Corporate Politics 2, plus 3 more at Rating 3

GANG LEADER

Uses: Information, muscle, connections with other gangs/organized crime
Places to Meet: Any street or back alley, especially in his gang's turf; neighborhood bar or cheap diner; gang safehouse, jail
Similar Contacts and Connections: Underworld street operative, ganger, smuggler, fence

You've probably seen the gang leader around, strolling down to the corner store flanked by a pair of bodyguards or driving by in a set of fancy wheels. On his own turf, he's king; outside it, he's likely a target. He's the boss of the local gangers, which means he has anywhere from five to fifty buddies who are his eyes, ears and foot soldiers. He knows about anything that's happening on his turf; depending on his connections, he may also know quite a bit about what's going on outside it. His gang may deal BTL for the Triads, or run protection rackets for the Mafia or they may be enterprising independents. He may not know all there is to know about his syndicate buddies, but he can point you toward a Mafia "made man" or a low-level Yakuza soldier who may be your ticket inside the shadowy world of the mobs.

Getting on the gang leader's good side also buys you protection, in more ways than one. If he calls you friend, his people won't hassle you. Prove yourself a good friend, and the gang may even bail you out of drek when you need it. Gangers can act as lookouts, create distractions, help you out in a firefight or even offer you a safe haven on their turf until the heat dies down.

Game Statistics

B	Q	S	I	W	C	E	R
5	5	4	5	4	4	6	5

INIT: 5 + 1D6
Combat Pool: 7
Karma Pool/Professional Rating: 2/3
Skills: Clubs 4, Edged Weapons 4, Etiquette 3 (Street 6), Intimidation 5, Leadership 4, Pistols 4, SMG 4, Unarmed Combat 5, plus one Vehicle Skill at Rating 4
Knowledge Skills: Police Procedure 3, Underworld Politics 5, Smuggling Routes 3, plus 2 more Sixth World or Interest Skills at Rating 3

MOB SOLDIER

Uses: Information, mob connections
Places to Meet: Any bar, nightclub, restaurant, Chinese laundry or other mob-owned business front; off-track betting parlor, casino, racetrack, bordello
Similar Contacts and Connections: Any similar individual from any other criminal organization, smuggler, pirate

Mafia made man or Yakuza enlisted man, Triad "sze kau" grunt or Seoulpa Ring stringer, the mob soldier is the street-level link with the big boys in organized crime. He takes care of whatever the higher-ups want done, from icing potential troublemakers to collecting extortion money to hiring outside freelancers when necessary. He's the lowest man on the mob totem pole, but he can be a gateway to connections higher up the ladder. He can also point you toward the people to talk to if you need information about syndicate doings. Just be careful what you ask him, or both of you could end up at the bottom of Puget Sound wearing cement shoes. The average mob soldier is loyal to his own organization, and is unlikely to offer much information about it unless he believes it will benefit both him and his syndicate in some way. He'll be much happier to spill the beans about a rival mob's activities, provided you convince him that no one will know where the info came from. However, he is likely to know less about other organizations than about his own employers.

Depending on his exact line of work for the mob, the mob soldier can also serve as a source of illegal or smuggled goods, from black-market weapons to stolen cyberdecks to BTL chips. Or he may be a gang leader, especially if he has connections to the Triads or Seoulpa Rings. All of the syndicates use gangs to a certain extent, most often as street muscle or as part of a smuggling network.

Game Statistics

B	Q	S	I	W	C	E	R
5	4	4	4	3	3	6	4

INIT: 4 + 1D6
Combat Pool: 5
Karma Pool/Professional Rating: 3/3
Skills: Car 3, Etiquette 3 (Mob 4, Street 5), Interrogation 3, Intimidation 4, Negotiation 3, Pistols 5, Shotguns 5, Unarmed Combat 3, plus any other Combat Skills at 3
Knowledge Skills: Area Knowledge 4 (gamemaster determines the mob soldier's territory), Local Politics 2, Rumor Mill 4, Smuggling Routes 2, Underworld Finance 3, Underworld Politics 3
Gear: Lined coat (4/2), heavy pistol

PARAMEDIC

Uses: Emergency medical treatment, medical supplies
Places to Meet: Any street where mayhem just went down, local medical clinic, fire station, DocWagon™ facility, diner
Similar Contacts and Connections: Street doc

The paramedic rides the ambulance or the med-evac chopper, ready to pile out and save a life while the boys with the guns provide covering fire. As part of a DocWagon™ rescue team or as an employee of the local fire station, the paramedic has one job: stabilize the patient with emergency treatment long enough to get him to the nearest hospital. If you get hurt bad in a firefight, the paramedic will be your best friend. Without him, you might not make it to the street doc or hospital alive.

The paramedic sees and copes with just about every kind of street mayhem, from pitched gun battles to whatever gets left behind by leg-breakers working for the mob. He can be an excellent source of medical supplies, especially medkits, stim or trauma patches, and anything else normally carried in an emergency vehicle. His connections with hospitals and clinics also enable him to deal in small amounts of drugs and other equipment that "fell off the back of an ambulance."

Game Statistics

B	Q	S	I	W	C	E	R
3	4	3	4	4	3	6	4

INIT: 4 + 1D6
Combat Pool: 6
Karma Pool/Professional Rating: 2/2 (3 when lives are at stake)
Active Skills: Biotech 5, Car 3, Etiquette 2 (Street 3), Pistols 2, Unarmed Combat 2, Stealth 3
Knowledge Skills: Biology 3, Cybertechnology 2, Magic Background 2, Medicine 6
Gear: Armor jacket (5/3), smoke grenade (1), medkit, patches (5 of each kind at various ratings)

PLAINCLOTHES COP

Uses: Information, cred for tips, criminal records, datawork on persons arrested (including tampering with same)
Places to Meet: Any street corner, local precinct house, neighborhood bar or donut shop
Similar Contacts and Connections: Detective, judges, local government officials, snitch, shadowrunners, beat cop

Like the company man, the plainclothes cop is the guy on the inside who also knows the outside. He's almost always the one in charge of investigating the murder, setting up the sting and so on. When any crime more serious than a purse-snatching goes down, the plainclothes cop will be involved, canvassing the neighborhood to find out who saw what. Tell him what he needs to know, and he'll look out for you in the future. He may even toss a little cred your way, if your information is worth his while.

The plainclothes cop can be a runner's best chummer. He knows things about the inner workings of the higher-ups—especially who's scratching whose back, and what that might mean for you. He also has easy access to criminal records, and can make certain parts of certain files go missing. Finally, the plainclothes cop has connections with the courtroom side of law enforcement. He can put in a word for you with his drinking buddy, the assistant D.A., or maybe steer your case toward a public defender who actually knows what she's doing.

Game Statistics

B	Q	S	I	W	C	E	R
4	5	3	4	5	3	4	4

INIT: 4 + 1D6
Combat Pool: 7
Karma Pool/Professional Rating: 3/3 (4 when lives are at stake)
Active Skills: Biotech 2, Car 3, Etiquette 4 (Law Enforcement 45, Street 7), Pistols 5, Unarmed Combat 5
Knowledge Skills: Police Procedures 5, Psychology 4, Sociology 3, plus 3 more at Rating 3
Gear: Armor jacket (5/3), Colt Manhunter, micro-transceiver, plasteel restraints

REPORTER

Uses: Information, various connections (reporters know everybody), publicity
Places to Meet: Trid station or newsfax offices; any bar, diner or 24-hour coffee shop; just about anywhere else that Big News is going down
Similar Contacts and Connections: Media entrepreneur, snitch, various street, governmental, and corporate contacts

The reporter is looking for a story that'll make him famous—and the juicier it is, the better he likes it. He goes anywhere and everywhere that his nose for news takes him, sniffing out the dirt and dishing it up for prime time. He lives or dies by the people he knows, and by what he can get them to say. This makes him a valuable resource for shadowrunners—the reporter may have any number of useful friends, some of them in higher places than the average runner could ever dream of reaching.

The reporter is also the man to know for runners who want to bust open a cover-up, expose some terrible wrong, or just make some cred selling a hot story. Publicity is the reporter's business; he knows exactly where to spread the word so that it reaches the maximum audience. He's also willing to pay for a solid tip or an exclusive, especially if it leads to a story that will help him stand out from the newshound pack. And if he works for a large news organization that has a protection program for sources, he can help the runners start life over with new identities if necessary.

Game Statistics

B	Q	S	I	W	C	E	R
3	5	2	6	5	5	4.2	5

INIT: 5 + 1D6
Combat Pool: 8
Karma Pool/Professional Rating: 2/2
Active Skills: Car 2, Etiquette 3 (Corporate 5, Political 5, Street 5), Pistols 3, Interrogation 6, Negotiation 5, Stealth 3, Unarmed Combat 3
Knowledge Skills: Conspiracy Theories 4, Local Politics 4, plus a specific topic the reporter works on at Rating 6, plus 2 Sixth World Skills at a Rating no greater than 4.
Gear: Armor clothing (5/3), Dodge Scoot, 30,000¥ of surveillance equipment
Cyberware: Datajack, headware memory (150 MP), headware telephone, image link, opticam

SNITCH

Uses: Information, street-level connections, cop connections
Places to Meet: Any bar or neighborhood diner, street corners and public parks where no one can listen in

Similar Contacts and Connections: Street kid, reporter

The snitch is a street rat with information to sell, usually to the highest bidder. Pay him enough and he'll tell you whatever you want to know. Nine times out of ten, his info is solid; he knows that if it isn't, you'll stop crossing his palm with credsticks. (As for the tenth time, hey—those are the breaks.) He has quite a bit to sell, too; intelligent and observant, he watches everything and everyone in his favorite haunts, knowing that just about any detail might be worth something to somebody. He makes it his business to know what's happening on the streets and who's making it happen. If you need to find a gunrunner or a dealer in hot high-tech merchandise or a reputable street doc in the snitch's neighborhood, he probably knows where to steer you.

The snitch works regularly with law enforcement, providing "anonymous tips" about criminal doings in exchange for cash. Keep him happy, or you may be the subject of his next report to Lone Star. For runners interested in making cop connections, the snitch can be an entry to the world of the boys in blue.

Game Statistics

B	Q	S	I	W	C	E	R
2	6	2	3	2	1	6	4

INIT: 4 + 1D6
Combat Pool: 5
Karma/Professional Rating: 1/1
Skills: Etiquette 2 (Street 4), Local Rumor Mill 6, Negotiation 4, Unarmed Combat 2
Gear: Armor vest, Walther palm pistol

STREET COP

Uses: Information, criminal records, datawork on persons arrested (including tampering with same)
Places to Meet: Any street corner, local precinct house, neighborhood bar or donut shop
Similar Contacts and Connections: Plainclothes cop, detective, metroplex guardsman

The street cop is the guy on the beat, the uniform in the squad car best known for stopping anybody with the wrong clothes or the wrong attitude. Unless he's on your side, that is. Give him a piece of your action, and the street cop just might let you walk on by, even when you're wearing heavy body armor and packing a pair of Ares Predators. Or maybe he wants to know who the *real* bad guys are in your neighborhood, like the thrill-gang that likes to slice people up or the BTL dealers in the park down the street, and is willing to cut you some slack if you keep him informed. Or maybe he half wants to be in your shoes, instead of working for a cop corp where the biggest crooks are the guys in the head office—so he takes it easy on you and your buddies, because your kind of crime doesn't seem so bad.

Street cops know what's going down at the local precinct house—which cops are on the take, which ones are gung-ho recruits fresh out of cop school and itching to bag some criminal scum, when the chief's going to order the next crackdown to make the department look good. He can tell you when to lie low and when it's back to business as usual. The street cop can

also "lose" pieces of datawork needed to book you or your buddies, or let you know who's in lockup and for how long. He might even have a friend or two who can make certain embarrassing pieces of your past disappear, if you give him a good enough reason.

Game Statistics

B	Q	S	I	W	C	E	R
4	4	4	4	3	2	5	4

INIT: 4 + 2D6
Combat Pool: 5
Karma/Professional Rating: 2/2
Skills: Clubs 4, Etiquette 2 (Corporate 4, Street 4), Firearms 4, Police Procedures 4, Unarmed Combat 3
Cyberware: Smartgun Link, Boosted Reflexes 1
Gear: Armor jacket (5/3), Colt Manhunter, micro-transceiver, plasteel restraints, stun baton

STREET DOC

Uses: Medical treatment, often cut-rate and without paperwork; cyberware installation; medical supplies
Places to Meet: Storefront clinic, public hospital in a lousy neighborhood, body shop
Similar Contacts and Connections: Paramedics, hospital staff, morgue officials, organized criminal syndicates, shadowrunners, smugglers

The street doc is your one-stop shop for anything medical you need done when you don't have a SIN or insurance. If you caught some flying lead and need patching up, or you want the latest lethal cyber-gadget installed, the street doc is the one to see. Choose your doc carefully, though. He may be anything from a top-notch surgeon with a social conscience to a quack that even the worst excuse for a public hospital won't let inside as a patient! Good, bad or indifferent, however, the street doc is the only provider of medical care that the average shadowrunner can afford. He's also the only game in town for runners who want bod mods on the cheap, or who need to have illegal cyberware installed with no questions asked.

The street doc knows the neighborhood where he works, and can tell you if any new faces have dropped in lately. If he has connections to a hospital, especially to one in a ritzier part of town, he may be able to tell you who to see for emergency treatment there, if you're unlucky enough to need it.

Game Statistics

B	Q	S	I	W	C	E	R
2	3	2	6	4	2	5.7	4

INIT: 4 + 1D6
Combat Pool: 6
Karma Pool/Professional Rating: 1/2
Skills: Biotech 7 (Cybertechnology Implantation 8, Surgery 8), Etiquette 2 (Street 3, Medical 3), Negotiation 4, Computer 3 (Cybernetics 5)
Knowledge Skills: Biology 6, Cybertechnology 8, Drugs 6, Medicine 6
Cyberware: Datajack, display link

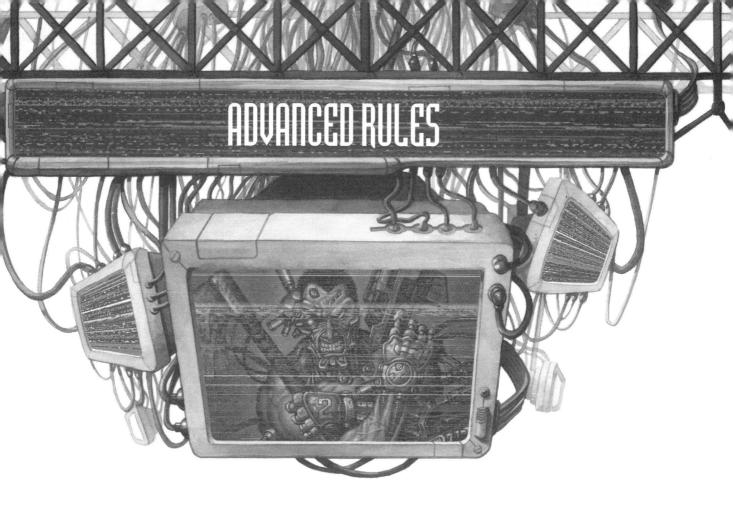

ADVANCED RULES

The *Advanced Rules* section provides new ways to look at existing rules. These rules expand and modify the uses of Karma, provide guidelines for designing appropriate opposition for player characters, propose a variety of ways for characters to retire and offer several miscellaneous rules that tweak specific areas of the current rules system.

KARMA

The *Shadowrun* game mechanic of Karma represents a character's accumulated experience and actions. By investing time and energy into certain aspects of his or her personal development or by performing good deeds, a character can earn Karma Points—a sort of cosmic "brownie points." In turn, these Karma Points improve the character's abilities and options. (See p. 242, *SR3,* for further information.)

BALANCING KARMA AND NUYEN

Most experienced *Shadowrun* gamemasters have faced the problem of balancing the amount of Karma and nuyen that player characters earn during a campaign.

The problem of too much or too little nuyen or Karma arises because different player characters may have radically different needs. On one hand, characters reliant on technology need nuyen to maintain their cyberdecks and implants and to buy all the latest tech toys. On the other hand, using magic generally requires large amounts of Karma, and characters who use magic often become "Karma vacuums," never having enough Karma to accomplish what they want to do. A few characters hover in the middle, requiring both Karma and nuyen to remain effective in their role on the team. Consequently, the gamemaster must carefully dispense cash and Karma so that players have enough for their needs but not enough to unbalance the campaign.

Though gamemasters can easily take excess money away from characters, keeping Karma under control can be a bit trickier. The Karma-for-Cash and Cash-for-Karma exchanges provide options for managing Karma assets.

Karma for Cash

Under the Karma-for-Cash exchange rule, the gamemaster provides opportunities for player characters to cash in Good Karma Points for nuyen or equivalent resources.

Such opportunities represent "lucky breaks" that come a character's way—someone paying off an old favor, a sudden windfall, an easy score, winning the lottery and so on.

Gamemasters should determine the amount of money/resources a character receives in exchange for Karma based on the average levels of nuyen characters possess in the campaign. For example, characters in a relatively down-scale campaign might receive 100 nuyen for each Good Karma Point they cash in. In a more up-scale campaign, a single Good Karma Point might be worth 1,000 nuyen. For random, infrequent windfalls, gamemasters can roll dice to determine how much money a character receives. For example, a gamemaster might determine the amount of a windfall by rolling 2D6 and multiplying the result by 10.

In any case, Karma Points that are cashed in for nuyen or other assets are permanently gone, in the same way as if the character had spent the points to buy a new skill.

Additionally, individual gamemasters should set their own limits on how frequently characters can cash in Karma and how much Karma they can exchange at any one time. Because the workings of Luck and Fate are unpredictable and mysterious, feel free to alter these limits throughout the course of the campaign, or set new limits for each exchange.

Cash for Karma

In the Cash-for-Karma option, a character may exchange nuyen for Karma Points. Karma bought in this manner counts as Good Karma only, and does not count for calculating when Karma is added to the Karma Pool.

Such exchanges may represent a character giving money to a church or charity, gambling it away in honor of Lady Luck (perfect for a Coyote shaman), spending it on a "magical lifestyle" that enables the character to perform daily devotions and rituals to boost her Karma and so on.

Individual gamemasters should determine the "nuyen cost" of Karma Points in their campaigns. Low nuyen costs will enable characters to more easily purchase Karma and may encourage player characters to take up magic. Higher nuyen costs will have the opposite effect.

Regardless of the temptation, players should avoid bankrupting their characters just to gain a couple of extra Karma Points. Having a lot of Karma does a character very little good when she can't pay her rent!

KARMA AND THE AMORAL CAMPAIGN

As a race, we humans like to believe that the cosmos rewards constructive and productive actions more readily than greedy or destructive ones. As is clearly indicated in the rules for Karma and the Karma awards suggested in every published adventure, the Shadowrun rules reflect this belief by rewarding characters who do good deeds and punishing those who fail to do the right thing. While history and fiction both provide numerous examples of people who live and act outside the law behaving in a heroic fashion, those same sources prove many times over that being bad can be a whole lot of fun. Rich and powerful people don't worry about the cosmos rewarding them; they have enough money and influence to create their own luck.

By definition, shadowrunners live outside the law. While that doesn't automatically make them evil, it also doesn't automatically mean that they act like Robin Hood. For every group of shadowrunners looking to make a difference in the world and change things for the better, there is a shadowrunning team willing to do anything for nuyen. Neither approach is the only right choice, because in roleplaying the right choice is the one that lets the group have the most fun. Though the Shadowrun rules encourage the heroic attitude, the Shadowrun universe seems custom-made for skilled opportunists, both player-characters and NPCs.

In those Shadowrun games where the player characters (and most NPCs) are amoral, if not downright immoral, gamemasters may use a variation of the Cash-for-Karma exchange system to allow characters to purchase Karma. This arrangement enables characters to obtain Karma Points to use for character improvement and growth without performing good deeds against their nature and inclinations. When using this system, the gamemaster makes no standard Karma awards during the campaign; player characters must obtain all Karma by purchasing it. The gamemaster sets any limits on the amount of Karma characters can purchase at any one time.

The player must first announce his intention to purchase Karma for his character, at which point the gamemaster determines the cost using the following formula: 3D6 x 100 = nuyen cost of 1 Karma Point. Keeping the cost of Karma unpredictable prevents players from keeping a running calculation of how much Karma their character can afford at any given time, thereby more closely matching the basically random system for receiving Karma under the standard rules.

Karma bought in this manner counts as "awarded Karma." Every twentieth point (every tenth point for humans) is added to the Karma Pool rather than to Good Karma.

FAVORS AND MARKERS

Favors and markers offer additional optional uses for Karma in Shadowrun. A favor represents the obligation of an NPC to perform a service or action for a player character. A marker represents an obligation of a player character to perform a service or action for an NPC. Favors provide a way for characters to spend Karma Points. Markers let them earn Karma Points. Favors and markers may be negotiated between characters and contacts, friends, neighbors, family, business associates or any other NPCs with whom the character regularly comes into contact; favors and markers might just as easily be bargained for with strangers who happen to be in the right place at the right time.

For 1 Good Karma Point, a player character can purchase a favor from an NPC. For the purposes of the favor, the NPC acts like a Level 1 contact and maintains a Friendly attitude toward the character for the purpose of Social Skill Tests (p. 92, SR3). If desired, gamemasters may give player characters the option to substitute favors for Karma awards at the end of adventures. This practice enables characters to store up a few favors that they can collect on when necessary.

When an NPC (never another player character) calls in a marker, the player character must perform the requested ser-

vice or action. If the player character performs the requested service, she receives at least 1 Karma Point. Gamemasters may increase the Karma Points earned if performing the service is especially difficult for the character.

Only players can agree to markers for their characters, though gamemasters may encourage the use of favors and markers by having NPCs negotiate for markers when dealing with characters ("I'll do this for you and you can owe me one."). Characters can also trade a marker for a future favor from an NPC.

KARMA POOLS

A character's Karma Pool reflects a character's accumulated "luck." Generally, Karma Pool Points give more experienced characters an advantage over less experienced characters with the same levels of ability, lending support to the maxim, "age and treachery will beat youth and skill every time."

The following rules enable gamemasters to expand the use of and more closely control Karma Pools in their games. The gamemaster and all players in a group should agree on any variant Karma Pool uses before incorporating them into their game.

Equalized Karma Pools

In *SR3*, the ratio by which new Karma is transferred to the Karma Pool differs between humans and the metahuman races. For humans, every tenth awarded Karma Point is added to the Karma Pool, while the other races add only every twentieth awarded Karma Point. This change was not made to reflect a difference in luck between the races, or to signify that humans are "favored by the gods." This distinction reflects the adaptability and versatility that allowed humans to survive into the twenty-first century. The metahuman races have only "existed" for fifty years. Humans, not metahumans, created the world the game is set in (for better or worse), and are simply better equipped to deal with it more efficiently. More rapid Karma accumulation serves as a human "racial" bonus, if you will.

Gamemasters may instead use the following optional rule for awarding Karma: For all characters, awarded Karma is added to Good Karma, except for every twentieth point, which is added to the Karma Pool. In other words, humans add to their Karma Pool the same way as other characters.

Staggered-Rate Karma Pools

In some cases, player characters may amass huge Karma Pools that enable them to escape dangerous situations with little effort. By limiting Karma Pools in their games, gamemasters can force characters to reduce their reliance on Karma Pools to escape harm.

Gamemasters may also use a staggered-rate system for increasing Karma Pools. Under this system, a character earns Karma Pool Points at the standard rate until the Karma Pool reaches 5. From 6 to 10, the character earns 1 Karma Pool Point for every 30 awarded Karma Points (every 20 for humans). When the Karma Pool reaches 10 points, the character then earns 1 Karma Pool Point for every 40 awarded Karma Points (30 for humans). The staggered-rate system makes acquiring very high

Karma Pools extremely difficult and tends to even the playing field between more- and less-experienced characters.

Permanent Karma Loss

Finally, gamemasters can limit the size of characters' Karma Pools by increasing the number of Karma Pool uses that result in permanent Karma loss.

Under the standard rules, a player character loses any Karma Pool Points he uses to buy test successes (see p. 246, *SR3*). These points are not replaced when the Karma Pool refreshes—the character must earn new Karma Points to replace them. Similarly, gamemasters can simply declare that other specific uses of Karma result in the loss of Karma Points. The gamemaster and all players should agree on any affected Karma uses before using this option in a game.

TEAM KARMA

This optional rule is intended for campaigns in which a regular set of characters are played over a lengthy period of time. In games where players tend to switch characters from week to week, Team Karma rules are not feasible.

Under this rule, just as a character has a Karma Pool, so can a shadowrunning team. Members of the team can contribute points from their personal Karma Pools to the Team Karma Pool. Once contributed, they are permanently gone from the character's personal Pool. Any member of the team can then use points from the Team Karma Pool exactly like points from a personal Karma Pool. The Team Karma Pool refreshes the same as personal Karma Pools. Any points from the Team Karma Pool used to buy successes (or otherwise burned) are permanently lost, just as they are from a character's own Karma Pool.

If a gamemaster chooses to use this optional rule, then when a team first gets together, they should make a list of the members, each of whom should contribute at least 1 point of Karma from his or her pool to the Team Karma Pool. Additional points can be added to the Team Karma Pool between encounters or adventures. Characters may not remove their given points from the Team Karma Pool unless one of the team members chooses to leave, or is asked to leave by the other members. In that case, one-half of the current Karma Points are permanently removed from the Team Karma Pool. The departing character does not take these points with him, and if that character ever rejoins the team, he must add new Karma to the pool before he can use it.

When a new member joins the team, he or she must contribute 1 point of Team Karma. No Team Karma is lost when a team member dies, and a replacement for that character is treated as a new character.

Team Karma is ideal for groups combining older and newer characters. The higher-Karma characters can contribute more to the Pool, improving the survival chances of the newer members and, at the same time, keeping their own Pools from becoming excessively large. Gamemasters should suggest a cutoff point for personal Karma Pools (such as 5 or 10 points), after which any Karma Pool earned by that character goes directly into the Team Karma Pool.

Gamemasters must carefully watch this use of Karma: Team Karma is not supposed to simply give the players more dice.

A character can be part of more than one shadowrunning team, but each team to which a character belongs counts against the value of his Team Karma contributions. The actual value of a Team Karma contribution is equal to the number of Karma Pool Points transferred, minus the number of additional teams to which the character belongs. For example, if a character is part of three teams and wants to contribute 2 points of Karma to the Karma Pool of one team, it costs him 4 Karma Pool Points (2 points for the contribution + 1 point for each additional team).

Characters should only be allowed to use Team Karma if they are acting with the team or on the team's behalf. If a character goes off on a solo run that has nothing to do with the team, he should not be allowed to use the Team Karma Pool. Likewise, characters may only draw points from the Team Karma Pool if a majority of team members agree that they may do so. All the characters on the team need not be present in an encounter for the Team Karma Pool to be used, but all the players present at the gaming session must vote on the use of the Karma. In the case of a tie, the gamemaster casts the deciding vote.

Karma and Defecting Team Members

Because a group's Team Karma Pool is reduced by half whenever a character leaves, team members may put pressure on their fellow player characters to remain with the team, and players may be reluctant to stop playing their characters for fear of putting the remaining team members at a severe disadvantage.

To lessen these pressures and make retirement a more desirable option for player characters, gamemasters may waive the Team Karma penalty when a character leaves a group on good terms. Instead, divide the total Team Karma Pool by the number of team members (round up) to determine each member's "share" of the Team Karma Pool. When a player character leaves, simply reduce the Team Karma Pool by his or her share. The defecting player does not receive the Karma Points—they are gone. If a player character leaves a team on bad or indifferent terms, the normal penalty applies.

NPC Team Karma

If a gamemaster allows player characters to use Team Karma, he should also use Team Karma for NPC teams. Any NPC group that acts together on a consistent basis, such as the Renraku Red Samurai, the Ancients go-gang, or enemy runner teams should have a Team Karma Pool to draw upon. The size of NPC Team Karma Pools should be detemined according to the player characters' Pool and the degree of threat the enemy group represents. See *Creating Prime Runners*, below, for suggested guidelines.

CREATING PRIME RUNNERS

Designing non-player character opponents that are powerful enough to genuinely threaten player characters yet vulnerable to defeat is one of the keys to running fun, engaging *Shadowrun*

games. There is no way to create a single set of game statistics for NPC opponents that will prove equally effective in all *Shadowrun* games, simply because the player characters in each game possess unique strengths and weaknesses. This section offers a method for creating the prime runners every shadowrunning team faces in the course of doing business and for tailoring the powers of known runners such as FastJack, Hatchetman, Argent, Talon and other high-profile runners to the level of their groups' teams.

The system provides frameworks for creating five broad types and ratings of NPC opponents: Inferior, Equal, Superior, Superhuman and Ultimate. The description of each type suggests statistic levels for the NPC that are based on the statistics of the player characters the NPC will face. In other words, the gamemaster will tailor the NPC prime runners to accommodate the relative strength of the player characters.

The description for each opponent level suggests a range of Karma Pool. Varying the Karma Pool of each opponent and occasionally increasing or decreasing the amount during the course of a campaign helps keep players guessing about the actual power of their opponents. Each NPC opponent should also possess a Professional Rating (see p. 248, *SR3*) to determine how the NPC reacts in a fight. For example, an Inferior/Trained opponent (Professional Rating 3) may possess lower Skill Ratings and abilities than most player characters, but she will take a lot of abuse before giving up a fight. On the other hand, a Superior/Average (Professional Rating 1) opponent may be highly skilled but will have little stomach for battle.

The following classifications may be useful for gamemasters creating enemies (see p. 68).

INFERIOR

An NPC rated as Inferior to the player characters may still be a prime runner. Power and influence can be measured in many ways aside from strength, intelligence, nuyen, equipment, contacts and all the other ways runners rank themselves against their peers. For example, an opponent who holds a piece of information that the player characters would find inconvenient to have revealed automatically ranks as a threat, even if that information is his or her only advantage.

Inferior NPCs possess Skill and Attribute Ratings 1–2 points lower than the Skill and Attribute Ratings of the average player character in a campaign. Under ideal conditions, a single player character is a match for 2–3 Inferior NPCs. Inferior characters may be very competent—they just aren't in the player characters' league.

Inferior characters have Karma Pools from 1 to 2 dice less than the average of the player characters' Karma Pools.

EQUAL

An NPC rated Equal to the player characters possesses Skill and Attribute Ratings roughly equal to the average Skill and Attribute Ratings of the player characters in the campaign.

These NPCs are the peers (and perhaps the rivals) of the player characters. They possess the same types of abilities and are capable of most of the same actions as the player characters. Depending on the player characters' general skill level and competence, they may have many peers or very few.

Gamemasters should give Equal NPCs a Karma Pool equal to the average of the player characters' Karma Pools.

SUPERIOR

Superior NPCs possess Skill and Attribute Ratings 1–2 points higher than the average Skill and Attribute Ratings of the player characters in a campaign. They enjoy an edge in experience, talent or just plain luck that makes them better than their player-character counterparts. Consequently, a single Superior character is an even match for two player characters.

Superior characters have Karma Pools from 1–2 dice greater than the average of the player characters' Karma Pools. Because they wield far more power than Equal or Inferior NPCs, Superior NPCs should show up only rarely in campaigns.

SUPERHUMAN

Superhuman NPCs possess Skill and Attribute Ratings 3 or more points higher than the average Skill and Attribute Ratings of the player characters in a campaign. These NPCs are the best at what they do, whatever that may be. They are the cream of the crop, legends of the streets, spoken of with awe. Superhuman NPCs make good foils for reminding player characters of their own mortality and limits, or good adversaries for a group of very capable characters. Usually, a single Superhuman NPC provides an even match for an entire team of player characters.

Superior characters have Karma Pools from 3 to 4 dice greater than the average of the player characters' Karma Pools.

ULTIMATE

The powers of Ultimate NPC opponents are off the scale. These opponents include great dragons, powerful spirits, ancient immortals, godlike AIs and other entities that are so powerful they don't need game statistics. Gamemasters simply determine their exact powers to suit the current campaign and

set an appropriate measurement to describe their characteristics as needed.

Because Ultimate NPCs are so powerful, they function more like plot devices than standard NPC characters. Player characters might be able to thwart some of an Ultimate NPC's plans and schemes, but no mortal has a prayer of surviving a direct confrontation with an Ultimate opponent.

Use Ultimate NPCs sparingly. They don't need Karma Pools per se—just keep rolling dice until they succeed. That's why they're called Ultimate.

STATE OF THE ART

The state-of-the-art (SOTA) optional rules provide game mechanics for simulating the steady advance of technology, the costs of keeping up with the latest technology and the disadvantages of not keeping up with technological innovations. In addition to helping the gamemaster convey the unstoppable rush of technological improvement that is an essential part of *Shadowrun*, the SOTA system provides a convenient way to reduce the amounts of nuyen and Good Karma characters possess and reduce overly powerful characters' skill and equipment ratings/bonuses.

While SOTA rules also apply to NPCs, gamemasters need not manage the details of every gamemaster character's relationship to the SOTA. He or she should simply keep in mind that the runners' opposition may also occasionally struggle to maintain the cutting edge and take care to not assume that all NPCs come equipped with the latest innovations and most recent discoveries in every field.

The *Virtual Realities 2.0* sourcebook provides SOTA rules for deckers. The following SOTA rules apply to other areas of the *Shadowrun* universe.

HOW IT WORKS

First, the gamemaster must determine how quickly the SOTA advances in her game. Gamemasters can advance the SOTA in their campaigns after each adventure, once per game-year, or at any interval in between.

Whenever a gamemaster decides the SOTA has advanced, she first makes a roll to determine what field the advances have been made in; see *Determining the Field of SOTA Advancement*. The gamemaster then consults the field entry under *SOTA Advancements* to determine the specific results.

Because these SOTA rules are abstract in nature, gamemasters are encouraged to fudge the results and roleplay out the changes represented. These rules should encourage game play, not reduce it to a bureaucratic nightmare.

Lifestyle Cost Reductions

To reflect the greater opportunities and advantages enjoyed by successful characters, any character who maintains a Luxury or High lifestyle receives an automatic SOTA cost reduction. A character with a Luxury lifestyle may reduce the final nuyen cost of a SOTA advance by 25 percent. A character with a High lifestyle may reduce the final nuyen cost of a SOTA advance by 10 percent.

Cyberware Costs

Alpha and standard-grade cyberware is subject to the SOTA costs described in the various fields of SOTA advancement. Beta and delta-grade cyberware is immune to the SOTA—for now. Characters who use cheap or second-hand cyberware must increase the SOTA cost by 20 percent.

DETERMINING THE FIELD OF SOTA ADVANCEMENT

To determine the field of SOTA advancement, the gamemaster rolls 2D6 and consults the SOTA Table. The *SOTA Advancements* section describes the effects of the advancing state of the art in each field, the resulting SOTA Factor, and the penalties a character suffers if he does not pay the SOTA Factor.

In addition to choosing the frequency of SOTA advances, gamemasters should customize the tables, adjust dice roll results, or otherwise alter the effects of SOTA advancements to better fit their own *Shadowrun* campaigns.

SOTA ADVANCEMENTS

Biotechnology

SOTA advances in this field represent innovations in biotechnology and medical treatments designed to address the injuries and illnesses related to the ever-increasing

SOTA TABLE

2D6 Roll Result	Field of Advancement
2	Biotechnology
3	Vehicles/Rigger Technology
4	Matrix*
5	Personal Armor
6–8	NERPS
9	Reaction Enhancements
10	ECM and ECCM
11	Electronics
12	Magical Theory

*Gamemasters who prefer to calculate Matrix SOTA advances separate from the general SOTA system can simply replace the Matrix entry on the table with a second Vehicles/Rigger Technology entry.

amounts of new drugs, cyberware and biotech on the streets. Consequently, a character who does not keep up with biotechnology advancements will find it increasingly difficult to effectively treat injuries and diagnose disorders.

The SOTA Factor for biotechnology advancements is equal to twice a character's original Biotech Skill Rating or twice the rating of his highest Biotech Specialization, whichever is higher. Each point of the SOTA Factor costs 500 nuyen. (This means that when your medkit goes out-of-date, it's cheaper to buy a new one.) Characters may spend Good Karma to reduce this cost; each Karma Point spent reduces the SOTA Factor by 1 point. (Biotechnology SOTA advances do not affect DocWagon contracts. Assume that DocWagon personnel automatically keep up with the SOTA.)

If a character does not pay the SOTA Factor, reduce by 1 point all of his Biotech Skill Ratings, including ratings for Biotech Specializations. The ratings of the character's Biotech expert systems, medkits and such are reduced by 1 point as well.

Vehicles/Rigger Technology

New cars with new gear have just hit the showroom floors (and the streets, of course). The gamemaster chooses which area of the field improves, the vehicle or the rigger gear.

The SOTA Factor for a vehicle SOTA advancement is equal to twice the original rating of the improved piece of equipment. Each point of the SOTA Factor costs 1,000 nuyen. Characters can spend Good Karma to reduce the cost; each Karma Point spent reduces the SOTA Factor by 1 point.

The gamemaster can consult the Major Systems Table on p. 86 of *Rigger 2* to determine a subsystem of a vehicle that has "improved."

If a character does not pay the SOTA Factor for an affected vehicle, reduce by 1 point one of the following ratings: Handling, Body, Armor or Pilot or, if you use the Major Systems Table, the Attribute that most closely links to that subsystem.

At the gamemaster's discretion, a vehicles/rigger technology SOTA advancement may occur in the area of vehicle-control rigs (VCRs) or rigger remote decks. The SOTA Factor for such advances is equal to 10 times the initial Reaction bonus provided by the cyberware (for example, 10 points for Level 1 VCRs and remote decks, 20 points for Level 2 items, and so on). Each SOTA point costs 1,000 nuyen. Characters can reduce the cost by spending Good Karma. Each Karma Point spent reduces the cost by 500 nuyen.

Characters that fail to pay these SOTA costs lose 1 point of the Reaction bonus provided by the vehicle-control rig or remote deck.

Matrix

For rules on SOTA advances in cyberdecks, programs and other Matrix technology, see the *Optional Rule: SOTA* on page 78 of the *Virtual Realities 2.0* sourcebook.

Personal Armor

Yet another new method for making cheap armor-piercing ammunition has hit the streets.

The SOTA Factor for this advance is equal to the Ballistic Armor Rating of each piece of armor a character owns. Each SOTA Factor Point costs 500 nuyen. (Generally, this cost makes replacement much more cost-effective than upgrading, except for heavy combat armor.)

Reduce by 1 point the Ballistic Armor Rating of all personal armor owned by a character who does not pay the SOTA cost.

NERPS

A SOTA advance in NERPS represents a new popular culture fad—anything from the new single by your favorite troll thrash band the Horns of Plenty to the new moving sidewalks in the Pike Place Farmer's Market.

These advancements have no game effect.

Reaction-Enhancing Cyberware

Reaction-enhancing cyberware SOTA advances represent innovations in wired reflexes and other reaction-enhancing cyberware.

The SOTA Factor for such advancements is equal to 10 times the initial Reaction bonus provided by the cyberware (20 points for Wired Reflexes 1, 40 points for Wired Reflexes 2, and so on). Each SOTA Factor Point costs 1,000 nuyen. Characters can reduce the cost by spending Good Karma; each Karma Point spent reduces the cost by 500 nuyen.

Double all SOTA costs for boosted reflexes; these systems can be tweaked but never properly upgraded.

For characters who fail to pay the SOTA cost, reduce by 1 point the Reaction bonus provided by the affected cyberware.

(For rules on VCRs and remote decks, see *Vehicles/Rigger Technology*).

ECM/ECCM

The gamemaster can treat ECM (electronic countermeasures) and ECCM (electronic counter-countermeasures) advancements as separate events or assume that any ECM improvement is automatically followed by a corresponding ECCM advancement.

For ECM SOTA advancements, the SOTA Factor is equal to 10 times the affected device's current rating. Each SOTA Factor Point costs 1 percent of the device's initial cost. For example, a Rating 6 maglock passkey would have a SOTA Factor of 60; the cost to keep it up-to-date would be 60 percent of its initial 60,000-nuyen cost, or 36,000 nuyen.

For characters who do not pay the SOTA cost, reduce by 1 the rating of any affected maglock key or electronic surveillance device (dataline taps, codebreakers, Scramble-breakers, signal locators and so on). Similarly, reduce by 1 the ECM rating of any affected vehicle or equipment.

For ECCM SOTA advancements, the SOTA Factor is equal to 10 times the affected device's current rating. Each SOTA Factor Point costs 1 percent of the device's initial cost.

For characters who do not pay the SOTA cost, reduce by 1 the rating of any affected maglock and electronic surveillance countermeasure (bug scanners, encryption systems and so on). Similarly, reduce by 1 the ECCM rating of any affected vehicle or piece of equipment.

Electronics

Electronics SOTA advances represent breakthroughs in circuit design or other innovations in electronics technology.

The SOTA Factor for such advances is equal to twice a character's Electronics Skill Rating or twice the rating of the character's highest Electronics Specialization, whichever is higher. Each point of the SOTA Factor costs 500 nuyen. Characters can spend Good Karma to defray this cost; each Karma Point spent reduces the SOTA Factor by 1 point.

Reduce by 1 point the Electronics Skill Rating of any character who fails to pay the SOTA cost.

Magical Theory/Practice

Magical theory SOTA advances represent new magical research findings that substantially revise magical theory.

The SOTA Factor of such advances is equal to twice a character's Magical Background Skill Rating or the rating of its highest Specialization, whichever is higher. Each SOTA Factor Point costs 500 nuyen. Characters may spend Good Karma to reduce this cost. For each Karma Point spent, reduce the SOTA Factor by 1 point.

Reduce by 1 point the Magical Background Skill Rating of any character who fails to pay the SOTA cost.

The SOTA Factor for a hermetic library is equal to twice the library's rating. For disk-based libraries, each SOTA Factor Point costs 100 nuyen. For chip-based libraries, each point costs 120 nuyen, for hard-copy libraries, 200 nuyen.

Reduce by 1 point the rating of the hermetic library of any character who fails to pay the SOTA cost.

FALLING BEHIND THE SOTA CURVE

Any character who fails to pay the SOTA Factor cost of a SOTA advance suffers the penalties described. The character may reverse these penalties by paying the appropriate SOTA Factor cost any time before the next SOTA advancement in that field.

If a character fails to pay the SOTA Factor cost for two consecutive SOTA advances in a field, she "falls behind the SOTA curve" and cannot reverse the penalty by simply paying the required costs. In addition to paying the required costs, the character must retrain in the affected field to regain the lost skill levels. Such training is subject to all the basic rules for skill upgrades and any rules the gamemaster wishes to apply from the *Optional Training Rules* section (p. 48).

ROLEPLAYING THE SOTA

The SOTA system primarily provides new roleplaying opportunities. For starters, gamemasters can inform players of a new SOTA advance in several ways—talk on Shadowland, a chance meeting with a contact who gives them the latest buzz, an eye-opening fight with a razorboy equipped with the new SOTA wired reflexes and so on.

Next, gamemasters can require that player characters do more than simply spend some nuyen to keep up with SOTA advances. Tracking down a new piece of hardware, finding someone who can teach the latest skill advances, or scamming a copy of the newest cutting-edge software are just a few examples of tasks that characters might have to perform to keep up. Additionally, gamemasters can consider SOTA Factor costs part of the resources—time, information, tools, equipment and so on—characters must spend to keep up with a SOTA advancement.

DEAD-END TECH OPTION

The dead-end tech option provides a way for particularly cold-hearted gamemasters to inflict additional SOTA penalties on player characters.

Under the dead-end tech option, the gamemaster can decide that characters must select between two or more upgrade options to keep up with a particular SOTA advance. (These competing upgrade options represent competing product lines manufactured by rival corporations.) At the gamemaster's discretion, any time a SOTA advance occurs in that field, one of the competing product lines may collapse. Characters who used the defunct product line must then pay double the standard SOTA Factor cost to maintain their ratings—which means re-training and big nuyen.

RETIREMENT

Most runners don't retire until shortly after they die. However, the lucky few who retire *before* they meet an unfortunate end will likely have contacts, skills and resources that make them valuable to the shadowrunning community.

Characters may retire for many reasons. Perhaps the player is simply tired of playing that character; maybe the gamemaster decides that a character has become too powerful or will not be able to play a useful role in the current campaign; perhaps the gamemaster and player initially agreed that the character would die at the end of a specific story line, but at the moment of truth neither really wants to let the character disappear from the game completely. In this case, the player may agree to hand over control of the character to the gamemaster, and the character may take on a completely new life as a friend or foe of the shadowrunner team.

Depending on the circumstances of their leaving the team, ex-runners may stand willing and ready to help their former teammates whenever and in whatever way is needed at a moments' notice. As a fixer or a Mr. Johnson, the character may serve as the team's primary resource for work, or may simply be a constant, inexpensive source of information and contacts. A character who chooses not to pursue a second career and decides to simply live on his or her savings may be persuaded to come out of retirement for "one more big score" or to get his old team out of a jam, especially if the team made very powerful enemies before the player character left ("Remember that comm line we tapped back in '55? Unfortunately for us, it turns out that that was Lofwyr's private LTG. He'd like us to come to a meet and discuss the consequences of our actions … .").

On the other hand, they may actively seek to aid the team's enemies and bring down their former chummers. An ex-runner may have been an agent of a team's enemy working from the inside, or some sort of misunderstanding might have turned the character against the team, leaving him or her ripe for recruitment by the enemy. In the best tradition of the spy genre (and *Shadowrun,* for that matter), gamemasters may spin a complex web of deceit, betrayal, double- or triple-crosses, regret and revenge that keeps the former player character involved in the campaign in newly sinister and morally complicated ways.

Retired runners can remain active in a campaign in several ways. Some may simply step back from the front lines and operate behind the scenes in relative safety. Others may come out of the shadows completely and put their experience to work in the civilian or corporate worlds. The following section offers some ideas for roles that retired runners can play in a campaign.

Regardless of the role a retired character assumes, all retired characters act as Level 3 contacts for their former teammates. Additionally, an ex-runner's contacts can serve as friends-of-a-friend for all team members. (See *Friends of a Friend,* p. 62, for more information about FOFs).

SECOND CAREERS

Ex-shadowrunners often have a wide variety of skills that enable them to earn a living in numerous ways. Some of the less traditional choices for a second career include: urban brawl player or combat biker, Matrix consultant, DocWagon employee, magical researcher, street doc, military advisor, talismonger, corporate wage slave and simsense star (an ever-popular choice).

Ex-runners may also choose second careers more closely related to the work they did as shadowrunners.

"Hello. I'm Mr. Johnson."

Usually, former shadowrunners are well-suited to act as "Mr. Johnsons." Typically, a former runner is intimately familiar with how a shadowrun is orchestrated, which can give such a character valuable insight into the potential risks and profits of a run. Ex-runners are also likely to know at least some of the shadowrunners operating in an area and be better able to pick the right people for a job. But perhaps most important, most shadowrunners will be more likely to trust an ex-runner rather than a Johnson who has spent his career behind a desk.

The same characteristics also make ex-runners well-suited to act as "talent agents" for shadowrunning teams. A character serving as an agent actively searches out the most lucrative jobs for her team and takes a percentage of the profits in return.

If an ex-runner character doesn't have a total of six contacts, the gamemaster and former controlling player can select additional contacts to bring the number to six.

"I Got What You're Looking For"

Any runner character who retires with some money may set himself up as a fixer. A former shadowrunner would likely

have the contacts needed to obtain hard-to-find pieces of equipment and to fence the kind of drek-hot paydata and trinkets that runners tend to collect. Furthermore, most retired runners have dealt with fixers often and are fairly familiar with that aspect of the business.

As a sideline, many fixers also arrange runners for independent shadowruns or act as intermediaries between corporations and runners. Such activities are practically required for fixers who deal primarily in information.

Any former runner who sets up shop as a fixer may select contacts to bring his total number of contacts to six. Fixers tend to specialize, so players may wish to select contacts that reflect the character's specialty.

"I Know How These Scum Operate"

Sometimes it takes a rat to catch a rat. Corporations recognize this fact, and often hire former shadowrunners to work as corporate security specialists, trainers, guards, security deckers and so on. Some ex-runners even set up private security consulting firms and sell their services to the corporations they used to run against.

"Hey, I'm Clean"

Any ex-runner who retires with a bit of cash can set up a "legitimate" business. (Some characters may even open a shop before they retire, though this involves a much greater risk in the event that their cover is blown.) Every legal business owner must have a SIN (even if it's just a counterfeit one), as well as the proper permits and registrations. Some popular businesses for ex-shadowrunners include weapons stores (for former street sams and mercs), talismonger shops (for former magicians), electronics/computer stores (for ex-deckers) and vehicle repair (for former riggers).

Opening any business requires an initial investment. The entrepreneur must buy base inventory and purchase or lease any required facilities. For most businesses, these costs can be determined by using the equipment and working gear costs listed in the gear tables at the end of *SR3*. Keep in mind that a character making legal purchases need not worry about the Street Index of legal items, facilities or shops.

Business and operating permits can cost anywhere from 100 to 1,000 nuyen or more, depending on the type of business—for example, a permit for a registered security agency will cost considerably more than a permit for a talismonger shop or a courier business. Individual gamemasters may set permit costs in their campaigns.

Finally, keep in mind that a "legitimate" business owner need not restrict herself to legal means to operate her business. "Hot" merchandise and alternative funding sources (loan sharks, bank heists and so on) are just two shady practices that may spell instant success (or eventual ruin) for a would-be business owner.

INTEGRATING NEW TEAM MEMBERS

Few gaming groups are willing to start a new campaign just to add a new player or player character. Every time a new player wants to join the game, however, or a new player character needs to join the team because a former character retired or died or because the team is lacking a necessary skill, the group must find a way to successfully integrate new characters into the existing shadowrunning team.

Using the team's contacts is perhaps the simplest way to introduce new characters to a group. A contact may introduce a new character at virtually any time and place.

Following the contact's introduction of a new character or in place of it, a team might hold a "trial run" to test prospective team members. Gamemasters can easily fill such runs with interesting and fun surprises, because the prospective member and the team will be unfamiliar with each other's skills, abilities, work methods, personalities and so on.

Finally, a chance encounter may bring together a new character and a group. Gamemasters can use nearly any element already present in their campaigns—Edges and Flaws, training, background stories, common enemies—to get a new player onto an existing shadowrunning team.

ADDITIONAL SECURITY SYSTEMS

The following material may be used by gamemasters to devise security systems. These systems complement the security systems described on pp. 232–37, *SR3*.

Trip Beams

Lasers or beams of high-intensity conventional lights serve as the equivalent of trip wires when fired across an area at a detector. Mirrors or reflectors may bounce the beam around an area before it reaches the detector, thereby increasing the amount of space covered and also creating an intricate web that player characters will find difficult to navigate. Interrupting the beam triggers an alarm.

Some trip beam emitters are placed obviously to be a visible deterrent. Others are concealed. To notice an intentionally obvious emitter and/or detector requires a successful Perception (2) Test with appropriate Visibility modifiers (p. 232, *SR3*). Note that in this instance, smoke will enhance the visibility of the beam, rather than reduce visibility. If the system is deliberately concealed, apply an additional +4 modifier. The old trick of spraying an aerosol into the area protected by the beam(s) to increase their visibility still works, but at the gamemaster's discretion may trigger certain sensitive alarm systems often found in

environmentally controlled interior areas.

To bypass trip beams, a player character can make a Quickness Test against a target number devised by the gamemaster (minimum 4), depending on the extent of the beam coverage. Player characters will, however, find it impossible to bypass some trip beams in this manner. Emitters and reflectors can be constructed to reroute the beam(s), but doing so requires knowledge of the system in advance, a steady hand and luck. A player character trying this tactic under the best possible conditions (possession of the trip beam's design schematics and plenty of time to study them) must make a successful Quickness (8) Test. The target number for this test rises to 12 if the character has only a picture of the system, and to 16 if the character has neither a picture nor the design schematics. The base time for coming up with a scheme and the necessary equipment to bypass a trip beam is 1 week.

The most common method of bypassing a trip beam is to create a proxy beam by aiming additional emitters of the appropriate type at the detectors. When the player character breaks the trip beam, the proxy emitter is sending sufficient beam wattage to the detector, fooling it into thinking everything is fine. Each proxy emitter costs 200 nuyen; one is required for each detector used by the trip beam. Setting up the proxy beam requires a successful Reaction (6) Test. If the test is unsuccessful, breaking the original trip beam triggers the alarm.

Pressure Mesh and Pads

Pressure mesh and pads are weight-triggered sensors usually concealed beneath the ground (pressure mesh) or flooring (pressure pads). Both are difficult to spot and easy to trip. The sensitivity of these pressure devices may differ, however, especially in areas where patrol animals or drones are used. The less sensitive the device, the easier it is to avoid tripping it.

To notice the mesh or pad, the player must make a successful Perception Test against the appropriate target number,

PRESSURE SENSOR SENSITIVITY TABLE				
	Perception Target		Sensitivity Level	
		Normal	Animals	Drones
Pressure Mesh	8	7	4	3
Pressure Pad	6	7	3	4

including any modifiers. If the test is successful, the character notices the sensor. If unsuccessful, the character steps on the sensor. The player then makes a second Perception Test against the same target number, with a –2 modifier. If the test is unsuccessful, the character trips the alarm. If the test is successful, the character knows he or she is stepping on a pressure sensor and can try to remove the pressure before it exceeds the device's sensitivity. To accomplish this, the character must make a successful Reaction Test against the appropriate sensitivity level, plus the character's natural Body Rating. Apply a +2 modifier if the character is running.

The sensitivity levels of pressure devices under various circumstances and the target numbers for noticing them appear on the Pressure Sensor Sensitivity Table, p. 89.

Vibration Detectors

Vibration detectors are small microphones affixed to doors, windowpanes, floors and so forth, which will pick up any noise or vibrations from movement and transmit them to a computer for analysis. Runners may use their Stealth Skill to attempt to move undetected through an area protected by a vibration detector. To determine success, make an Opposed Test using the character's Stealth Skill against the vibration analysis software's rating. A single net success means the character avoids detection for the turn. The character may move only half a meter per turn when trying to avoid detection. Characters who want to move 1 meter per turn must add +3 to the target number of the Opposed Test. Characters who move faster than 1 meter per turn automatically set off vibration detectors. Because vibration detectors pick up such low movement rates, defeating this type of system is difficult.

Typical analysis software algorithms are Rated from 6 to 10+.

Gas Delivery Systems

Because timing is everything when determining the effectiveness of a gas-dispersal system, the gamemaster should use the following rules to determine how quickly the gas spreads, how quickly the characters notice it (if at all), and how quickly they can take action.

Dispersal systems can fill an area of 30 cubic meters in one Combat Turn (3 seconds). No simple way exists to determine exactly how quickly the gas spreads, but the following guidelines should serve in most cases. Gamemasters should feel free to make any on-the-spot modifications necessary.

The gas will spread at a rate of about 10 cubic meters (roughly 2 meters high, 2 meters wide, by 2.5 meters deep) every second. Approximate this by having the gas spread 10 cubic meters each Initiative Pass, up to a maximum of 3 Initiative Passes per Combat Turn.

The gas starts spreading at the end of the Initiative Pass in which it was triggered, and always goes last during each Initiative Pass. Characters who have Delayed Actions may make a Perception Test at the time of exposure to recognize the presence of the gas by rolling a number of dice equal to their Intelligence against a Target Number of 10, using the appropriate Perception Test modifiers. Characters equipped with a gas detection system (see p. 293, SR3) may be alerted by their gear.

See p. 250, SR3, for details on various gases and how they will affect characters.

Note that gas-based security systems are difficult to detect and react to, and give players little or no chance to deal with a bad scene. Gamemasters should always try to provide the players with some sort of solution to a situation. No-win is no fun.

Chemical Detection Systems

Chemical detection systems (see p. 292, SR3) are "sniffers" that analyze molecules in the air. Specifically designed to detect explosives or ammunition propellant, they are rarer than magnetic-anomaly detector-based systems, but are generally more effective. Available in Ratings from 1 to 8, hand-held systems are available only up to Rating 3. The base Concealability Rating for architecturally based systems is 4.

To determine if a chem-sniffer detects explosives or ammo, roll a number of dice equal to the detector's rating against a Base Target Number of 10. Modify the target number according to the total amount of explosive being carried, per the Chemical Detection Modifiers Table. These modifiers are cumulative.

Mau-Mau the street samurai is packing his fully-loaded Ares Predator (10 rounds) plus an extra clip (10 rounds), and two frag grenades. Blissfully ignorant of the risk, he wanders through a chem-sniffer in the MCT skyraker. Twenty rounds of non-explosive ammo modifies the Detection Test target number by –3. Two grenades provide an additional modifier of –2, for a total modifier of –5.

The Base Target Number for a chem-sniffer is 10, and so the modified Target Number is only 5. Odds are, Mau-Mau's in deep drek.

DOCWAGON

DocWagon is the UCAS's premier private, mobile and armed health-care provider. As described in *DocWagon Contract* (p. 303, SR3), they offer contracts for four different classes of on-call medical service.

CONTRACTS

Acquiring a DocWagon contract requires the purchaser to pre-pay for at least a year's service and to file tissue samples and voice prints with DocWagon.

CHEMICAL DETECTION MODIFIERS TABLE

Situation	Modifier
For each 8 standard rounds (or portion thereof)	–1
For each 6 explosive rounds (or portion thereof)	–1
For each 1 concussion or fragmentation hand grenade	–1
For each 2 smoke or flash grenades	–1
For each 3 mini-grenades (any type)	–1
For each 30 grams of standard (non-plastique) explosive	–1
For each 100 grams of plastique	–1

Purchasers are given a sealed-band, direct-dial wristphone (Rating 2) through which they can contact DocWagon. Rupture of the band triggers a DocWagon response immediately.

Basic Service (5,000¥/year) guarantees the arrival of a trauma team within ten minutes, or the immediate medical care is free. Basic service contract holders are also liable for other incurred medical costs, as listed on the DocWagon Service Costs Table. In the event a High Threat Response (HTR) is necessary, contract holders are charged 5,000 nuyen and are billed for any medical costs incurred by DocWagon employees, including death benefits.

Gold Service (25,000¥/year) provides the same level of service as basic. Additionally, Gold clients receive one free resuscitation per year, plus a 10 percent discount on acute and extended care. The base cost for HTR service also drops to 2,500 nuyen.

Platinum Service (50,000¥/year) provides basic service along with free HTR service, though the client is still liable for death benefits and innocent victims. In addition, they receive four free resuscitations per year, and a 50 percent discount on acute and extended care.

Super-platinum Service (100,000¥/year) is not advertised by the company. In addition to Platinum service benefits, Super-platinum clients are not liable for death benefits for DocWagon employees, and they receive five free resuscitations per year. The Super-platinum wristphone also contains a bio-monitor that will trigger an audible alarm and alert to DocWagon if lifesigns ever stray beyond "safe parameters." In such an event, DocWagon immediately scrambles an HTR team.

DOCWAGON RESPONSE TIME TABLE

Enforcement Rating

AAA–AA	–2
A–B	–1
C	—
D	+1
E	+2
Z	+3

Type of Response

SRT	—
CRT	+1
HTR	–1
Ground Vehicle	—
Air Vehicle	–2

Beyond city limits

Less than 10 miles	+3
Less than 25 miles	+5 (if at all)

DOCWAGON SERVICE COSTS TABLE

High Threat Response*	5,000¥
Employee Death Benefits	20,000¥
On-site Resuscitation	8,000¥
Acute Care**	
Basic	500¥/day
Intensive care	1,000¥/day
Extended Care (3+ weeks)	2,500¥/week

* This is the base charge. The client may also be responsible for these additional charges: ammunition, equipment damage, health-care costs for injured employees and bystanders, and death benefits.

**These figures do not include additional costs for specific medical procedures.

Calls and Responses

All calls for aid to DocWagon are screened by personal identification number (PIN) or wristphone serial number and the client's voice pattern. Once verified, the customer may request Standard, Crisis or High Threat Response (and they will be billed accordingly). If the customer cannot specify service, DocWagon responds with HTR service. If either an SRT or CRT is fired upon during service, they will immediately withdraw and call in an HTR unit.

Standard Response Teams (SRT) include four lightly armed and armored paramedics (see the *Paramedic Contact*, p. 76). They will arrive in either a DocWagon SRT ambulance or helicopter (see p. 153, *Rigger 2*), each capable of carrying two clients.

Crisis Response Teams (CRT) are dispatched to incidents where there are too many clients for a single SRT to handle: large accidents, earthquakes, fires, bombings, gang wars and so on. CRTs are composed of eight SRT personnel, and arrive in a CRT ambulance or air unit (see p. 153, *Rigger 2*), each capable of carrying four clients.

High Threat Response (HTR) units are composed of three paramedics and four heavily armed and armored "threat response personnel." HTR units travel in either a DocWagon Citymaster, WK–2 Stallion helicopters or Osprey II tilt-wings (see pp. 153–54, *Rigger 2*).

Response Time

To determine a DocWagon unit's response time, first determine the type of unit responding to the call. Then roll 1D6: For SRTs and CRTs, the unit will be in a ground vehicle on a result of 1–4, or in an air vehicle on a result of 5–6. HTR teams will respond via Citymaster (1–3), Stallion (4–5) or Osprey (6).

Next, roll 3D6 and modify the result according to the DocWagon Response Time Table. The result is the number of Combat Turns before DocWagon arrives.

The Enforcement Rating refers to the Lone Star Security rating of the area from which the call originated. See *New Seattle*, p. 108 for a complete listing of Lone Star ratings and definitions.

Note that DocWagon will not respond to calls originating from extraterritorial corporate or government property without first obtaining express permission from that agency or government to do so.

Responses to calls originating from any area with a Z security rating are automatically exempt from the ten-minute response guarantee.

RUNNING THE GAME

A *Shadowrun* gamemaster acts as referee, host, actor, director and storyteller—all at the same time. Consequently, becoming a skilled gamemaster takes experience and practice. This section provides ideas and guidelines to help gamemasters develop their skills. Much of the information applies to gamemastering any roleplaying game, and some information applies to running *Shadowrun* in particular.

Gamemastering can be one of the most enjoyable aspects of playing roleplaying games, and everyone should try it at least once—if only to gain a better appreciation of the work that their gamemaster puts in! If you're a gamemaster, encourage your players to try their hand at gamemastering. If you're a player, give gamemastering a try—you might like it.

THE ROLE OF THE GAMEMASTER

The gamemaster's job is to oversee a game or campaign—in other words, to get the ball rolling and then keep it moving along. The gamemaster must act as moderator and guide. He or she is the final authority on rules in his or her game, and he or she must provide all of the "extras" in a game or campaign. The gamemaster must keep the game together and on track. Players often get caught up in the roles of their characters and may forget where the story is supposed to be going. The gamemaster must keep an eye on the progress of the story and give things a little nudge when needed to keep the story moving and fun for everyone.

Though gamemasters wield enormous power in their games, gamemasters are not gods (despite what some of them may believe!). No gamemaster can create a truly interesting game without the cooperation of his or her players. The gamemaster's job is not to lord his or her power over the players and put them in situations where they have no chance of succeeding. The gamemaster's job is to work *with* the players to create the most satisfying game play for everyone.

The secret of successful gamemastering is actually quite simple—keep the game fun for everyone involved. Everything else is secondary. The best gamemasters have fun while gamemastering and do their best to make sure their players enjoy themselves, too. Rules and systems and such are intended to help create fun and satisfying games—they are not ends in themselves. Don't get so caught up in game mechanics that you lose sight of the most important goal—having fun.

BREAKING THE RULES

If you played cops and robbers as a kid, you probably remember playing pretend as a lot of fun, just like roleplaying. You're also likely to recall at least one argument along the lines of "I shot you!" "Did not, you missed!" "No I didn't!" and on and on. Roleplaying games are just a more sophisticated versions of cops and robbers—the main difference is that roleplaying games provide rules to help determine whether or not your shot really did hit.

All roleplaying rules are simply guidelines to help reduce arguments over what really happened during a game. They help us to visualize and experience events in the story as they unfold. But sometimes the rules can trigger arguments, hinder creative players and gamemasters, and otherwise get in the way of everyone's enjoyment of the game.

That's when gamemasters need to fall back on the old adage, "rules are made to be broken." Slavish devotion to the rules of the game is not always the best way to have fun. If a particular rule doesn't work for a particular scene or action, feel free to ignore or modify it. Many groups even develop "house rules" over time, rules that are uniquely tailored to the group's needs and style of play.

Stay flexible about the rules—they are designed to serve the game, not the other way around.

KEYS TO A GOOD ADVENTURE

Shadowrun is an adventure roleplaying game and the player characters, whether they are shadowrunners or not, take the roles of active figures in the Sixth World. They go out and have the kind of adventures that would make for a good action novel or movie. (The point of roleplaying is to step outside the roles we play in real life. There's not much point in playing a librarian, lab technician, mechanic or retail clerk in *Shadowrun*.)

This section provides suggestions for creating satisfying adventures. Each subsection—*The Premise, The Goal, The Opposition* and *Complications*—focuses on a single component of a well-designed adventure.

Note that *Keys to a Good Adventure* and the section that follows, *Plotting a Shadowrun Adventure,* do not present a step-by-step adventure creation system. Gamemasters and players may create and assemble the various components of their adventures in any order they like.

THE PREMISE

The premise is the "story behind the story" of the adventure, the basic plot that gets things going before the player characters get involved. It describes the scale of the adventure, creates the setting of the adventure and hints at the adventure's theme.

The scale of the adventure is the size of the story. A large-scale adventure might consist of the runners taking on a worldwide conspiracy, while a small-scale adventure might involve taking on a single individual based in one city. The scale of an adventure is important because taking on Lofwyr and Saeder-Krupp will be very different from taking on a mid- or small-level corp.

The setting is simply where the main action will take place. The setting consists of one or more locations—such as Seattle, or perhaps various locations around the world—and a *milieu*. The milieu of a setting is simply the surroundings and environment. For example, the milieu of an adventure centered around efforts to steal or protect a new prototype cyberdeck might be filled with deckers, techno fixers, computer designers, lots of Matrix hardware, plenty of decking and so on. The milieu of a search-and-rescue mission in Bug City might be filled with insect spirits and shamans, ex-military personnel, loads of big guns, vicious fire fights, narrow escapes and other action-packed events.

Once the premise has been set, an NPC may hire the players to involve them in the story, or the players' personal goals or contacts may prompt them to become involved on their own initiative.

Gamemasters can make adventure premises as specific or as general as they like. For example, a gamemaster designing a specific premise may decide that a certain corporation (Corporation A) has developed some breakthrough technology for cybereyes. A rival corporation (Corporation B) wants to steal the research on the new discovery so that it can complete the design and sell it first. The runners will become involved when an NPC from Corporation B hires the players to break into and steal the new technology from Corporation A.

By using a general premise, a gamemaster can give players more control over the direction of the game or campaign. For example, a gamemaster might decide that the players' attempts to destroy a particular corporation (preferably a corp they already have reason to hate) will be the general premise of a campaign. The gamemaster will have to create some events to get the players involved—perhaps the corp geeks some of their friends—and provide the players with information about the corporation and its major characters. From there, the players are free to decide how they go about their task; the gamemaster simply fills in the details as events unfold.

For examples of plot premises and how they work within adventures, look at any *Shadowrun* adventure. Sourcebooks, supplements and novels also provide plenty of information for creating general premises for adventures and campaigns.

THE GOAL

Stealing some important data, staying one step ahead of the corporate hit team—every adventure needs a goal for the player characters. Clear-cut goals give the players something to shoot for and help keep an adventure on track.

Gamemasters can set adventure goals themselves, let players set goals, or work with their players when creating goals. In any case, the adventure goal should always reflect the personalities and personal goals of the player characters. In fact, the personal goals of player characters are an excellent basis for the overall premise of an adventure. In the corporate-downfall premise, for example, each player should clearly define why his or her character wants to see the corporation destroyed. Personal vendettas, a desire for profit, a hatred of corporations in general, a sense of moral outrage at the corporation's activities—any of these represent valid personal goals.

Player characters' personal goals and motives provide a good indication of what kind of actions the characters are inclined to take. By noting these motives, the gamemaster can create adventure or campaign opportunities for the players to successfully roleplay their characters' personalities and lifestyles.

After determining the adventure goal, the gamemaster must provide some possible ways the players can achieve the goal. Players often lose interest in an adventure that offers no clear paths to reach the goal. At the same time, don't try to force the players into a particular plan. Offer them a few alternate avenues so that they can decide themselves how to achieve the goal. And don't spell things out for them. The players don't need to know exactly how they might accomplish their task—they simply need to be aware of the possibilities. Prepare for the unexpected—players sometimes devise very strange strategies to achieve a goal.

THE OPPOSITION

Every story needs one or more antagonists, or "bad guys," and *Shadowrun* contains a broad range from which gamemasters can choose. The antagonist is simply the main obstacle between the player characters and their goal. An adventure antagonist can consist of one or more individuals, a group or organization, a great dragon, and so on.

Don't settle for one-dimensional, "cardboard" villains—the antagonist is the main source of conflict and drama in an adventure, and so make your NPC antagonists full-fledged characters, with distinct personalities and motivations. Be thorough and careful when creating the antagonist's abilities and goals.

Complex personalities and motives allow antagonists to act in unpredictable and unexpected ways. Additionally, player characters might be able to exploit an antagonist's personality or motives during their attempts to overcome the opponent.

Creating a personality and goals for an antagonist will also help the gamemaster decide how powerful the opponent is and what types of methods the opponent will use to achieve his, her or its goals. Some opponents may use subtle plots and tricks, even brainwashing others to use as tools against the runners. Other opponents may try to kill the runners outright. An antagonist such as Lofwyr might "befriend" runners and spare their lives—so that he can call in his favor in the future when he needs someone to perform a suicide mission or take the rap for a failed operation.

Finally, keep in mind that NPCs represent only the "traditional" *Shadowrun* opponents. Anything that acts as an obstacle to the players or threatens them can serve as an antagonist—non-metahuman, even non-sentient beings, creatures, systems and so on. A highly sophisticated security system, a hostile and Awakened wilderness, paranormal critters, even normal animals can be used as antagonists. Using non-traditional opponents provides both players and gamemasters with opportunities to stretch their skills, abilities and imaginations.

COMPLICATIONS

If all shadowruns were as simple as gathering allies and blasting through the opposition, they wouldn't be very exciting for long. Heck, if it were that easy, adventures would take

an hour and *Shadowrun* would have gone the way of the dodo. Complications are unexpected twists and turns that help keep things interesting and force the players and characters to stay alert.

Throw in one, perhaps two, three, or more complications in every adventure. A complication can be as simple as a piece of equipment failing or as complex as the adventure's goal turning out to be something other than what the players originally believed. For example, a team performing a run in a Trans-Polar Aleut nation with all the stealth technology and secrecy they can muster might be attacked by a marauding gang—a "gang" that just happens to have the standard-issue weaponry of a corporation the runner's fixer works with on a regular basis. The runners should realize that something's rotten, and they'll have to change their plans accordingly. Or perhaps halfway through a corporate extraction, the targeted research scientist starts mumbling a mysterious name. Just as the runners are about to deliver him to the Johnson, the scientist—who was supposed to be a willing extraction—pops something into his mouth and dies moments later. Time to investigate him, the job, and their employer. Maybe the runners perform a simple burglary, only to discover that the item they've stolen belongs to a dragon's treasure hoard.

Finally, gamemasters can always rely on that old stand-by, the double-crossing Mr. Johnson, who might lie about what corp he's from (if he's from one at all), set the runners up to be killed, not pay them, decide they know too much, pay them in traceable "screamer" credsticks that transmit their locations to the cops, or otherwise use them and "screw them over."

Complications are the main way to inject the unpredictability of "real life" into adventures, keep them interesting for players and provide the "intrigue" that is one of *Shadowrun's* distinguishing characteristics. Like everything else in *Shadowrun*, however, use complications judiciously. If you throw too many complications at players, they'll begin to feel like they have less and less control over their characters' lives, and your game may become frustrating and boring rather than enjoyably complex.

PLOTTING A SHADOWRUN ADVENTURE

When plotting a conventional story, a writer looks at the goals of the main characters and then provides obstacles to those goals to create dramatic tension. *Shadowrun* adventures are plotted in basically the same manner, except that the player characters serve as the protagonists.

For this reason, custom-designed adventures can often be more fun than published *Shadowrun* adventures. A gamemaster knows his player characters better than anyone else, and that knowledge can enable him to accurately tailor adventures to those player characters and their goals.

GETTING STARTED

Every adventure starts with an idea—a seed from which the story grows. Fortunately, there's no lack of sources for adventure ideas. Any *Shadowrun* book—adventure books, sourcebooks and even rulebooks—can provide ideas. In fact, certain sourcebooks, such as *New Seattle* and *Corporate*

Downloead, contain adventure hooks specifically designed to help gamemasters create adventures from the material provided in the book. The "black information" posted by shadowrunners in the various books is especially rich with adventure ideas. This black info, posted by members of the shadow community, often describes various hooks, clues, vendettas and prior runs that can be converted into usable adventures. If a published adventure does not suit your group, it might contain useful plot elements, NPCs and other ideas that can be used in custom-designed adventures.

Even a group's own past games or campaigns can provide adventure ideas. Loose ends and unresolved plot lines from old adventures can serve as ideas for new adventures. Bring back an old adversary that everyone thought was dead or introduce a "successor" intent on carrying on the adversary's schemes. Call in some of the old favors that the player characters owe their contacts and allies or have one of them ask for a favor from one of the characters.

With a little imagination, nearly anything can provide suitable adventure ideas—films, novels, other roleplaying games, TV, video games, news media and magazines, even events at work or school. Try keeping a notebook or a journal handy and jotting down anything you see or read that sounds like it might have potential use in an adventure story. When you're looking for ideas for a game session or campaign, you can review your notes and choose a single event or concept, or combine several related items into a complex, intriguing story line.

CHOOSING THE CAST

Choosing a cast for the adventure—the NPCs, organizations, groups and opponents involved in the story—provides yet another way to shape the adventure. Different "actors" have different motives, goals and operating methods. Using characters that play a part in published *Shadowrun* books helps tie an adventure to the larger *Shadowrun* world.

A gamemaster can choose the cast of an adventure at any point while creating an adventure. Some may prefer to do so after deciding on a premise. Others may want to start by casting the major "actors" in the adventure, then establishing a premise based on the interests and previous actions of the people and organizations to be involved in the story.

The actors in an adventure can be individuals, small or large groups or organizations, or any combination of the "players" of the *Shadowrun* universe. An actor may play his part on the stage or behind the scenes. Generally, big actors and big adventures go hand in hand. For example, a war between local gangs can seem fairly routine to some runners. But if the Triads are backing one gang and the Mafia is backing the other, a bigger and potentially more dangerous scenario begins to take shape. Now, if that same war takes place near a secret Saeder-Krupp research facility, Lofwyr himself might take notice and really heat things up.

The following entries offer a few suggestions for potential actors based on descriptions of various individuals, groups and organizations in published *Shadowrun* books, though this list is by no means exhaustive. Many *Shadowrun* sourcebooks also include descriptions of specific NPCs and organizations, and suggestions for using them in adventures and campaigns.

Corporations

Big megacorporations such as Ares and Mitsuhama have been fiercely competing with one another for decades. With the recent rise of mid- and small-sized corps in the *Shadowrun* universe, business has become more cutthroat than ever.

Organized Crime

The Mafia and yakuza come to mind immediately, but don't forget the Triads, Seoulpa Rings, t-bird smugglers and pirates. All of these organized crime groups prey on innocent people, not-so-innocent people and on one another. Deadly power struggles are common between and even within these groups. Any community that would be reluctant to take its problems to law enforcement makes a tempting target for organized-crime protection rackets, and mobsters continue to control a cornucopia of crime industries, ranging from smuggling to BTL production to sexual slavery.

Cops

Lone Star, Knight Errant, Hard Corps, Wolverine, Eagle, Thugs with Guns—who and what do the law-enforcement organizations in the *Shadowrun* universe really serve and protect? Are they clean or corrupt? Where do their jurisdictions end?

Law-enforcement types share a natural, mutual hostility with shadowrunners, and there's no better cover for a racket than a police badge.

Gangs

Shadowrun gangs run the gamut from mutual-protection clubs of friends to groups of street punks who joytoy for money to RV-equipped go-gangs that roam the interstate highways to syndicates of hardened criminals with drugs, guns and connections. There's also the old-fashioned biker gangs that hang in heavy-metal bars and provide security for concerts just to make ends meet, and a hundred other specialty gangs.

Military/Para-Military Groups

The land, sea and air forces of any country possess military resources that most corps can't match, including submarine fleets, entire divisions of soldiers, novahot tech toys and major mojo. Nearly every modern military contains air, armor and recon branches, as well as those nifty Special Forces. The GI Joes and Janes of the Sixth World are usually called in to handle seriously weird magic situations or unexplained phenomena (such as Bug City), but the militaries of nearly any combination of countries (the Ute Nation and Tír na nÓg, CAS and ... another faction of the CAS) might face off over matters of "vital national interest" in the world of *Shadowrun.*

Conflict might also come in the form of the Seattle Metroplex Guardsmen and other civil policing groups sworn to control riots and otherwise keep order in Seattle.

Politicians and Policlubs

Politics is a dirty business, so it's not surprising that shadowruns can become particularly messy when they're politically motivated. City councilmen, mayors, governors, senators, even folks no one thinks about, such as Supreme Court justices and the Surgeon General, may hire shadowrunners to act as bodyguards, gather information on their opponents or conduct "dirty tricks" campaigns.

Policlubs also present a wide range of roleplaying possibilities. Metahuman and human rights, secessionists, abortion, the death penalty, gun control—name any cause or prejudice you can think of, and the odds are there's a policlub espousing or condemning it.

International Opponents

Megacorporations may have usurped much of the power once wielded by national governments, but that hasn't lowered the stakes of international geopolitics and it hasn't reduced the number of international spies, wheeler-dealers and terrorists running around. The CIA, Interpol, the successors of the KGB, the Tir Paladins, international fixers, arms dealers and general troublemaking terrorists are just a few potential international actors that can play a role in an adventure.

Media Types

Media types can add a dash of glamour, danger and good old-fashioned sex appeal to an adventure. Trid networks, radio, simsense, music, sports and flatscreen movie theaters remain big business in the Sixth World. From simple radio interviews to Desert Wars, from pirate trideo broadcasts to desperate rockers faking their own deaths, the media types of the *Shadowrun* world will go to any lengths to boost their ratings and sales. Muckraking investigative reporting shows, daytime talk shows, combat-game shows, professional wrestling, sim-porn, music trideos—they all generate billions of nuyen each year, and the assorted stars, has-beens, producers, media conglomerates and organized-crime types involved in the business fight tooth-and-nail for their share.

Shadowrunners and Other Shady Characters

Player characters need not be the only shadowrunners involved in an adventure. Shadowrunning teams operate more loosely than organized-crime groups and corporations and generally consist of individuals with greater skills and more highly developed talents than those that make up gangs. By definition, shadowrunners do the work that no one else can or will do. The profession generally attracts the marginal types who just don't fit in with twenty-first-century militaries, corporations, organized crime groups and other "acceptable" societal norms. Consequently, NPC shadowrunners provide an excellent way for gamemasters to introduce wild, outlandish and colorful characters into adventures. Furthermore, runners are a notoriously competitive bunch, and no one makes a better match for a shadowrunner than another runner.

Ordinary People

Ordinary people are the folks you deal with during your "normal" daily life—bank employees, the clerks at the Department of Motor Vehicles, insurance adjusters, temporary employee services, caterers, janitors, garbage men, vidphone solicitors, college professors, lawyers, squatters, girlfriends, boyfriends and so on. All these people have a place in the *Shadowrun* universe, too. Watch television for two hours. Design a run that involves a member of a profession portrayed on a program or commercial, or a scene that requires runners to put on the hat of an ordinary person for a little while. Interaction with ordinary people might not create great drama, but it might generate some light comic relief, remind the runners who gets hurt when they act carelessly, develop new contacts or add a little metahuman interest to an otherwise corp-focused story line.

Odds and Ends

The *Shadowrun* world offers a mix of science fiction and fantasy that generates a wide range of individual beings and organizations unique to the universe (or distinct from similar groups in other mythos), such as ancient elves, free spirits, dragons, Things Man Was Not Meant to Know, ghosts, vampires, werejaguars and initiatory groups, not to mention whatever's bouncing around in the Matrix. A member of any of these species or groups can serve as an actor in a campaign, or gamemasters can create their own unique life forms based on these types.

THE DECISION TREE

Published *Shadowrun* adventures use a "decision tree" format. Unlike a single, linear plot line, the decision-tree format describes several courses of action player characters may take. The players' decisions, in turn, determine the adventure's outcome. By using the decision-tree format in your own adventures, you can provide player characters with the same flexibility and decision-making power.

Start by thinking of your adventure plot as a flow chart with two points. Point A represents the beginning of the adventure, the point at which the players become involved. Point B represents the end of the adventure, at which the player characters achieve the adventure goal. A linear plot would have a single path from Point A to Point B. In the decision-tree format, however, multiple paths, or "branches," connect the beginning and end of the adventure.

To create each different path, simply start at Point A and write down the possible courses of action the characters might take at that point. For example, if they are meeting with a Mr. Johnson who offers them a job, they have two obvious choices—accept the job or reject it. Depending on the player characters, they might also take other actions, such as starting a fight with the Johnson. Once you've determined the character's likely choices, start a plot line for each choice. The next point on Plot Line 1 will cover what happens if the runners accept the job offer. The next point on Plot Line 2 will cover what happens if they reject the offer. Plot Line 3 would cover what happens if they attack the Johnson.

Continue this process at each event in the different plot lines. Simply ask yourself, what are the characters likely to do, and what will happen next because of their choice? Make notes about the NPC opponents the characters are likely to encounter along each plot line, important locations where the action will take place, and so on. These notes prepare you to run each encounter as it occurs, regardless of the path the characters follow. Be sure to note any complications you intend to throw at the players (see *Complications,* p. 95, and *When the Drek Hits the Fan,* below, for more information)

Keep in mind that different plot lines can merge and intersect. The characters' decision at one point may lead them back to another plot line, or various plot lines may lead back to one main line. Additionally, some scenes in an adventure can be arranged so that they can take place in a variety of orders without affecting the overall plot of the adventure. For example, some scenes may simply describe different locations characters can visit while doing legwork; the characters can visit the locations in whatever order they choose without changing the effect of the information they discover.

No matter how many different "branches" you plan for your decision tree, players tend to surprise you with unexpected plans that take them along paths you didn't predict. In these cases, simply stay flexible and modify your planned material to suit the new direction.

For examples of the decision-tree format, look at a few published *Shadowrun* adventures and outline the various plots. You'll quickly recognize the different branches of the decision tree used in each adventure.

WHEN THE DREK HITS THE FAN

Besides injecting the unpredictability of real life into adventures, complications make convenient turning points to change the direction of an adventure and keep the player characters from proceeding directly to the adventure goal.

Usually two or three major complications are enough to get the adventure off and running. After that, keep an eye out for the complications that the players themselves will provide for you and learn to use them to your advantage. For example, if one character badly fails a Stealth Test and is captured by corp security while the other runners escape, weave that complication into the story. Will the corporation get information from the captured runner? What will it do with that information? Will the captive runner's companions try to rescue him or hang him out to dry? If they abandon him, how will the captured runner react? Even one or two complications can spawn numerous new plots and subplots.

See *Complications*, p. 95, for more information.

Allies

Allies are contacts and NPCs who can help player characters achieve their adventure goal. Though they need not function as a deus ex machina, the fact remains that allies are often most helpful as tools to get the runners out of an impossible situation and back on track in the adventure.

Like antagonists, allies should possess their own personalities and motives. They shouldn't simply wait around to offer help when the player characters need it. Every ally should have his, her or its own reasons for helping the player characters. Some might help the runners out of mutual respect or friendship. Others may offer to help for their own selfish reasons—usually because they are opposed to the antagonist as well. Still others may help because the player characters' success will further their own plots. Consequently, characters may want to keep a close eye on their allies as well as their enemies—because an ally who is helpful one day may abandon or even turn on the players the next day.

The most fickle ally of any shadowrunner is Fate—also known as Lady Luck, Fortune, Chance, kismet and many other names. Fate provides gamemasters with a convenient way to give player characters lucky breaks when needed to keep an adventure moving along. Unfortunately, what Fate giveth, Fate also taketh away—runners who benefit from sudden good fortune may run into unexpected complications later on (when such complications suit the gamemaster's plans, of course).

AFTERMATH

Once the characters achieve the adventure goal or give up trying, it's time to wrap up the adventure. Consider a variety of endings for the adventure. Try not to fall in love with one particular ending or climatic scene. The decisions of your player characters are likely to change your plot early in the adventure, and an ending that doesn't flow naturally from earlier events will seem contrived. Simply keep the scene in mind in case an opportunity to use it arises in another adventure.

The consequences, or aftermath, of different endings may also affect which ending you choose to present. Events that happen in one adventure can be used in future games to provide continuity and richness to your campaign. Jotting down answers to the following questions is an excellent way to determine likely directions for the aftermath of an adventure:

· Did the players leave any loose ends hanging? If so, would any of them be fun to pursue in later adventures?
· Did the runner's actions hurt or anger any NPCs, corporations, or other groups (specifically, anyone who might want revenge)?
· Which NPCs and player characters were the major "actors" in the story? Which ones acted memorably?

· Did the runners' actions attract any media attention? If so, would this attention mark the runners as targets?
· Did the runners create any Enemies for themselves?
· Did other parties notice the runners' actions?
· Did the runners leave evidence behind? If so, how much? (Runners may be SINless, but if corporate security forces and cops repeatedly find the same unidentified fingerprints and lots of shell casings at specific break-ins, they're going to start a file on the people who left those prints and casings.)
· What's the real identity of the Johnson? Have the runners worked for him or her before? If so, are the two runs connected somehow? Why is the Johnson interested in the runners? Is there anyone who might pay for a run against *this* Johnson?
· Is it time to let a player character achieve the personal goal that she's always dreamed of—and will it happen in the way she expected?

PAYMENT AND REWARD

The end of a successful run means it's time to count the nuyen. How much money is an appropriate fee for a team of runners? The gamemaster ultimately decides, based on the risk of the run, the employer's ability and willingness to pay and the runners' reputations, but the following guidelines may help set appropriate fees.

First, keep in mind that player characters will average about one shadowrun per month. A good starting point for an individual runner's payment is one month's living expenses, plus the cost of gear needed for the run. If the player characters on the team have different lifestyles, use an average of the characters' lifestyle costs to determine their living expenses.

As a general guideline, gamemasters can also use the Baseline Shadowrun Payment Table, p. 100, modifying the figures to select a payment range that seems appropriate. The fees listed can be considered the low-end rate for certain kinds of runs; if the run requires more work or risk, or the target or runners themselves are of a higher-than-normal caliber, the rate should go up. The rates given are for the task alone and do not take into account the number of runners; teams with more characters can generally expect more. The rates also do not necessarily cover expenses, "hazard pay" or "death benefits." Remember, the rates given are only a benchmark figure, and will likely need to be adjusted to fit your particular style of play.

An occasional big windfall serves as a great campaign tease. Windfalls make excellent pay-offs after hard-fought campaigns or excellent stepping stones for new campaigns. Keep windfalls rare—they should reflect the difficulty of the campaign that's just finished or the difficulties likely to afflict the upcoming campaign. As a rule of thumb, a windfall should equal roughly six months of the character's lifestyle cost. Windfalls always come from unexpected sources.

Runner fees and windfalls need not be briefcases filled with credsticks. In fact, alternate payment methods are a great way to enable player characters to survive and continue to perform runs without accumulating fortunes. Instead of nuyen, payment may take the form of valuable data, individuals, equipment, paid expenses, time in a magic-research facility or special Matrix access. SIN numbers also make good alternate payment, as do DocWagon contracts and cyberware implants. For more ideas, look in the Equipment Tables at the end of the *Shadowrun* rulebook or other *Shadowrun* books. These sections contain numerous items that most characters can't afford but would willingly accept from a grateful Johnson.

Double all base fees and windfalls if you're running an amoral campaign in which the player characters are more concerned with making money than doing the right or honorable thing (see *Karma and the Amoral Campaign*, p. 80). Adjust fees and windfalls to match the needs of your game.

ARCHETYPAL ADVENTURE PLOTS

Experienced *Shadowrun* players may find their characters caught up in certain "classic" adventure plots again and again, each time struggling against a different variation on a theme. This section describes several of these archetypal adventure plots and provides ideas for using them as models for your own unique adventures.

Remember that variety is the spice of life—and of *Shadowrun* adventures. Every new plot or twist on a familiar story creates fond memories and keeps players coming back to the table. Keep your players' interest by mixing things up. Change the specifics, or "variables," of an adventure to keep the mood, tone and focus of adventures fresh. Sure, a dragon or powerful elf that's pulling the strings during an adventure is fine—once. Maybe even twice, but your players are going to get bored if they continually see the same old face.

ASSASSINATION

The employer wants someone dead. Variables include:
- Level and types of security around the target (magic, Matrix and physical security measures)
- The events triggered by the target's death
- The conditions for the assassination. Trying to make someone's death look like an accident or a specific type of accident (run over with a garbage truck, heart attack, electrocuted by a power line, random violence) is a lot tougher than simply blowing the target away.

BLACKMAIL

The employer wants evidence that the target is doing something wrong. Not only that, he wants the runners to let the target know that someone's on to

BASELINE SHADOWRUN PAYMENT TABLE	
Run	**Bottom-line Fee**
Assassination	5,000¥
Bodyguard/Security Duty	200¥/day
Burglary	2,000¥
Courier Run	1,000¥
Datasteal	20% value of data
Distraction	1,000¥
Destruction	5,000¥
Enforcement	1,000¥
Encryption/Decryption	200¥ per MP
Extraction	20,000¥
Hacking	1,000¥ x Host's Security Value
Investigation	200¥/day
Smuggling Run	5,000¥

him and to collect hush money from the target. Generally, blackmail jobs require long-term employment and extra levels of secrecy on the part of the runners.

BODYGUARD

The player characters are hired to keep a subject alive or undamaged. Variables include:
- The subject's lifestyle and health
- The resources, intentions, knowledge and expertise of his would-be killers

COURIER/SMUGGLING

The team must pick up a message or transport cargo from one location to another. Variables include:
- The point of origin and destination—Redmond, Tir Tairngire, a remote spot in the desert, a crippled submarine, Maria Mercurial's penthouse, a restricted military base and so on
- The number of borders that must be crossed
- The mode of transport—foot, train, car, boat, panzer, ultralight and so on
- The nature of the cargo—a person, chip, suitcase, 500 underfed security dogs, communications suite, nuclear bomb, magical focus, red rose and so on
- The legality of the cargo

DATASTEAL

The shadowrunners have to snatch data from a highly secured location. Variables include:
- The target location—for example, CIA headquarters, a remote experimental lab in the Amazon rain forest, the Zurich-Orbital bank, a flophouse in downtown Seattle
- The form of the target data—for example, computer data hooked up to the Matrix, off-line computer data, hard copy, ideas in someone's head
- The nature of the target data—for example, research plans, names and locations of undercover cops, Things Man Was Not Meant to Know, kiss-and-tell info on the president
- What happens if the runners scan the data—for example, they discover their employer is betraying them, an ancient curse boils their brains, Mr. Johnson sends goons to silence them, they find out they should give it to someone worthier, they find out the identity of their father

DISTRACTION

A duplicitous Johnson hires the runners to perform a mission. Unknown to them, they are really serving to distract attention from some other nefarious activity. Variables include:

- Who the runners are impersonating—shadowrunners, uniformed Lone Star cops, eco-terrorists, Johnny Whocker and the Guitar Trogs and so on
- The goal of their mission—break into an embassy, beat protesters senseless on camera, attract media attention by blowing up an oil refinery, play a concert and attract an assassin's bullet and so on
- The real story—another shadowrun across town, interrupting the first five minutes of a TV sitcom to prove a point, giving the Mr. Johnson time to escape, Johnny wants out of the music business and so on
- Whether or not the characters know they are only a distraction for a larger plot

DESTRUCTION

The employer hires the team to erase, wipe out, or otherwise destroy a target. Variables include:

- The target itself—for example, a datafile, North Sea oil rig, ritual sample, biohazard, "indestructible" magical focus, graveyard, a centimeter of a summoning circle
- How many targets exist—for example, ten copies, two linked rigs with a narrow bridge, seventeen hairs
- Whether or not the job endangers innocent bystanders

ENCRYPTION/DECRYPTION

The employer wants something decoded or secured. The job can serve as a quick shadowrun in itself, be tacked onto another shadowrun, or serve as a complication.

ENFORCEMENT

The runners are hired to "send a message" to someone. Variables include:

- How the message is delivered—for example, a stern warning, nailing a dead cat to the target's door, planting a bomb in the target's refrigerator, tattooing the message on the foreheads of the target's kids
- How publicly the message is delivered—switching the simsense chips on the target's bedside table, kicking down the target's front door, broadcasting a ten-minute death threat over every major network and so on
- The size and power of the target—for example, a single person, a family, a group of protesters, rowdy folks at a bar, Ares Macrotechnology

HOAX/COUNTERFEIT

The runners must use their creative talents and connections to stage a hoax or create a counterfeit item. Examples include faking a death, creating a false charity or bank that will attract deposits from a target, falsifying records or "framing" someone for a crime.

INVESTIGATION

The runners are hired to gather information on an event or person. Variables include:

- The nature of the information. "Low-stakes" information includes evidence for messy divorce cases, missing persons,

who was present when a robbery took place and so on. "High-stakes" information includes photo reconnaissance for a military strike, political secrets, enough evidence for the police to bust a drug ring.

- The means of gathering the information—for example, interviewing witnesses, infiltrating a weapons-smuggling ring, Matrix searches, "test-driving" an experimental combat vehicle or weapon system

EXTRACTION (KIDNAPPING)

The employer wants someone bodily picked up and taken somewhere. This is usually known as an "extraction," because the target can be willing or unwilling. Variables include:

- The target—for example, a dangerous parole violator, simsense starlet, researcher who wants to defect from his corporation, ornery elephants
- How long the target must be held—1 day, 3 months and so on
- How the target should be treated—like a queen, don't break more than two bones and so on
- The size of the target—for example, one individual, a group of six people, all the passengers on an airplane
- Additional instructions—keep the target captive on his private cruise liner, deliver him to another team, brainwash her, execute him, write the ransom note, escort the target to the personnel department at Corporation X and so on

PLANT

The runners are hired to plant an object somewhere. Objects might include electronic listening devices (bugs), remotely controlled or timed bombs, microfilm or datafiles for later pick-up, and restricted milspec weapons.

RETRIEVAL OF OBJECT

This is the classic "go get the secret prototype" mission. Gamemasters can vary it by substituting different items for the prototype—a powerful focus or magical weapon, a symbolically significant item such as the Holy Grail or the sword of the employer's grandfather, and so on. Other variables include the security around the object and other people intent on "retrieving" it for themselves.

SECURITY

The employer needs someone to provide security. Variables include:

- Item/subject to be protected—for example, a ritual magic circle, vacuum-sealed vampire, entire rock concert, your fixer during a BTL deal, a corporate facility, a storehouse of food
- Whether or not the runners know the true nature of the item or the real identity of the subject
- Type of security to be provided—physical, magical, Matrix, any combination of those and so on
- Restrictions on the level of force the runners can use. Remember, drunk bar patrons sue, black-ops teams don't.
- The threat from which the team is protecting the item/person—for example, petty criminals, other shadowrunners, heavily armed mercenaries, corporate hit teams

TAILCHASER

This adventure plot creates a specialized sort of double-cross. The employer has two or more goals that the runners may fulfill either by succeeding in their task, failing in their task, being captured by the opposition, dying in the attempt or participating in any number of other outcomes. Whatever the runners accomplish or fail to accomplish provides the employer with a certain amount of desired information, and he, she or it walks away from the run satisfied with the results. The primary effect of this type of run is to demoralize the player characters—no matter how well or how poorly they perform their task, the employer is equally pleased with the outcome, forcing the characters to accept that their actions just didn't matter. This type of adventure can be particularly devastating if the team loses a member or two in the course of the run.

WAR

The employer wants a *lot* of people hurt, intimidated, ruined or killed so they can no longer harm his interests or hinder his plans. The runners may start slowly and gradually escalate their tactics or simply begin with a full-scale conflict.

WILD THINGS

The runners are hired to observe, track, capture and tame, or hunt and kill a particular critter or critters. Variables include:
- The target critter(s) itself—for example, wolf pack, troglodyte, nomad, wraith, dragon
- The innate intelligence of the target critter
- The critter's natural habitat

CAMPAIGN CONSIDERATIONS

A campaign is a linked series of adventures that form a larger overall story, like individual episodes of a television show or the chapters of a novel. Characters develop and change over the course of a campaign, just as they do in other stories. A campaign also allows a gaming group to tell many different stories with the same set of characters.

A successful campaign, like a successful adventure, requires some planning. This section describes the various considerations a gamemaster should take into account while planning a campaign and includes suggestions for creating fun and interesting story lines.

PLAYER CHARACTERS

The player characters themselves are probably the most important consideration of creating a campaign, because the player characters' interests and abilities will determine the most satisfying type of campaign for the group to play. For example, if all the players want to play magician characters, the gamemaster should create a campaign specially tailored to provide plenty of opportunities for them to use magic. If the players want to run a team of cyber-solider mercenaries, the gamemaster can go for an over-the-top action-oriented campaign. Gamemasters may even wish to use one of the specialized alternate campaign types provided in *Alternate Campaign Concepts*, beginning on p. 109, to create a challenging campaign tailored to their players.

In addition to selecting an appropriate campaign type for the player group, the gamemaster should try to devise a campaign that provides each individual player character with opportunities to use his or her unique abilities and "grab the spotlight."

Creating the Team's Characters

Players have two options when creating a team. They may develop their characters as a group, or each player may develop his or her character without any input from the other players.

Designing characters as a group helps ensure that they will fit well together as a team. Players can provide their characters with common enemies, give them previous adventures together or connect them to each other with ties of friendship or blood. By working together, players can ensure that their characters represent a variety of different specialties and abilities, enhancing the versatility of the group as a whole and reducing the number of characters possessing similar skills and abilities. Designing characters as a group also enables the gamemaster to tailor his adventures and campaigns to the skills of the characters more easily and provide enough situations for all of the characters to get in on the action.

Creating characters as a group, however, also takes away the element of surprise that adds to the fun of discovering things about your teammates. By designing their characters without input from the rest of the group, players can give their characters background, contacts, Edges and Flaws and abilities that they keep secret from their teammates. Such secrets can serve as jumping-off points for unexpected events and opportunities for roleplaying. The drawback to individual character generation is that it may produce ill-matched or unevenly balanced teams. When team members have little in common, simply getting along with one another can become an adventure for the player characters.

Assembling the Team

The gamemaster can assemble the individual player characters into a team in a variety of ways. Providing the player characters with a common contact (fixer, Mr. Johnson, mob boss and so on) is probably the easiest way. In this case, the contact has a job that requires the specific skills of each character.

Giving the team members a common purpose may produce the most cohesive group. The common interest may be as simple as staying alive and making a fast nuyen on the mean streets of the Sixth World or something more involved. Generally, the more invested each character is in the common purpose, the more likely the runners are to work together, though that doesn't mean that the characters have to like one another. The *Shadowrun* universe contains plenty of individuals who don't like each other but are willing to put aside their mutual dislike to achieve a common goal.

Defending against a common enemy or opponent offers one example of a common purpose. In this example, if time allows, the gamemaster can even run a few preliminary mini-adventures with one or two player characters at a time to introduce or foreshadow the enemy's interest in each character.

Fostering Team Spirit

Assembling a team is only one of the challenges facing a gamemaster and his or her players. Keeping a team together can prove even more difficult.

Both players and gamemasters share a responsibility to tolerate one another and find ways for their characters to work together as teams, but gamemasters have the greatest stake in keeping things together—simply because gamemasters spend so much time preparing adventures and campaigns.

Assembling a group of players who get along in real life is a simple way to increase the chances that the player's characters will get along in the fictional universe. However, the power to roll dice and tell someone you've killed their character can produce tensions between even the best of friends.

Gamemasters can promote "team spirit" among characters by emphasizing the characters' non-business relationships. Characters that hang out and relax with one another are more likely to work out their disagreements peacefully than characters who are mere business acquaintances, because roleplaying non-business time gives characters chances to learn about one another. For example, the appearance of a new troll teammate who went berserk and killed every single person in the Aztechnology building might prompt characters to call the cyber-psycho squad. However, those same characters might have a different view of their new teammate when they learn that Azzie goons killed the troll's sister first—and in a particularly unpleasant fashion.

Isolating a team of characters from the rest of the world can also help foster team spirit. Isolating a team forces the members to depend on and trust one another. For example, if you dump a Seattle-based team in the middle of the Mojave Desert or drop a team of human runners into the Ork Underground, they will need to rely on each other simply because they won't be able to trust anyone else. Even the simple act of putting street runners into unfamiliar corporate territory can encourage them to work together.

A common enemy or opponent—an individual, group or entity that the characters can defeat only by banding together—may also force characters to work together and foster team spirit. Running a game session only when all the players are present may also promote team spirit. If characters are always hired as a unit, they are likely to feel like a team. Conversely, if new characters are constantly coming and going, the player characters may view themselves more as individuals than as a team.

Finally, listen to your players and try to give them what they want. Players who are happy with the game and their characters are more tolerant of their fellow players' idiosyncrasies and mistakes than players who are unhappy with a game. Similarly, everyone enjoys a chance to play the hero every now and then, so give each player character opportunities to do so. This will reduce jealousy and rivalries among player characters and make player characters more supportive of one another.

Team Tensions

While playing together as a cohesive, trusting team offers many advantages, occasional tensions and suspicions among teammates can provide great roleplaying opportunities. Team tensions can inspire impassioned arguments and conversations among characters and memorable nights of roleplaying for players. For the sake of enjoyable gaming, however, it's probably best to develop players' team spirit and group cohesion before introducing team tensions. A group consisting of five ork street sams and a Humanis decker is likely to lead to a quick fight and a dead character. But characters who learn that the new teammate who saved their lives last night is a former terrorist may be willing to get along despite deeply felt, contrasting beliefs.

Keep in mind that some issues are more volatile than others. Characters who might forgive a new teammate's questionable past may not be willing to accept a racist character or one who acts specifically against them.

THEMES

The overall themes of a campaign may determine the direction and tone of the campaign as well as specific adventure plots. For example, adventures for a campaign based on themes of revenge will be quite different than adventures for a campaign based on themes of greed.

Other themes include heroism, redemption, fighting the good fight, making as much money as possible without getting caught, improving the living conditions of a neighborhood, protecting children, wiping out prejudice, wiping out another race, saving or destroying the earth and so on.

Certain themes may also provide common purposes for groups of player characters. For example, characters in a revenge-themed campaign may want to settle a score with a common enemy. Characters in a redemption-themed campaign might join together to perform a mission to redeem themselves or others.

MORALITY

Players and gamemasters should also consider the moral tone of their campaigns. Are the player characters heartless mercenaries who would do anything for nuyen, or are they knights in shining chrome and leather? Most characters fall somewhere in between, but gamemasters and their players may still want to establish some campaign ground rules early on. These types of ground rules will let players know what is expected of their characters and prevent unpleasant surprises later in the game.

Some groups prefer principled characters who avoid unnecessary violence and killing. Other groups prefer plenty of combat and have no problem with geeking any opponents who come along, as long as the money is right. The *Shadowrun* universe has room for both types of players and everyone in between. Each player group must decide for itself what kind of team it wants to play.

SCOPE

In a roleplaying adventure, the player characters are always at the center of the story. The scope of a campaign is simply how far out from that center the characters' story extends. How much impact will the characters' actions have on

the rest of the world? Are they just cogs in the big machine of the metroplex, unable to really change the way things are, or are they visionaries with the power and influence to shape the fate of nations? The scope of the campaign can determine its stability and direction, as well as how it will change and grow over time.

Campaigns with limited scopes are usually best for beginners, because attempting to comprehend and react to all of the events of the *Shadowrun* universe can be quite daunting. A small scale also allows the gamemaster to control the campaign more easily, though it limits the players' options a bit as well.

More experienced players may find small-scale campaigns too confining, while others find them very comfortable. The players of an individual group should decide if they prefer to move on to larger-scale adventures. Players should also consider their relative skill, ability and power levels when selecting the scope of their campaign. Characters who aren't capable of tackling world-class threats may want to stick to small-scale campaigns lest they find themselves hopelessly outclassed. On the other hand, a global-scale campaign may present the ideal challenge for experienced runners who want to topple or protect governments, megacorps or other powerful and influential figures—and are ready to take on very powerful opponents.

LOCATION, LOCATION, LOCATION

The Sixth World offers a broad range of adventure settings, from urban sprawls to Awakened wilderness areas. Gamemasters should consider the settings that will be used in a campaign while planning the campaign, because the choice of settings can have a great impact on the story. Gamemasters should ask themselves questions such as: Will a campaign's adventures take place in a specific metroplex or nation? Which locales will the characters frequent? Which corporations have the most influence in those places? What is the local shadow-community like? What are the local laws?

When planning campaign settings, gamemasters should avoid the common temptation to send their players bouncing all over the globe during a single campaign (unless, of course, the players' group is a jet-setting, globe-hopping team of high-priced runners). In many cases, players in globe-hopping campaigns start feeling that nothing in the campaign is permanent or important.

THE FIRST RUN

The first run of any campaign is very important, because it sets the tone of the campaign to follow and establishes the overall themes and premises of the campaign. Like the first line in a short story or the first scene in a movie, the first run of a campaign must grab the players' attention or they may soon lose interest in the game. Additionally, it should "hook" the player characters without overwhelming them; it should provide the basis for spin-off adventures and encourage the players to continue pursuing a campaign. It should provide time for the different characters to develop without becoming overly long or boring. It should reveal enough to keep the players involved without giving away too many mysteries.

Perhaps the best way to ensure that a first run does all these things is to incorporate into the first adventure the various elements discussed in this section—opportunities for each player character to shine, an exciting and climactic plot, an external threat that brings the players together as a team, and so on.

CHARACTER ADVANCEMENT

Gamemasters can control the speed of character advancement in their campaigns by adjusting the size of Karma awards for adventures, providing opportunities for the characters to use their accumulated Karma, controlling payment for runs and adjusting the runners' expenses as necessary. Larger Karma awards enable player characters to advance and gain power quickly, while smaller Karma awards slow character advancement. Similarly, higher fees for runs will generally enable players to buy more equipment, though gamemasters can exert control over player characters' wealth by raising or lowering their expenses.

For more information on handling Karma and character advancement, see the *Advanced Rules* section, p. 79.

KEEPING IT FRESH

Over time, any extended campaign may become a bit stale. However, inventive gamemasters and creative players can take several steps to revitalize campaigns and keep them fresh and interesting.

Simply taking a break from the campaign and setting it aside for a time may be enough to rejuvenate a campaign. A break gives the gamemaster's and the players' creative "batteries" time to recharge and may inspire renewed interest when the gamemaster and players return to the campaign. Every group must determine the appropriate length for a break. Some groups may find that a few weeks is enough, while other groups may want to take a few months off.

Alternatively, an ongoing campaign might need something to shake it up a bit and get things moving again. The gamemaster might want to change the campaign's theme or focus to help breathe new life into the story and the characters. For example, one *Shadowrun* campaign that had been running for several years had reached a point where the player characters were highly capable shadowrunners with extensive backgrounds, resources and abilities. The players no longer found the "typical" shadowruns challenging or interesting, and they had begun to grow tired of their characters. To shake things up, the gamemaster set up a new series of adventures in which the player characters were framed for the murder of an important political figure and sent to a UCAS federal prison. An influential fixer sprang the shadowrunners from prison within a relatively short period, but during their jail time the runners lost most of their contacts and resources, and their reputations took a serious beating. The characters found themselves on the streets with little more than the clothes on their backs, in debt to a mysterious fixer and looking to clear their names and avenge themselves against the people who framed them. The campaign was off and running again.

The *Underworld Sourcebook, New Seattle, Corporate Download* and other sourcebooks all offer plentiful twists that can help change the direction of a campaign and spark new interest among players.

BLUEBOOKING

"Bluebooking" is an excellent roleplaying and story-development tool for campaigns.

Players who use a bluebook simply keep records of their characters in notebooks. A character's bluebook is like a diary—it can include everything from personal recollections to private conversations between characters. They can be used to record character stories and background and between-adventure activities.

Using bluebooking to record private conversations between characters or between characters and gamemasters enables characters and gamemasters to keep secrets from other players. This use makes bluebooking an ideal tool to inject paranoia, conspiracies, or simply a bit of mystery into a game. To use bluebooking for secrets, a character simply writes down the secret message or information in his notebook, then shows the notebook to the gamemaster or the character with whom he wants to share the secret.

Gamemasters should carefully control bluebooking in their games, however, because players may begin to conduct nearly all of their interactions by bluebooking (which is not necessarily a bad thing, as long as it's intentional) and abandon active roleplaying.

ENDING THE CAMPAIGN

Gamemasters can devise dramatic, "blaze-of-glory" endings for campaigns or simply allow their player characters to go their separate ways and break up the team. In either case, the events and fallout of the old campaign can be used as source material for a new campaign. Friends and foes alike can resurface in the new campaign, along with unfinished business or other loose ends. If, for any reason, the players are no longer interested in playing their characters at the end of a campaign, that need not spell the end of the player characters. See *Retirement,* p. 87 for suggestions on using old characters in continuing games.

SOLUTIONS TO COMMON PROBLEMS

Most experienced gamemasters face the following common challenges when gamemastering *Shadowrun* (and other) games and campaigns:
- controlling "power gamers," players who create super-characters so powerful that they dominate the game
- maintaining overall game balance
- satisfactorily involving deckers and other unique character types in games
- effectively using the overwhelming amount of *Shadowrun* information available

This section offers advice on dealing with these difficult situations.

POWER GAMING

Power gamers, sometimes (unkindly) referred to as "munchkins" or "Monty Haulers," are players who create "super-characters"—magicians with Initiate grade ratings in the double digits and truckloads of foci and bound spirits, street sammies with so much cyberware they become virtual walking tanks, deckers with Computer Skills of 12 and cyberdecks that make the Fairlight Excalibur look like an abacus and so on.

Well, there's nothing wrong with power gaming. (Despite persistent rumors, FASA does not maintain a cadre of game police ready to kick your door in, confiscate your rulebook and drag you before the game Inquisition for violating the unwritten laws of *Shadowrun*. Well, actually there are game police—

but they're too busy checking on *BattleTech* rules violators to bother with *Shadowrun* groups.) Seriously, FASA couldn't be more pleased to hear that you're enjoying *Shadowrun,* no matter how you play it.

However, if power gaming starts killing the fun in your game, then it's a problem. Generally, such discrepancies can be avoided by meeting with your players and deciding on the general power levels you want in your campaign before you start — a low-powered "street-level" campaign versus a wild and wahoo power game of super-characters, for example. Even conscientious planning may not prevent a player character from amassing a superhuman power level that begins to spoil the fun for everyone else. Gamemasters may use the strategies described in *Obnoxious Characters* to control such players.

OBNOXIOUS CHARACTERS

Sometimes, players and/or their characters simply get out of line and begin spoiling the group's fun. Players can be quite creative when it comes to spoiling a game—some may simply create characters that overpower everyone and everything else in the game, while others may insist on following their characters' own wacky plans or their own interpretations of the rules, regardless of their fellow players' wishes. The simplest way to deal with such a character is to kill him or her—the character, not the player, of course. However, *Shadowrun* provides gamemasters with a variety of other, less-drastic ways to control such players.

Reason with the Player

Take the problem player aside and talk to him. Tell him that he's creating a problem and how you think the problem can be fixed. Reasoning with a problem player is always better than simply punishing the player's character. The player may not understand why his character is catching the drek or may decide that the gamemaster is picking on his character for no reason.

If the player is not willing to change his or her behavior for the benefit of the group, then it may be time for the player and the group to part ways. If reasoning with the player fails, most of the other measures described here won't work much better.

Put the Character in Jail

A stint in one of the prisons run by Lone Star or the government can go a long way toward improving a character's attitude. If the character is SINless and lacks powerful connections, the authorities may even want to try some experimental new "rehabilitation" techniques on the character.

Ruin His/Her Reputation

Reputation is everything in the shadows. A character who develops a reputation as a troublemaker and unreliable or uncontrollable on runs will eventually run out of people willing to work with him or her. Such characters must shape up and take a few low-paying, hazardous runs to rebuild their reps— or find themselves sliding right to the bottom of the shadow food-chain to get chewed up.

Give Him/Her Bad Karma

Karma is a useful gamemaster tool for rewarding characters who have done well in an adventure. Similarly, gamemasters can punish troublesome player characters by penalizing them via Karma Points. Penalized characters will have to shape up if they ever want a chance of advancement in the future.

Take It Out on His/Her Contacts

Characters who frag off the wrong people may find that those people decide to take out their anger on the character's friends, contacts and even loved ones. Contacts are not going to continue to work with a character who spells such trouble, and any character with a shred of conscience should feel badly about bringing trouble down on their friends and loved ones.

Take Away His/Her Toys

If a character's main problem is too many toys—cyber or magical—the gamemaster can always take a few away. Gamemasters can relieve characters of excess cyberware or magical gear in a number of ways. For example, certain authorities might confiscate equipment—especially if the character is imprisoned. Alternatively, items can be stolen, disabled or simply suffer system failures. A character's enemies may also destroy the character's assets to deprive him or her of the advantages they provide.

Give 'em What They Want

If a character really wants an outlandish advantage or toy, let him or her have it—along with all of the trouble that comes with owning it. Characters with exotic gear and other powerful advantages tend to attract powerful enemies. Additionally, a powerful item or advantage can attract a continual stream of thieves, ambushes and saboteurs, hopefully creating more trouble than the item or advantage is worth.

MAINTAINING GAME BALANCE

Maintaining a balance between the power of player characters and their NPC opponents is one of the most important tasks of the gamemaster. By keeping the NPC opponents slightly more powerful than the player characters, the gamemaster forces the player characters to rely on their brains and teamwork, rather than simple firepower, to prevail. On the surface, maintaining such balance seems simple enough. However, the whole purpose of maintaining game balance is to keep play as fun as possible. Consequently, the gamemaster must strive to maintain game balance in ways that don't reduce the fun of the game. In other words, the gamemaster shouldn't sacrifice the players' freedom to use all the cool weapons and spells available in *Shadowrun* and also shouldn't simply create overpowering opponents whenever it's convenient. Maintaining game balance and fun in a game requires some thought on the gamemaster's part, but understanding a few basic principles can make it an easier, more rewarding task.

Power Is Relative

The first principle to remember is that game balance is determined by the power of the player characters and the power of their NPC opponents—not the power of one side alone. Instead of denying your players a minigun for their starting characters, simply remind them that their opposition will also have miniguns—and the enemy will probably have a slightly better version. The player characters' opponents need not be so totally overpowering that the runners never have a chance. They just need to be strong enough to keep the player characters from easily defeating them. As long as the opponents always challenge the runners, your players eventually will realize that no matter how strong their characters become, there will always be somebody bigger and badder, someone with a bigger budget, better tech toys, older and more experienced, with greater magical training and experience—someone they can't defeat in a straight-up fight.

Firepower Is Not Everything

Increasing the strength of NPC opponents is not the only way to maintain game balance against power-hungry player groups whose strength continues to grow. With a little imagination, gamemasters can devise shadowruns and opponents that can't be defeated using little more than firepower and combat spells—situations that force the player characters to use brains and teamwork.

For example, a Johnson might hire a team of runners for a run where secrecy is of the utmost importance, a run that no one must ever know about. Obviously, the team can't simply blow away anyone and anything in its path—that would draw too much attention. They'll have to come up with a strategy that gets them to their goal with a minimum of fuss and muss.

Keep "Gamebreakers" Rare

"Gamebreakers" are pieces of equipment, spells, or other items that can destroy game balance and "break" a game. What constitutes a gamebreaker varies depending on the power levels of a game or campaign. For example, even a submachine gun might be a gamebreaker in a campaign full of gang members armed with light pistols and baseball bats. The same gun would be no big deal in a campaign full of folks packing assault rifles, heavy machine guns and other heavy-duty goodies.

Keeping potential gamebreakers rare is the most effective way to prevent such elements from ruining a game.

For example, consider the Panther assault cannon. The cannon's basic cost is a mere 7,200 nuyen, so most starting characters can buy a case of them—one for the den, the car, the bedroom and so on. Sounds like a game-balance disaster waiting to happen, neh? But let's just say that the Panther is rare—not just "no-starting-character-can-have-it" rare, but "no-one-has-seen-one-or-really-knows-about-it" rare. Contacts scoff if you mention the "magic gun," the so-called Holy Grail of the street.

Suddenly, the "gamebreaker" no longer threatens game balance. Runners will have a hard time locating one. And if they do, everyone's certainly going to notice them. In fact, people will be screaming and running away or trying to cack them from behind and steal the thing.

So by making the Panther rare, rather than forbidding the players from obtaining one, the gamemaster has not restricted their freedom. He hasn't reduced the "coolness" factor of the

weapon—it will still blow a hole through that Azzie hitman's heavy body armor (as well as her body, the car parked behind her, and the brick wall behind the car). He hasn't made the weapon commonplace by equipping all the Lone Star cops with Panthers to keep things even. But he's maintained game balance.

INCORPORATING DECKERS

Every *Shadowrun* group has probably experienced it at some time. The decker goes off to do something in cyberspace and the rest of the players go out for pizza or play a video game or simply sit and chat while the gamemaster and the decker's player do their thing. Though the new Matrix rules in *SR3* and *Virtual Realities 2.0* speed up decking in the game, they do not entirely solve the problem of handling decker characters during the game. The following options suggest ways to better integrate decking with the rest of the action in a game and keep it from slowing things down.

NPC Deckers

NPC deckers enable gamemasters to dole out information for a fee as needed. A gamemaster can quickly determine the results of an NPC decker's Matrix run and report that information back to the player characters. NPC deckers give gamemasters a great deal of control over the information players acquire and greatly speed things up, but they also greatly reduce the game opportunities provided by the Matrix.

Two-Pronged Attack

In a two-pronged attack, the gamemaster plots two simultaneous shadowruns in which the decker goes online and works "behind the scenes" to disable security measures and monitor the progress of the run itself while the other characters do the physical work of the run. Published *Shadowrun* adventures and fiction contain numerous examples of such runs.

Simultaneous Gamemastering

Under the simultaneous gamemastering approach, the gamemaster works with the decker to play out the Matrix run and guides the other characters through their own activities at the same time. The gamemaster must switch between scenes quickly enough to keep all the action moving, maintain dramatic tension and keep the players busy, but this difficult task can be accomplished successfully with plenty of advance preparation.

Assistant Gamemaster

The gamemaster may also choose to appoint a player to be the assistant gamemaster with the primary task of handling Matrix runs with the decker's player. This arrangement frees the gamemaster to devote his full attention to play with the rest of the group. This approach requires some coordination between the gamemaster and his assistant, but it works well for data runs that are not directly connected with the action that the other characters are experiencing.

Solo Matrix Adventures

Gamemasters can conduct some Matrix runs as short solo adventures for their decker characters before the main game

session starts. In this case, the gamemaster simply uses the results from those Matrix runs as they are needed during the main game. This approach greatly speeds up play but may reduce the amount of continuity between Matrix action and the rest of the game. For example, a decker might learn something during the main game session that would have affected his Matrix run that evening.

Computer Skill Test

In some cases, gamemasters can represent a Matrix run with a single Computer Skill Test, modified by the effects of the decker's applicable programs. Gamemasters should use this option sparingly, if possible. A player may become bored quite quickly if his decker character never does anything other than make Computer Tests.

AVOIDING INFORMATION OVERLOAD

Each new *Shadowrun* book that hits the shelves adds to the vast amount of *Shadowrun* information already available. Understandably, gamemasters and players often want to incorporate as much of this information as possible into their version of the game, which can lead to "information overload" and can bog down play. Gamemasters and players simply may need to find a way to narrow their focus and incorporate only the information important to their campaigns at any given time. The following suggestions are designed to aid this process.

Latest-and-Greatest Syndrome

The Sixth World is an incredibly rich setting that becomes richer with each successive *Shadowrun* book. Naturally, many gamemasters and players want to use every new rule, weapon, spell, opponent, setting or idea that comes along. However, doing so can quickly turn a campaign into a long string of tricks, gimmicks and unconnected plots that don't really hold together. Fortunately, gamemasters can avoid this pitfall and still satisfy their players' and their own appetites for new ideas by simply exercising some patience and doing a little creative gamemastering.

Perhaps most important, gamemasters should consider carefully the appropriateness of any new idea based on the scope of their campaign, their players' abilities, and the likely effects of the new idea on their games. Not all options are well-suited for all campaigns. Depending on the current direction, power level and story line of his or her campaign, a gamemaster may want to modify or even prohibit certain options. Remember, just because an option has appeared in a FASA-published book does not mean that the gamemaster has to allow it into his individual campaign. All of the material in *Shadowrun* books, including the *Shadowrun Companion,* are *options* for gamemasters—not required elements that gamemasters must use.

Rather than modifying or prohibiting new options, gamemasters may incorporate new material into their campaigns gradually. For example, revolutions in bioware, cybertechnology or magical research shouldn't happen overnight. Gradually adding innovations from sourcebooks such as the *Magic in the Shadows, Man and Machine, Rigger 2* and *Virtual Realities 2.0* not only mimics the dispersal of technological innovations in the real world—it provides the players and gamemasters time to adjust to the new options. Additionally, gamemasters may prohibit starting characters from using such options. This provides the gamemaster with greater control over the use of a new option.

THE SECRETS OF FASA

Occasionally, *Shadowrun* players and gamemasters complain that they just aren't getting the whole story behind every new development in the *Shadowrun* universe. Well, it's true FASA does have some secrets. But we have good reasons for keeping those secrets.

Our continuing effort to keep the *Shadowrun* universe vital and growing is the main reason for keeping some things to ourselves. To keep things fresh, we need to put out new material all the time. Consequently, we have to hold some ideas back to develop for future products. Additionally, we have to make sure that each new idea fits with the existing universe. And finally, new options—and your reaction to them—have a way of suggesting even more directions for the universe. Given these factors, we simply cannot fully describe every nook and cranny or completely explore every new direction in the game universe. That's why no one will ever know *everything* about the continuing *Shadowrun* saga.

Of course, this situation need not stop gamemasters from creating their own unique twists on elements of the Sixth World. Have a great plot line about the truth behind the Lone Eagle incident or the Crash of '29? Feel free to elaborate on it and use it in your campaign. If it clashes with something published by FASA at a later date, simply adjust the campaign or ignore the FASA concept or find a way to make the two stories meet somewhere in between. We feel fairly confident, however, that FASA's story lines and the story lines of *Shadowrun* gaming groups will rarely overlap in an inconvenient way. All *Shadowrun* sourcebooks provide a multitude of adventure and campaign plot hooks, and only a few of them will be explored in future books—leaving plenty of room for gamemasters to play with the possibilities of the universe without worrying about FASA stepping on their toes.

Don't limit the possibilities of your *Shadowrun* world by hedging your bets against FASA's version of the universe.

ALTERNATE CAMPAIGN CONCEPTS

The world of *Shadowrun* is rich and varied, but most players never get to see more than its grimy underbelly. Spending all their time doing the corps' dirty work and trying to survive on the mean streets, typical shadowrunners never get more than a glimpse of the larger world they inhabit. Gamemasters who want to explore other aspects of the *Shadowrun* universe, or players who simply want a change of pace, might consider running game sessions or even campaigns in which the characters are something other than shadowrunners.

These alternate campaigns follow pretty much the same rules as the *Shadowrun* you know and love, with a few changes that reflect the different situations player characters will face as cops, gang members and so on. This section briefly describes several non-runner campaign concepts, each outlined in the terms given in *Keys to a Good Adventure,* p. 94. This material offers the gamemaster springboards for building new campaigns based on any one of these themes, using the techniques outlined in this book. Though many of these concepts take the campaign beyond the "shadowrunner team" and into other areas of the Sixth World, all of them still focus on the unique blend of science fiction and fantasy elements that make *Shadowrun* exciting.

Gamemasters interested in these alternate campaign concepts may wish to take a look at the *Missions* collection, which features four adventures based on the campaign suggestions below.

WHERE DOES IT HURT?

Altruistic-minded players might want to try playing a DocWagon High Threat Response team. Just think: all the dangers of shadowrunning, a regular salary and your own VTOL! This type of campaign may appeal to players who want loads of action without a lot of setup—HTR teams only get called in when the action is hot and heavy. Of course, there's a lot more to being a DocWagon tech than pulling people out of dangerous situations—just watch any TV hospital drama for a whole host of ideas.

For more details about DocWagon HTR teams and their equipment, see p. 90.

CHARACTER CREATION

Create DocWagon player characters using standard *Shadowrun* rules, plus the following guidelines as appropriate. The team should consist of a rigger (to drive the ambulance, medevac chopper or other appropriate vehicle); a mage or shaman for magical healing and fire support (note that HTR shamans tend to be followers of Bear and Snake because of the healing bonuses conferred by those totems); one or two medical specialists who do most of the actual patching-up of victims; and additional fire-support personnel (anything from adepts to troll muscle to heavily cybered combat specialists). Deckers don't usually come along for the ride; they stay at the local headquarters and keep track of all the tactical information, as well as notifying local police, governments, businesses and other services of what's going down. Other types of characters with no knack for medicine or defensive combat will have little place in this kind of campaign.

The gamemaster may rule that no DocWagon characters can take Resources as Priority A or B during character creation, as DocWagon will supply most of the team's non-implanted equipment. (Besides, anyone who can afford that kind of gear must be making a lot more than DocWagon pays!) Each character should have a minimum Biotech Skill Rating of 3; medical specialists should also have some biology and/or cybertechnology skills. Because HTR teams respond to high-threat situations, combat skills will also be useful, though the team should be concerned about saving the custom—um, patient first and kicking hoop second.

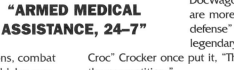

"ARMED MEDICAL
ASSISTANCE, 24–7"

ADVENTURE IDEAS

The daily duties of a DocWagon HTR team involve rescuing badly injured DocWagon customers from situations too dangerous for standard medical teams. One obvious example is a firefight, wherein an innocent bystander or even a participant with a DocWagon contract gets hit and needs attention. Charging into a gun battle is a dangerous proposition, particularly when Lone Star or heavily armed shadowrunners get involved, or when participants in the fight might not want to see a particular victim survive. In addition, the gamemaster has numerous ways of making things even more interesting for the players. What if the DocWagon customer is a shadowrunner, and the rest of his team carries him along as they flee the scene or continue with their run? The HTR team is contractually obligated to help their customer, and so may follow along and get mixed up in all kinds of shadowrunning mayhem.

Gun battles are not the only source of serious injury. Natural disasters, terrorist activity, paranormal animal attacks—all of these situations are prime candidates for an HTR team, and may put the medics in as much danger as the patient. These types of scenarios, where numerous lives are endangered, can also be used to tweak the characters' consciences. If a terrorist bomb wounds fifty people and only three are DocWagon customers, will the characters be able to make themselves ignore the other wounded while performing their duties? Where does an employment contract give way to conscience?

The HTR team's job will be complicated by the fact that they are carrying huge amounts of drugs and extremely expensive medical equipment, not to mention firearms, all of which makes them prime targets for thieves. Particularly daring thieves have been known to injure a DocWagon customer and then set an ambush for the HTR team. Though HTR teams are better equipped to deal with such situations than the average paramedic squad, they are by no means immune to disaster.

Finally, DocWagon player characters may well have to deal with the problem of competing medical organizations. DocWagon is the largest company of its kind, but by no means the only one, and many smaller medical companies will try just about anything to preserve their market share—including attacking DocWagon teams if both companies respond to calls in the same area. Theoretically, the first priority of DocWagon personnel is to insure their customers' safety and health. But many DocWagon teams—especially HTR teams—are more than willing to engage in "active defense" against rival companies. As the legendary DocWagon HTR pilot Jim "Doc Croc" Crocker once put it, "The Hippocratic oath don't apply to the competition."

CAMPAIGNING WITH DOCWAGON

The following section complements the *Archetypal Adventure Plots* section, p. 100 of *Running the Game*, by fleshing out some of the concepts presented in that section.

The Premise

Most DocWagon campaigns will be limited to a single city or district that DocWagon serves, though the characters can occasionally be "loaned out" to other DocWagon branches for training, demonstration of new techniques and so forth. The gamemaster can create some interesting variations by setting the campaign in a place that offers other challenges than gunfights, such as a MediCarro campaign in war-torn Aztlan or a DocWagon adventure in an uneasy border town like Denver.

Medics working for DocWagon aren't likely to be physical or magical powerhouses. The characters should be competent at certain combat and self-defense skills as needed, but their primary purpose is to save lives, not beat people to a pulp. The player of such a character can channel the Skill Points and Resources that he might ordinarily have used to create a combat monster into additional medical and social skills and abilities that can help the character in his or her line of work.

with groups or opponents likely to target a medical organization: eco-terrorists, ghouls, organ-smugglers, rival companies and, of course, shadowrunners looking to heist a DocWagon vehicle for cover (what shadowrunning team hasn't tried this at some point?).

While a certain amount of violence might be permissible when a DocWagon crew is trying to get to a client, that doesn't mean the characters can blaze away at anyone in their path without having to answer to the law for it. Most of the violence likely to occur in a DocWagon campaign will be after the fact; this gives the players an interesting opportunity to see the frequently gory results of a "simple" shadowrun. For example, an HTR team may get called to a corporate site where a group of shadowrunners have mowed through the guards and defenses; immediately on arrival, the player characters must treat all the hapless guards who are still alive. They might find a clue that could nail those lousy shadowrunners, and they may well feel inclined to use it.

Complications

A search-and-rescue campaign allows the characters to go into all kinds of dangerous and exciting situations with plenty of backup at the home base. It also provides sanctions for high-speed vehicle action and last-minute saves, and can send a refreshing breath of heroism into the darkness of the Sixth World; for once the characters are helping people and saving lives rather than grubbing up nuyen. The gamemaster should make each DocWagon mission feel like a hour-long TV action drama.

On the other hand, heroic do-gooding may not be everyone's thing—especially for players who aren't interested in medicine. Adventures can sometimes become routine, and maintaining a variety of stories and opportunities for a DocWagon campaign is more difficult than for the standard shadowrunning game. Players may be frustrated by the lack of combat, lower power level or lack of financial reward for their heroism (though they should net a fair amount of Karma to compensate).

In addition to the player characters, other important characters in a DocWagon campaign include the doctors and medical personnel back at the hospital/clinic/home base, who may often be in touch via the Matrix to offer assistance. Player characters may also have to deal with company administrators, the local authorities (police and others) and the occasional street doc or healer whom the characters may befriend and help out on the sly from time to time. A final complication is the person being rescued—how does he, she or it feel about it? Did DocWagon stop an extraction team from taking the patient unwillingly, or did he or she want to go with them? Has the patient become an employee without a corp? Did the patient get into trouble because he or she intended to go out in a blaze of glory, and the DocWagon team prevented a spectacular suicide? Did someone set up the patient to be murdered? The patient alone can lead to multiple adventures for the rescuers.

The Goal

The player characters are members of an ambulance crew or search-and-rescue team that gets sent out to help a variety of people in need of medical attention, almost always in highly dangerous situations. The characters' first job is to see to the safety and health of their patients—in this case, to save lives, so the campaign should have a moral tone. The characters are doing difficult and dangerous work for little or no reward (by the standards of many people in the Sixth World) and so they must be devoted to their jobs. Though DocWagon characters may get involved in the shadier side of the medical business—organlegging, drug smuggling and so on—it makes for a better campaign if the characters try to maintain the moral high ground. They may touch on the problem of corruption while trying to root it out of their own organization, for example.

The life of the patient is the most important consideration. Characters risk themselves to save lives because that's their job. Sometimes they need to break rules to get that job done. And sometimes you don't manage to save the victim—so you try harder next time.

Opposition

Much of the opposition that characters face in this kind of campaign will be natural, impersonal forces: disaster, fire, disease, street warfare and so on. They might also have trouble

SMILE, YOU'RE ON CAMERA!

In the 2050s, information is the purest kind of power. Therefore, corporations and governments spend a great deal of time and money attempting to keep it to themselves. But one group exists that is dedicated to taking information from the Powers That Be and giving it to the common man—the news media. Much like today, the media hounds of the 2050s are the ones who dig up the skeletons in the closets of the rich and powerful or shed light on the secrets that the megacorps don't want anyone to know. It's a dirty job, but somebody has to do it—why not your players?

Most of the big media outfits in *Shadowrun* are controlled secretly or openly by the megacorps, and so the characters will probably be working for the bit players. They may be from a pirate trid station, stealing bandwidth from authorized stations to broadcast their sound bites and fleeing before security shows up. Or maybe they're stringers, scrabbling for anything newsworthy and selling it to the highest bidder. Or they may work for a small local station with a shoestring budget, fighting off hostile takeovers while broadcasting the news that the major studios can't or won't touch.

CHARACTER CREATION

You can create newshound characters with the standard *Shadowrun* rules or the optional rules in *Character Creation* (beginning on p. 6). Players should also keep the following guidelines in mind. A pirate trid station would definitely need a decker/electronics expert to wire up their broadcasting equipment to override legitimate media traffic. In fact, a decker's unparalleled ability to track down data and uncover hidden information makes him or her especially useful in any media-related campaign. Unless the team works solely for the datafaxes, they will want at least one high-Charisma "face" person to make the actual broadcasts. The rest of the team can be camera people, technicians and security people, all of whom will surely have other talents they can use to keep the team alive and effective. Combat skills may not be the team's first priority, but newshound characters should definitely have them; uncovering corruption in the megacorps and governments of the Sixth World is a good way to get dead if you can't defend yourself. Mage characters can be useful to a news team if they have masking, invisibility and other "stealth" spells. A good rigger, who can get you the heck out of trouble when the drek goes down, is also an asset.

Anyone who might appear on camera or have to deal one-on-one with sources should definitely have high Charisma; in addition, good Etiquette and Negotiation skills are crucial when tracking down leads. Stealth is also handy when trying to surreptitiously record scandalous meetings or covert operations, and Interrogation is great for hitting those corporate mouthpieces with a barrage of revealing, rapid-fire questions. But the most crucial part of a newshound character is his contacts. A newshound should have plenty, from as many different walks of life as possible to give him or her the best leads fast.

ADVENTURE IDEAS

News media adventures can start from almost any premise: an overheard conversation, an anonymous tip or the reporter's ever-popular "gut feeling." Any sign of corporate cruelty, government cover-ups, shadowrunning activity or other ratings-grabbers will surely draw reporters like flies on drek.

In most media campaigns, the characters' primary goal is to get incriminating evidence on film, then broadcast it so that the public at large knows about the dirty deeds being done. Whether that means following chemical tankers as they dump toxic wastes on a wildlife preserve or recording a meeting between a mayoral candidate and a Mafia don, these jobs will require excellent investigative skills, subtlety, stealth and (if discovered) the ability to flee at high speed. Of course, broadcasting the story doesn't end the adventure; the megacorps and other powerful miscreants are not known for their "live and let live" attitude toward those who reveal their dirty laundry to the public. The characters must either maintain a high profile and hope that the targets of their exposés won't dare take action against them, or drop out of sight until the heat cools off.

If the characters develop a large public following, an unscrupulous corporation (pretty much all of them) might decide to use the characters to frame an appropriate victim. With an "anonymous tip," the corp puts the characters on the target's trail and then uses illusion magic, disguises or high-tech trickery (whatever is at their disposal) to give the characters "proof" that the target is doing something shady. The characters take the bait, the target is publicly crucified, and if the frame-up job comes out it'll be up to the characters to prove they were innocent dupes instead of co-conspirators. (And even proving that has its price—what media hound really wants the public to know he can be fooled?)

The characters may also occasionally be hired by shadowrunners who are investigating some manner of cover-up and want concrete proof of their findings. An interesting way to use this type of adventure is to have the runners alert the news team of their suspicions, then get mercilessly slaughtered as they commence their investigation. Now the newsies are the only people who know the deadly secret that the corp (or whoever) is hiding, and they must decide whether or not to risk their lives by taking up where the dead runners left off.

Finally, for a gamemaster who wants to get his players involved with the Sixth World's real media movers and shakers, both legit and not-so-legit, see p. 20, *New Seattle*. An unknown source constantly sends the characters clues to major news events that are about to happen, giving them just enough time to arrive on the scene and record the historic happenings. The characters may wind up covering a lot of things that the Powers That Be prefer to be forgotten, and any number of people will wonder where the characters get their information—including the characters themselves! This premise could be the basis for an interesting, high-action campaign that reaches its climax when the characters finally think they've figured out who their source is (and then must decide what to do about it).

CAMPAIGNING WITH MEDIA TEAMS

The following section complements the *Archetypal Adventure Plots* section, p. 100 of *Running the Game,* by fleshing out some of the concepts presented in that section.

The Premise

The player characters are all part of a team working for a major or pirate media network, or else they are freelance news hounds. They specialize in handling the hot stories that often put them in the line of fire; they also dig up the dirt on the world's megacorporations and governments, often information that these powers do not want broadcast. The pirate news station KSAF makes a useful basis for this type of campaign; useful equipment appears in *SR3,* beginning on p. 288.

This type of campaign can vary greatly in scale depending on the desires of your players. A news team might confine most of its reporting to a single metroplex, or the team might travel all over the world to track down the hot news and top stories. Generally, the larger the news organization for which the characters work, the more influence their stories will have (and the correspondingly greater risks they must take to get the story out).

This type of campaign can take place in a wide variety of settings. The player characters can go anywhere a potential news story may break, from corporate boardrooms to the harsh back alleys of the Barrens and more.

The Goal

It is possible to uncover the truth. The public has a right to be informed, and information must be free—especially in the Sixth World, where control of information means control over people's lives. Many people in power prefer to conceal their activities from the media's eye, or want to distort the truth for their own ends. Reporters must therefore remain objective, but also must always struggle with the Powers That Be to get their stories out.

The moral questions of a media campaign can range far beyond the simple issues of mercenary work and violence. The player characters must make decisions about what types of stories they will cover and how. Because so much of the media in the Sixth World is censored by government or corporate owners, the characters will have to deal with the consequences of that censorship in one way or another—working with a pirate network or within the structure of an existing "legit" network. A media campaign, which gives player characters a chance to influence events through their reporting, can have an entirely different tone from the typical shadowrunning game. Gamers interested in the complex, behind-the-scenes plots of the Sixth World will find a media campaign an interesting opportunity to explore those kinds of stories. Conspiracy and investigation buffs can have a lot of fun, and the gamemaster can also give the characters a chance to hobnob with some of the major players of the *Shadowrun* universe.

Few media hounds are physical or magical powerhouses. A media character's power lies in entirely different directions than that of most shadowrunners: information and influence. A talented and respected reporter character can wield considerable power without having wired reflexes or a massive Combat Pool. Though newshound characters are likely to need some combat skills and abilities to handle the dangerous situations they will tend to encounter, a media campaign is likely to be less combat-oriented than most other campaigns in *Shadowrun.*

Opposition

The major antagonists for a media campaign are rival news organizations working to get the best stories and information first, and the people who don't want their affairs exposed by a bunch of pushy newshounds. The characters can easily fall into a situation where they know too much to be allowed to live, much less report what they know.

Though reporter characters are likely to cover violent incidents, they rarely engage in violence themselves. Most media teams will use violence only in self-defense, and any group as subject to dealing with the authorities as a local news team must answer for any violent acts they commit. Media characters must therefore carefully consider the actions they intend to take. In a media-team campaign, the pen is often truly mightier than the sword.

Complications

An investigative media-based campaign can be frustrating to players who are looking for combat action. The restrictions under which a media team must operate are vastly different from the ground rules that apply to a typical group of shadowrunners, and some players might find working (mostly) within the law a serious cramp in their style. There is also the danger that the reporter character or characters might overshadow the other supporting characters in the campaign. To avoid this, the gamemaster should flesh out various NPCs that the player characters will work with—the news team's editor or producer—and the workings of the player characters' network should be described in detail. The gamemaster should also flesh out all the newshounds' contacts and informants, as well as the important people that the player characters might be interested in investigating. A media campaign requires a proactive gamemaster who is willing to let the mystery unfold over the course of the game.

TRAINED TO BE GHOSTS

Most countries have an elite group within their militaries who go through rigorous screening and training programs to become the top-secret arm of the government assigned to taking on the missions that are too weird, too dangerous or too controversial to perform openly. These special-forces characters spy on others, steal or copy confidential data, eliminate key problems, blow stuff up, help "freedom fighters" and assassinate national leaders of questionable morality. Sound familiar?

Special forces are essentially the government's topnotch shadowrunners. They perform many of the same functions for the corps, for largely the same reasons, as do ordinary street runners. They are officially employed and so are not quite as deniable as the average runner if something goes wrong, but their training ensures that what they lose in deniability they make up in talent and loyalty.

CHARACTER CREATION

Create special-forces characters according to the standard rules, but do not use the optional rules for enemies (p. 68). Though special-forces characters can certainly create enemies by the dozen during game play, simply having a lot of money or cyberware doesn't automatically make people kill you in the real world. Special-forces characters can also ignore the Availability optional rule when procuring weapons and armor. The characters are on their government's tab; if the mission requires a Panther assault cannon, the taxpayers make sure that the characters have one. (On the other hand, getting BTLs on a military base can be tough.) The characters' two free contacts are automatically their commanding officer and quartermaster (the person who manages their equipment). Any additional contacts must be purchased. Characters will also receive an annual wage of 75,000 nuyen—enough for a Medium lifestyle and some extras. Obviously, the Sixth World's governments need all types of shadowrunners from deckers to riggers to muscleboys, and most will hire all types of metahumanity. Possible exceptions are governments of a specific race—for example, the elven nation of Tir Tairngire, whose members prefer to hire fellow elves whenever possible (though they might find trolls and orks perfectly acceptable as cannon fodder).

ADVENTURE IDEAS

Military campaigns can involve regular soldiers, but special forces are the type of character closest to shadowrunners. They work in small units and are extremely well-equipped; for example, a government will actually spend a million nuyen on a special-forces operative to make him the ultimate cybered machine, as opposed to a regular soldier who gets a smartgun link and an armored jacket. Finally, special forces are required to keep their operations classified.

Gaming groups are likely to know and want to use varying levels of detail about special forces. As an example of a typical special-forces team, a UCAS Delta Force twelve-man "A-Team" is commanded by a captain (CPT) who changes every three years; the rest of the team stays together for life. The second-in-command is the Chief Warrant Officer (CWO). This character must at some point have been a non-commissioned officer (NCO) with one of the following specialties: Operations and Intelligence, Medical Technician, Communications Technician, Weapons Specialist, or Demolitions Specialist. Magic is considered a subset of these specialities, depending on its use. The rest of the team are non-commissioned officers.

Each team will have as its senior NCO a Master Sergeant (MSG-E-8). This character is the Operations and Intelligence specialist who gets his hands on the required intelligence to plan the mission. The Sergeants–First Class (SFC E-7) are a well-trained medical technician and a demolitions expert. The medic is qualified to perform certain types of surgery and authorized to carry controlled narcotics for medical purposes. The demolitions expert can use all known forms of explosives, whether manufactured or improvised, and usually carries any such materiel on a mission.

Staff Sergeants (SSG E-6) include the communications officer, who knows how to operate his own and the enemy's communications equipment. He can also create communicators of some kind from whatever happens to be handy. Another SSG is the weapons specialist, trained in the use of almost all known light or medium weapons. This officer should be able to use field artillery and even tanks if necessary. The remainder of the team are additional Staff Sergeants and Sergeants (SGT E-5). All of the specialties described are suggestions for assigning skills, histories and appropriate equipment to various characters; none of these provide a game bonus unless the gamemaster chooses to assign such an advantage. Before embarking on any mission, the special forces personnel are isolated for at least three days.

Special-forces missions often involve travel, frequently to hostile nations where the characters carry out threats and assassinations or aid rebellious freedom fighters. Characters can also perform intelligence-gathering missions, datasteals, interrogations and spy missions against foreign governments or against "undesirables" in their own country. They can function as an elite unit sent to handle the most dangerous jobs during a war, or perform the ever-popular mission where "something weird happened to the last group we sent in, and you've got to stop whatever's going on."

CAMPAIGNING WITH SPECIAL FORCES

The following section complements the *Archetypal Adventure Plots* section, p. 100 of *Running the Game*, by fleshing out some of the concepts presented in that section.

The Premise

A special-forces campaign resembles a regular shadowrun—but with certain important differences. Most special-forces campaigns will not be centered around legwork—special forces are trained to act decisively, not chase clues around—and so contacts become a less important aspect of the game. The characters will have the same "Mr. Johnson" every time—their commanding officer—and they must cultivate his trust and respect in order to stay on the team. If the gamemaster wants to start the characters out in boot camp and roleplay their selection and training, that can significantly intensify the relationship with their CO.

The Goal

When playing a special-forces game, emphasize the characters' loyalty to their country. That country need not be the UCAS; imagine a Tir Ghosts or Sioux Wildcats campaign. The characters are not freelancers; though they do get paid for their work, they should do it primarily out of patriotism and loyalty. They must succeed in their missions at all costs and they rarely have any input into their orders. To a special-forces character, the job is an honor and the goal is to succeed for the glory or well-being of his country. If a character doesn't want to play that game, he or she should leave for the more lucrative life of a shadowrunner.

Opposition

The opposition for any special-forces team is likely to be another special-forces team: an opposing government's hit squad, corporate security on red alert, or even freelancers out to make a name for themselves. Terrorists also make excellent villians for a special-forces campaign. For less military, more spy-oriented missions, the primary "opposition" may be the sheer difficulty of infiltrating the target area or organization and then getting out alive. These missions are extremely danger-ous for many reasons; they are usually long-term, an agent involved in one may well go "over the wall" and join the other side, or the agent may get caught and simply disappear.

Complications

Special-forces characters must learn to work together. Unlike ordinary shadowrunners, they cannot choose whom to work with or kill a teammate they dislike. This arrangement can be good for group harmony as players learn to work out in-character differences. The characters must also concentrate on teamwork to make sure their missions remain secret. If they are ordered to assassinate a dictator and they hose it, they can't just pack up and run the way a shadowrunner often can. They must answer to the rest of their unit and their government.

Also, military/special-forces characters are more likely to have normal lives than shadowrunners. Such characters may have spouses, children, parents and siblings whom they talk to and care about, or friends outside the military. Gamemasters should take this element of their player characters' lives into account when the campaign needs a change of pace. For example, if characters are used to calling the president for the mission plan and necessary equipment, they might have to think hard about what to do when they hear from an old friend who needs their help because he's gotten on the wrong side of the mob. They have the skills to accomplish what needs to be done, but the necessity of operating outside their orders might force them to reevaluate their careers in terms of their dedica-tion to country or to family. They would also need to decide whether to operate outside the sanctions of the government, ask their superior officer for help, "borrow" equipment from the "office," and other moral dilemmas.

I AM THE LAW

Playing corporate security or police officers, whether from Lone Star, Knight Errant or smaller outfits, offers players a dif-ferent look at the Sixth World. In many ways these characters resemble shadowrunners; they have many of the same skills and abilities, some of the same interests, and often the same functions. Both types of teams include varied characters—deckers, magicians and combat-types—and get involved every day in the down-and-dirty, take-your-life-in-your-hands aspect of the Sixth World. And security specialists or law enforcement characters live with almost the same level of danger as shad-owrunners—in fact, they're the ones that the runners come after. There are some significant differences, however. For one thing, corporate guards and cops spend more time on intra-corp competition, bragging to improve their reputations and actively soliciting the interesting jobs. No one wants to go from

being one of Knight Errant's golden boys this week to elemen-tary-school lunch duty next week because a jealous rival spread rumors.

CHARACTER CREATION

Creating cop and corporate-security characters is a little different than creating runners. To reflect the extent of corpo-rate and law-enforcement discrimination, metahuman charac-ters should be exceedingly rare—usually no more than one in any group. Among the few metahumans, elves and dwarfs are more common than trolls and orks. Skills must be at least C Priority, reflecting the fact that the characters have had training, and each character must have at least two Academic or Background Knowledge Skills to reflect the fact that they've had some sort of education. If you are using the point-based system (beginning on p. 13) to create your character, you must allocate at least 24 points to Active Skills. As corpsec person-nel and Lone Star cops, the player characters should make a high enough salary to maintain a Medium lifestyle.

Unlike shadowrunners, for whom a wide variety of spe-cialties on a team is necessary, cops and corp security are more likely to work in one field. For example, everybody might play deckers who are Fuchi's front line of defense for a campaign set entirely in the Matrix. If all your players want to play magical characters, they may be the "point team" for astral defense at the local Lone Star's magical division.

Cop and corporate-security characters should have at least two enemies at character creation. One should be a Rank 1 enemy, the other Rank 2. The characters' two free contacts must be employees of their corporation or fellow cops at their precinct. Purchased contacts may be of any type.

ADVENTURE IDEAS

Cop and corporate-security campaigns offer opportunities for more roleplaying and social interaction than the average shadowrun. Characters must work reasonably within the law, and so will almost always try to solve things by talking before resorting to violence. Despite Lone Star's brutal trid image, any cop who consistently shoots before speaking will find himself in court or on the streets pretty quickly. Cop and corporate-security characters also have to work within a corporate struc-ture, answering to higher-ups, working together or competing with contemporaries and mentoring newbies. This offers opportunities for social interaction beyond contacts from whom characters get weapons and information, and also for enemies who subtly attack a character's career and ego rather than his physical person.

When running cop/corp campaigns, keep in mind that when the dangerous drek goes down, the first thing most cops do is call for backup. This action may be realistic, but it isn't much fun for the players to know that their characters will always have fifty fellow cops ready to cover them should they screw up. The gamemaster must make sure that the characters can get into high-suspense situations where a lot depends on a few moves made only by the protagonists. In other words, look more to cop movies for inspiration than to "real-world" police operations. Encourage characters to have moral codes, doing the right thing even if the chief has been bribed to look the other way, or to use their contacts and skills to help a group on the side of "good" but not on the side of the law (metahuman rights, ecoterrorists and so on).

Another technique is the "nobody ever goes in or comes out" ploy. The characters may not be able to call for backup for some reason—for example, they've been kidnapped and their radios taken, or they're inside a barrier like the Bug City containment zone. Alternatively, backup may not be able to reach them—terrorists may control the building they're in, or they started exploring some mysterious sewer tunnels and now they don't know where they are. Techniques like these put the story into the hands of the player characters, making for a more exciting and memorable game.

The cop character has an ambiguous relationship with the streets. He or she may have come from there, his or her most interesting work takes place there, and yet the people of the streets most likely despise and fear the cop. Nonetheless, cops must be able to work with people in the shadows. When conducting an investigation, having contacts is as helpful for cops as for shadowrunners. Cops tend to use their contacts much more actively to "get a feel" for what's happening on the street. The Negotiation rules (*Spilling the Beans*, p. 67) can make these interviews interesting. Some contacts may also have a hold over the character; for example, a Yakuza oyabun who helps a cop out with the occasional bit of information may successfully blackmail that same cop to open a smuggling channel into a local prison.

When running a cop campaign, the gamemaster should have a plausible reason for involving a small group of people rather than a large team. Creating specialty teams or SWAT teams is one way to do this; having a big event occur elsewhere that drains all the NPCs away so that the player characters are the only ones left is another. This type of campaign also works well if you have a very small group of players (1–3) and would like to run an intimate game that requires a lot of investigation rather than combat.

Corporate security functions in the same way as cops for the most part, save that they have an even more limited range of operations. Most often they stay on the grounds of their parent corp. To keep the game varied, consider sending corpsec characters on undercover missions or varying the types of security crises (a gang attack, an assault by chromed-to-the-teeth or magically powerful runners, an internal-affairs investigation, a rampage by wild paranormal animals, a wageslave gone postal and so on). You can also create campaigns around personal friendships and enmities, or have the characters inadvertently uncover their corp's dirty secrets. Starting out with characters who work for Aztechnology with no idea of its reputation, then having them stumble over increasingly clear evidence of blood magic and sacrifices, can lead up to an emotional climax as the characters decide whether to continue working for the corp they now know is evil or risk everything they have to do what is right. (If they leave, of course, they can go directly to traditional *Shadowrun*.)

Corporate characters often have shaky relationships with their street contacts. Most often they are either bribing the contact for information—and they'd better keep up the payments in the game or suffer the consequences—or they are personal friends from before the corp character went legit, in which case the character must consider how deeply he or she wants to drag a friend into trouble.

Corp/cop adventures do not center around making money, and characters can't really steal and/or loot bodies because they have no access to a black market through which to sell their pickings. An easy way to make the campaign tougher is to slash the corporate or precinct budget; this means the characters may not be able to get their hands on the best equipment, or even equipment that works, and they may also not have the cash to grease all the palms that need it. As with special-forces campaigns, corporate and cop characters are more likely to have normal lives than shadowrunners. If a character's whole family is tied up with the corporation, might he or she think twice about leaving after finding out about Aztechnology's questionable experiments? Or if a cop spends months tracking down some piece of shadowrunner scum only to find out that the runner is her little sister who ran away two years ago, how will she react to that discovery?

Going Undercover

An adventure in which an individual or group must go undercover is difficult to pull off and poses some obvious problems, such as the short life expectancy of an undercover character if his or her cover is broken. Also, the gamemaster must create a complete undercover environment for the character or the group. Finally, an undercover adventure is likely to be high on social skills and sweet talking, and low on combat action. If well-roleplayed, however, an undercover campaign can create an interesting story and loads of opportunity for character interaction.

When playing an undercover character, design him or her as if the character actually is the person he is disguised as (shadowrunner, organized-crime member, gang member). The character must also have a Skill Rating of at least 3 in Etiquette, and should probably specialize in the type of Etiquette most needed to succeed at his or her undercover profession.

If the players are willing to risk it, an undercover campaign can lead to some intense and memorable scenes when a character's cover is broken and he must break the law in order to prove his loyalty to his new bosses. A super twist is to have an undercover cop be a member of a shadowrunning team. Keep in mind that no matter how well the character plays his or her runner role—or even if the character decides he prefers his runner buddies to being a cop and ultimately takes to the street himself—other players and their characters don't like feeling foolish. When the character's cover is broken, as it will be eventually, that character will have to do some quick and convincing talking to stay alive, and even then the enraged runners may kill the character out of spite.

CAMPAIGNING WITH THE LAW

The following section complements the *Archetypal Adventure Plots* section, p. 100 of *Running the Game*, by fleshing out some of the concepts presented in that section.

The Premise

The characters are trying to hang on to the moral high ground in a world of chaos. They stick to the ideal of the law, if not always the letter of it, and must often face corruption in their own organization. This premise makes an interesting change from most campaigns, where the characters are "criminal scum" (shadowrunners); cop characters might even find themselves outsmarting and hauling in a few shadowrunners from time to time!

Law enforcement characters try to uphold the ideals of "good cops" and deal with crime and corruption in their jurisdiction as well as within their organization. The player characters are members of a single crime squad, or perhaps an elite unit such as a Lone Star Fast Response Team. They work together all the time, and form the kind of bonds that people only form with those who save their necks on a regular basis; there are no loners in a cop squad. The unit may include magicians and adepts as magical support, though such characters must answer to the magical specialty division of the organization for which the characters work. Most cop squads also include a decker to provide needed technical support.

The characters work in a distinct locale, dealing with criminal activity in their particular city or precinct if they're cops and keeping tabs on the corporate site to which they've been assigned if they're corpsec. Though they may have to deal with their company's or organization's home office at times, most of their attention is confined to the local area.

Cop/corp campaigns lend themselves to any good-sized city or metroplex like Seattle. The gamemaster can create some interesting variations by choosing cities outside the UCAS or CAS and focusing on those cities' unique aspects and problems, such as Los Angeles, Denver, Vancouver (in Salish-Shidhe) and Portland (in Tir Tairngire).

The Goal

To a cop character, being a "good cop" is the most important thing in the world. Without good people to uphold the law, anarchy reigns and people get hurt. There is nothing worse than a bad cop, because a bad cop corrupts the law. People deserve protection from crime, and so sometimes you have to bend the rules a little to put criminals away. But you can't bend the rules too much, even if sometimes that means letting the bad guys go. Cop and corpsec characters have an immediate reason for working together and clearly set goals for dealing with criminal scum; they also have enough leeway to act on their own initiative. They have fewer worries about getting gear than the average shadowrunner character, and the gamemaster has more control over character advancement. The cop/corp campaign shows players "the other side of the street" and lets them be on the side of law and order for a change.

Opposition

The player characters have plenty of ready-made opponents in the criminal element with whom they must deal daily. Organized crime offers quite a few powerful adversaries; the characters are also likely to tangle with small-time criminals such as gangs, smugglers, gamblers, con artists and shadowrunners.

Other interesting opposition may be corruption within the characters' organization or precinct. Bad cops, corrupt political officials, political pressure from higher-ups and the like can be much more difficult for the characters to fight than simple street scum. Cop characters might also have trouble from rival police or security organizations, especially if a contract dispute is going on or some other company wants to muscle in on the police business in the player characters' city.

The campaign is likely to see plenty of violence with characters who work the mean streets every day, but the mayhem is of a different kind than most shadowrunners encounter. Cops are bound by the law and company regulations about the use of deadly force; sensational trid stories to the contrary, they should never deal with a problem by shooting first and asking questions later. Cop and corpsec characters will have the advantage of the best modern weapons and armor that nuyen can buy (unless their department is underfunded, as many are); however, they should still be careful. Shadowrunners can be tricky opponents, after all.

Complications

Some players may find the rules and restrictions of working in a police organization—especially the limits in equipment and advancement—too constricting. Certain "square peg" character types such as shamans might have a tough time fitting into the campaign. Also, the players can become complacent and lazy if all their characters' activities are dictated by their superior officers.

Unless the characters are part of an elite group like an FRT, they probably aren't cyber-gods or Nth-grade initiates; they're most likely just ordinary cops trying to do their job. The characters have the advantages of professional training and whatever backing and equipment their organization provides, so they shouldn't have to worry much about scrounging for gear unless they want something that isn't regulation.

Magician characters will have free access to the organization's magical equipment and resources, and may also have an in-house initiate group to teach them the higher mysteries at some future point. Decker characters will have the chance to play with a number of systems legitimately (for a change), and they also have free access to their own organization's hi-tech systems.

The company rules and regulations offer a plausible rationale for the gamemaster to control character advancement and any new cyber or magical abilities that players want their characters to acquire.

As a general rule, the player characters stay in one area most of the time, leaving only when transferred to a different unit. However, such transfers may be as frequent as the gamemaster desires. Corp security teams come up for review fairly often in the fast-paced economy of the Awakened world, and so player-character teams could be transferred to anywhere in the world. They may be ordered to shore up existing security, request a transfer upon realizing that their superiors are corrupt or inefficient, or arrange for their own disappearance to another corp or the shadows.

DOUBLE, DOUBLE, TOIL AND TROUBLE

The magical campaign puts an interesting twist on a *Shadowrun* game because it revolves around encounters with, research into and exploration of the eerie and often formidable mystic powers of the Awakened world. From uncovering the truth behind Aztechnology to discovering the real purpose of the Atlantean Foundation or the ultimate scheme of the Illuminates of the New Dawn, magical investigations have an otherworldy feel that players may find appealing. Less like shadowrunners and more like scholarly investigators, characters in a magical campaign face all kinds of dangers—especially the fear of the unknown.

CHARACTER CREATION

Most or all of the player characters in a magical campaign should have some kind of magical ability, though the occasional mundane character can be added to make things interesting. This type of campaign works best if all the player characters are members of the same magical order or lodge or other initiatory group; this automatically gives them a history together and will likely give them a goal as well. Many of the characters' activities must remain hidden in order to conceal the order's secrets from mundane humanity. The group may work toward the goals of their order, lodge, government or organization, or may work against another organization. The magical campaign offers a perfect opportunity to use the adept characters that appear in many *Shadowrun* products.

A magical campaign can be more aggressive on all levels if its members are working for someone else, preferably a powerful backer. In this case, not all the team members need be magically active. The Dunkelzahn Institute for Magical Research (pp. 33–34, 102 of *Target: UCAS*) is an excellent organization for this type of campaign.

ADVENTURE IDEAS

The world of *Shadowrun* is full of magical sites, items, people, creatures, spirits and organizations. Most are secret; some are so secret that the only evidence of their existence is the occasional whispered rumor. A magical campaign can easily take on the feel of a regular shadowrun—for example, sneaking into the local Aztechnology facility to find out what magical research is going on there. Others may feel like an archaeological expedition—such as investigating a power site, mana line or magical anomaly like the Mojave Desert. Still other adventures may cast the player characters as astral investigators looking into the metaplanes. And of course, an ongoing covert war against another magical group or society is always a good adventure hook.

CAMPAIGNING WITH MAGIC

The following section complements the *Archetypal Adventure Plots* section, p. 100 of *Running the Game*, by fleshing out some of the concepts presented in that section.

The Premise

Characters in a magical campaign travel wherever they must for their work. They might hit the Bermuda Triangle one week, Egypt the next and Glastonbury, England the week after that. This type of campaign lets the gamemaster offer a wide variety of exotic and magical settings for adventures, but also makes it extremely important for the characters to have a stable "home base" with their organization so that they can deal with regular recurring NPCs.

Magicans as a group tend to feel that they have a greater stake in the workings of the universe because magic is neither good nor bad—that judgment applies only to specific uses of it. And "bad magic" is almost always very, very bad. Therefore, magical campaigns tend to be large-scale, with far-reaching implications for at least the characters' magical order and possibly even the world.

The Goal

This type of campaign is ideal for players who want to explore different aspects of magic in the Sixth World, including the metaplanes and the many different types of spirits and paranormal critters. It also offers the chance to use different exotic locations. The tone of a magical campaign is open to interpretation, but assumes that the player characters are all seeking knowledge and truth (however they define it) and have plans for using that knowledge. If the players can handle the complexity, their group might even have a mixture of goals and motivations. Some characters might seek knowledge for its own sake, some might be looking for magical power, and others may be seeking to protect mundane humanity from various magical threats.

The moral tone of the campaign, whatever it may be, can be strongly expressed through the strictures of the magical group to which the characters belong (see *Magic in the Shadows*). This setup gives the campaign some added weight because a character who violates too many strictures can be expelled from the order. If this happens, the character would most likely have to leave the group.

Opposition

The major opponents characters are likely to face in this type of campaign are members of rival magical orders. Knowledge is power, and magicians seek knowledge above all else. Rival groups working at cross purposes may contend with each other to get their hands on some valuable magical lore, or to snatch a hidden magical treasure from some ancient site or ruin. Groups such as the Illuminates of the New Dawn, Aztlan blood mages, the Black Lodge, Winternight and the Atlantean Foundation are all possible rivals for the player characters. Individual magicians such as toxic shamans can also provide hefty challenges.

Other major antagonists for a magical order are powerful spirits: free spirits, insect spirits and even the mysterious Enemy, if the gamemaster so desires.

Though the magical campaign is primarily investigative, it has the potential for some truly spectacular magical battles, as well as grand-scale physical conflict on the astral plane and the metaplanes. Mundane characters may be most useful in this type of campaign as bodyguards for the less brawny magicians in the group. If desired, the characters might be members of a physically oriented organization, such as a martial arts dojo. Such a campaign would be well-suited for adept characters.

Complications

The campaign's focus on magic can be its greatest weakness as well as its greatest strength. For players not especially interested in magic, a magical campaign can quickly grow tiresome. Also, a magical campaign's narrow focus can tend to make all the player characters seem the same; they all know the same spells, have similar magical skills, and so on. To avoid this pitfall, the gamemaster should encourage players to create more specialized characters than a typical *Shadowrun* magician.

Player characters are likely to develop considerable magical power as the campaign progresses, and so gamemasters are advised to keep a close eye on how characters spend their Karma for advancement. Remind your players that non-magical skills and abilities are useful in various situations, and encourage the players to buy them. The gamemaster may also wish to set an upper limit on magical skills such as sorcery and conjuring so that no character grows out of control.

THIS IS OUR TURF, MEAT

Shadowrun makes an ideal environment for a gang campaign. This type of campaign allows players to play characters who don't have it all under control. They're just above squatters on the food chain and have to fight for every inch of ground they get. They can't fight without thought because there are predators a lot bigger and meaner than they are on the streets. So if gang characters want to survive, they have to think. A last-resort home of sorts for people who've been used and abused by the system, a gang is a social club, shadowrunning group, terrorist organization and law enforcement (of a sort) for their home turf. Usually led by a charismatic leader, gangers tend to belong to disenfranchised groups: racial, ethnic or economic. They band together and form mini-societies with their own rules, attitudes, prejudices and goals.

A gang campaign offers an immediate means of getting a group of characters together and keeping them that way by forging bonds of cooperation and loyalty between them. The campaign also allows for a lower power level so that the players and gamemaster can concentrate on character development and personal interaction rather than simply accumulating various toys.

The following campaign notes apply to small neighborhood or area gangs, not city-wide or national forces.

GANG CREATION

Forming a gang gives outcast individuals the protection of numbers and the advantage (physical and psychological) of backup when on the offensive. They also provide the only way for a shadowrunner wannabe to have something to hold onto in a world gone crazy. The gang gives him a group of friends his own age, to whom he is loyal and who are loyal to him. He gets to feel a part of something bigger and more powerful than his own insignificant self. He gets status within the gang that he could never have outside it, which attracts girls and makes him look tough to other guys. To reflect these factors, all gangs have the trappings of an initiate group; they must maintain rituals, know codes and undergo initiations.

Using the following guidelines, the gamemaster should develop the concept for a gang before the players create their gang characters.

Gang Focus

The gang focus is the reason why this group of individuals got together. Because gang members are all like-minded individuals, the gang focus is usually narrow and frequently based on hatred of something or someone. The most common gangs are those in which the members are all one race: trolls, elves, humans and so on. The flip side is almost as common—multi-racial gangs whose focus is mutual hatred of one race in particular. If a gang's focus is to unite all the neighborhood trolls, then obviously all of the gang members will be trolls. If a gang's focus is hatred of trolls, people of any race aside from trolls can join. A gang's focus might also be to fight a mega-corp whose activities or products have been killing "our kind"; these types of gangs are especially common in Oakland, California Free State. Gangs like this will accept recruits of any race who pledge to help bring down "the enemy." Still other gangs are generally anti-corp, anti-government, and so on.

Initiation Rituals

These rituals can be anything that a ganger must undergo to become a member. The ritual can include personal pain, a particular mission, hazing, tattooing or scarring and so on, and usually also involves an oath or vow. The initiation ritual to become a lieutenant may be different than the ritual to become a member; the ritual might change with a gang's leader, or a new leader might require the gang members to renew their vow or oath to show loyalty to him or her. Upon successfully completing the ritual, a new recruit is considered a full-fledged member of the gang.

Uniforms

Known commonly as colors, gang uniforms can be anything from red bandannas and red socks to the complete uniform of the New York Yankees baseball team circa 1918. Everything from a particular piece of clothing worn to a type of weapon used may be part or all of the uniform. Uniforms let people know exactly what gang a gang member belongs to, and gangers consider it dishonorable to remove their colors for any reason.

Symbol

A gang's symbol is used to mark their territory; gangers may also wear the symbol as a tattoo or a logo on their jackets.

Territory

Territory is the gang's home turf, its boundaries usually marked by their symbol. Any given gang's turf is usually in one area of a city and is patrolled by the gang members. Patrols are especially likely if a gang shares a border with an enemy gang. Territory is a gang's ego reflected; members of other gangs are rarely allowed to cross a rival's territory, though a gang's turf may include limited "free" or "safe" zones such as the local street doc's clinic or a school. A good rule of thumb for determining the size of a gang's territory is to make it a number of city blocks equal to the number of gang members (including NPCs). Keeping within that limit should make it possible for the gang to patrol its turf.

Operations

Operations are the gang's main cash cow (or cows). The gangers may be front men for the Yakuza, roughing up businesses that don't pay their protection money on time. Or they may run their own protection racket. They may sell BTLs, smuggle contraband, strip cars, or anything else likely to earn them money to live on and to finance their particular war.

Uniqueness

Each gang has a unique style; maybe they only fight with katanas, or maybe they're all orks. Go-gangs are a unique type of street gang because they only ride cycles; one of the more unique go-gangs is the one that only deals in highway robbery between Seattle and Portland. They rarely kill anyone and always take the customs papers for the border. Other gangs are known for the type of shadow businesses they take on, as well as how they perform that business. Names, pets, main squeezes, hobbies and fighting tactics may all define a gang's uniqueness. The only limits are the players' imaginations and the gamemaster's approval.

CHARACTER CREATION

No gang character may start with more than 90,000 nuyen. If you are using the priority system of character creation, that means the character cannot make Resources Priority A or B. Depending on the gang's make-up, a character's race may or may not matter.

Gang members usually aren't a well-educated bunch. Many have not completed high school and extremely few have gone to college. To reflect this, no ganger can have starting Knowledge, Technical or Magical Skill ratings above 3, including Sorcery, Conjuring, Magical Theory, Demolitions and Computer Skills. In addition, any Edges relating to education are double the standard cost. The point of a ganger campaign is to have fun without being the best at anything.

Gangers tend to have less money than other types of characters and they don't know very many people with money. This means they can't always get their hands on what they want, even when they have the nuyen. To reflect this, gangers cannot have any starting gear with an Availability higher than 5.

It is assumed that the player characters' gang will include NPC gangers, but the players must pay for them during character creation. For every 50,000 nuyen sunk into the gang during character creation, the player characters gain 1D6 extra NPC gang members. Each NPC ganger is considered to have standard Attributes of 3 (modified by metatype) and Skill Ratings of 3. Gang members created this way are NPCs that the gamemaster may allow the players to control. These gangers belong to the entire group, not to any individual gang member

or leader, and do not count as contacts for character creation. All gangers are assumed to know others in their gang; aside from that, ganger characters get the normal number of contacts per standard rules. Gangers are not likely to have non-Street contacts; if they do, there should be an interesting story behind the friendship. For more information on generating a gang, see *Gang Creation*, p. 120.

Because most gangs lack resources and funds, they rarely boast mages among their number. Cyberware is also a relative rarity, though the less-expensive stuff trickles down to the back streets. Deckers are the rarest characters in a gang because of the cost of equipment and most gangers' lack of training and cyberware. Many a gang member sports a datajack, but actual Matrix access is uncommon. Riggers, by contrast, are common. Taking vehicles and borrowing parts to jury-rig faster or more powerful vehicles are a part of life for many gangs.

Whichever character sunk the most nuyen into buying extra NPC gangers is the gang leader at the beginning of the campaign. If a player cannot roleplay a charismatic leader, don't expect the other player characters to be willing to listen to him. NPCs may stay loyal for a little longer, but they won't stick by a complete frag-off either. Gangs are nothing if not disorganized, and a leader who can't keep his followers' loyalty won't last very long (see *Leadership Battle*, p. 123). The rest of the player characters are lieutenants, to differentiate them from NPCs and regular gangers. Because of his or her position of power, the leader gets a second Rank 1 enemy. (It's tough at the top.) Gamemasters may wish to bolster the leader by awarding him a Karma bonus (10 Karma is usually sufficient) before game play begins, to represent his fledgling Reputation.

The gang as a whole gets a single Fixer Contact at Level 1. This contact is established when the gang is created, and does not count as an individual contact. The fixer fences the gang's booty (if any; see *Earning Money*, p. 123).

All gangs have enemies, most of them other gangs. To find out how many gangs are enemies for the player characters, the gamemaster should divide the number of gang member player characters by 2 (round fractions up). (The bigger you are, the more people want to take you down, right?) For gamemastering purposes, treat all rival gangs as Rank 2 enemies. Each player character will also have an individual Rank 1 enemy: a member of a rival gang, a squatter, a BTL dealer, a prostitute or other street person whom the ganger has slotted off, a corporate wage slave that he has inadvertently (or intentionally) hurt, even a member of his own gang who dislikes him because of some past slight. These enemies will often prefer to humiliate the character rather than kill him outright.

Gang Options

The character creation rules above apply to the "typical" street gang; by using a few variations, the gamemaster can create several other gang types.

The basic concept behind an all-elf gang might be a bunch of bored kids convinced of their own superiority. Unlike other gangs, they aren't fighting for their lives; instead, they're out to destroy their "inferiors." If they so choose, they can be backed by "elven interest groups" (with no connection to Tir Tairngire government officials, of course), meaning they would have more money and prestige than a regular street gang; it would also mean that they have to dance to their sponsor's tune. Characters in elf gangs that choose this elven-backed option can have up to 400,000 nuyen (Priority B to Resources) as starting money. Mages are more common in all-elf gangs than in regular gangs, and the members are generally better educated. On the other hand, elf gangs have twice as many enemies as a regular gang, and must maintain at least a Medium lifestyle.

The tribesmen gang is not the usual urban gang; this type of gang operates between cities or on very localized turf. Tribesmen are almost always human Native Americans; metahuman members must also be from NAN lands or have Native American blood. The tribesmen follow the standard rules for street gangs, except that one character—usually the leader—must be a shaman. Whether or not the shaman is the leader, his or her totem will be part of the gang's symbol. Deckers and riggers are scarce in tribesmen groups. Only the leader will have City or Street contacts; all other contacts should be Rural or Tribal.

The decker gang is a specialized type of gang whose leader must start the game with 1,000,000 nuyen (Priority A to Resources). Whichever character buys the leadership position also pays for random jackpoints that he has set up in at least ten locations (determined by the gamemaster and the player running the leader character) and two hidden microtronics shops. The leadership fee in this case serves as a recruitment tool. Decker gangers have no cash or education limits, though only the leader should have any Street contacts. The rest of the gangers have contacts via the Matrix. The gamemaster determines if a given Matrix contact is the real deal or a Matrix poser.

ADVENTURE IDEAS

Gang campaigns operate on a different scale than shadowruns; they usually boil down to helping your own gang, hurting a rival gang, or internal power plays. Because gangs function in many ways like miniature crime families, most gang campaigns should use the *Karma and the Amoral Campaign* rules (p. 80). Gangs run small smuggling and theft rings, protection rackets, BTL deals, even prostitution rackets. The point of playing a gang is to fight the gang's enemies, and in order to do that the gang needs nuyen to equip themselves for their ongoing war. The economics of the gang's operations is determined by the gamemaster, but keep in mind that the average small-time street gang usually acts as middlemen (see *Special Rules*, p. 123).

Gang wars are the bread and butter of a gang's existence. Gang wars can run the gamut from bragging and posturing to fist and knife fights to blazing firefights and all-out destruction. Many gang wars are one-on-one battles; for the character being "called out" in this way, even a knife fight can be as intense and suspenseful as a war. Gang rivalries are also dynamic; an exciting mini-campaign might involve the characters needing to make peace with a rival gang, and having to convince both sides to sit down and do it.

Ganger campaigns can often be humorous. Without

money or training, they aren't going to be good at much, and the kindest thing the gamemaster can do is to keep the opposition at a manageable level. The point of the game is to have fun, so if the players come up with an in-character creative solution, give it to them even if it's not quite plausible. Gang campaigns can make a nice break from other campaigns or other games. The weight of the world is not on the characters' shoulders in this type of campaign; they shouldn't feel much pressure to do things right, and no matter how dumb, clumsy or inept they are, they know that others are worse.

If you want to showcase the dark side of the streets of the future and the bleak life of the poor, a gang campaign is perfect for that, too. Gang characters have nothing; they have to watch their friends and family suffer without much power to help them. Most NPCs treat them like dirt, and when they try to earn some money shadowrunning, people take it as confirmation that they are nothing but worthless killers.

CAMPAIGNING WITH GANGS

The following section complements the *Archetypal Adventure Plots* section, p. 100 of *Running the Game*, by fleshing out some of the concepts presented in that section.

The Premise

The characters are all part of an urban gang or tribe trying to survive and prosper in the Barrens or similar abandoned areas of the metroplex. They must deal with all the challenges of the mean streets, but have few resources to call upon. Any major metroplex can serve as the setting for a gang campaign, with different settings offering different atmospheres and story opportunities. Choose a setting with which the gamemaster and the players are comfortable; most of the campaign's stories will take place there and so the gamemaster needs to generate a large amount of detailed information about the setting. The characters' turf should be especially well-defined. Many of the campaign's stories will have a personal tone because they deal with small-scale events.

The Goal

The gang is family and tribe, and so loyalty to one's fellow gang members is the most important quality. Never show weakness in front of another gang. Answer all challenges to your gang's turf and honor. Never cooperate with "the man" or anyone else in authority from outside your gang. Oh, and survive until tomorrow. Simple, eh?

Opposition

Major antagonists for a gang campaign are other gangs who want to cut into the characters' turf and squeeze them out. Conflicts between various gangs in the campaign can also be influenced by corporate interests working behind the scenes for their own purposes.

The hardware and resources available to shadowrunners rarely fall into the hands of a bunch of scroffy gangers. Therefore, conflict between gangs and the fight for day-to-day survival in the urban jungle offer plenty of opportunities for violent conflict, as much to get money and gear as for any other reason. Gang violence often erupts in large-scale combats between two gangs, but can also show up in small-scale brawls and challenges between individual gangers. Finding ways to solve problems without violence can be posed as an interesting challenge to characters in this type of campaign.

Complications

The restrictions on power may prove frustrating to some players; also, constantly tending to the needs of the gang may take over the campaign and leave no room for other types of stories.

SPECIAL RULES

The rules below answer some major questions and offer strategies for dealing with some of the problems that may arise when running a gang campign.

Earning Money

Shadowrun is usually a do-the-job-get-paid world. In a gang campaign, however, characters aren't working for Mr. Johnson, so there usually isn't any pay for their efforts. Gangers do what they do for pride, honor and the amount of pain they can inflict on those they hate. That said, gang members must still earn cash to live and improve their lot in life. Therefore, gangs usually run a moneymaking operation of some sort— nothing big, but enough to keep them flush.

Most gangs get their cash by acting as middlemen in small-time criminal deals—say, BTL dealing or selling illegal weapons. A simple way to figure rates of pay for this work is to assume that the gang pays 10 to 60 percent of an illegal item's price and then sells it for the prices listed in various *Shadowrun* products. For example, a gang selling BTL chips at approximately 50 nuyen apiece might purchase them for 25 nuyen from their fixer; this nets the gang a 25-nuyen profit per chip. As always, the gamemaster can simulate the randomness of real-world economics by basing the percentage that the gangers pay on a D6 roll. The gamemaster can also add or deduct an extra 5 or 10 percent, depending on whether or not the gang won its last turf war or completed its most recent mission.

Gangs can also make money by stealing vehicles. Assuming they don't steal the vehicle to use (which saves them money because they don't have to buy one), they can sell it or strip it. If they keep it, they can do anything they want with it—repaint it, smash it into buildings, live out of it, whatever. If they decide to sell it, they can net up to 50 percent of the listed price. If the characters decide to strip the vehicle and sell the individual parts, they will get the full price for the vehicle as listed, but cannot collect until a number of days equal to the total of the vehicle's Body and Armor ratings has passed.

The Sploches steal a Mitsubishi Nightsky out of a parking lot near Dante's Inferno. They weigh their options. They can keep the kick-butt car and use it against the Zero Hours, with whom the Sploches are at war. But the Sploches need nuyen. If they sell the car whole, they can (maybe) get 125,000 nuyen—enough to keep the gang in arms, BTLs and synthohol for a long time. If they strip it,

they can get the entire 250,000-nuyen purchase price, but the cred would take 8 days to arrive (Body 5 + Armor 3 = 8). The Sploches can't be sure the Zero Hours won't attack in those 8 days, so they decide to sell the car (after hitting a cash register or two on the way back to their home turf).

Reputation and Leadership

Essentially, a gang's leader *is* the gang. The leader is the glue that keeps the gang together, and the leader's rep is the gang's rep. The leader of a gang relies on a combination of fear, reputation and honor to retain his authority, rather than the standard Leadership Skill. To determine a gang leader's (and therefore the gang's) Reputation Rating, use the following Reputation rules.

In his or her home town, a character's base Reputation Rating is equal to their Total Karma ÷ 10, rounded down. In another city or country, a character's base Reputation Rating is equal to their Total Karma ÷ 20, rounded down. This number represents the leader's notoriety; the higher the number, the more people have heard of him or her.

To calculate a target number for Etiquette or Street Knowledge Skill Tests to determine whether a particular opponent, contact or group of people knows (and fears) a character, subtract the base Reputation from 20. For example, someone asks their contact if she has ever heard of Shetani. Shetani has 150 Total Karma, making his base Reputation 15. The gamemaster calculates the target number as (20 – 15 = 5) for the test to recognize the gang leader.

The gamemaster may modify the base Reputation number to reflect the character's recent activities. For example, if Shetani mows down an entire enemy gang with a few well-placed fireballs or gets busted for child pornography, the gamemaster may modify the leader's Reputation by +2 to account for his current notoriety. The new calculation for the target number is 20 – 17 = 3, making it easier to succeed at the Etiquette Test, and therefore more likely the person will have heard of Shetani. On the other hand, if Shetani's been laying low for a few months, the gamemaster may modify his base Reputation by –2 to reflect this inactivity, creating a higher target number and so increasing the difficulty of succeeding at the test to recognize his name.

A gang leader's Reputation can be crucial to defeating an opponent and winning over other gang members in a leadership battle (see below).

Leadership Battle

Gangs get involved in infighting more often than gang wars. Invariably, a gang member will challenge the leader for control of the gang in a one-on-one battle. Rules for a leadership battle are determined by the gamemaster and the player or players controlling the character or characters making the challenge. The fight can be unarmed combat, a "one knife, two fighters" combat, an old-fashioned duel or any other known or imaginary version of single combat. The battle and the results can be humorous or a bloodbath. The fight can be to the death or to humiliation (which many gangers consider far worse). The winner becomes (or remains) the gang leader.

In a leadership battle between the leaders of two gangs or the leader of a gang and an outsider trying to take control of an established gang, one "contestant" may have a lower base Reputation than the other. The gamemaster may also modify either or both leaders' Reputation Rating before the leadership battle per the rules above. For every 2 full points a character's Reputation is higher than his opponent's, that character receives an extra Karma die for the duration of the leadership battle. This represents how a character's Reputation can daunt his opponent, especially when cheered on by those on the sidelines.

The winning gang gets the losing gang's assets and turf. At that point, each member of the losing gang makes an Intelligence Test against a target number equal to the new leader's Reputation minus his Charisma, but plus their own Willpower. Those who succeed are swayed by the new top dog and become his supporters. Those whose tests fail will walk away, either forming their own gang to exact revenge against the leader or becoming that character's personal enemies.

Red, the leader of the Ladies from Hades, decides to take on Goldy, the leader of the Medusas. Red wins. Red's Reputation is 12 and her Charisma is 6, and so the nine surviving Medusas (each with Willpower 3) each make an Intelligence Test against a Target Number 9 (12 – 6 + 3 = 9). Five of the Medusas make successful tests. The remaining four take off, to form a new gang or seek revenge.

Gang Creation on the Fly

When a group forms a gang, the opposition is usually another gang. To create an entire gang out of whole cloth, the gamemaster should use the *Creating Prime Runners* rules (p. 83). The gamemaster should also make sure that the rival gang's numbers match those of the player-character gang, or at least come close. No matter how tough its members, a smaller gang will always lose to a larger one in the long run, and so the gamemaster should aim for a roughly equal balance of forces. Gangs have one of four possible ratings: Inferior, Equal, Superior or Superhuman. There are no Ultimate gangs. All gangs follow the standard rules for ganger NPC statistics.

If an Inferior gang has double the numbers of the player characters' gang, they are considered Equal. An Inferior gang should have fewer lieutenants than the player characters' gang.

If an Equal gang is twice as large as the player characters' gang, consider them Superior for purposes of Threat Ratings and Dice Pools. If an Equal gang has less than half the numbers of the player characters' gang, treat them as Inferior. An Equal gang should have the same number of lieutenants as the player characters' gang.

If a Superior gang has double the numbers of the player characters' gang, they are considered Superhuman. If such a gang has less than half the player-character gang's numbers, consider them Equal for determining Threat Ratings and Dice Pools. A Superior gang should have more lieutenants than the player characters' gang; the exact number is up to the gamemaster.

A Superhuman gang follows the standard rules for NPC statistics, but usually wins its battles no matter how much smaller they are than the player characters' gang. The Superhuman gang has at least twice as many lieutenants as the player characters' gang.

A Superhuman or Superior gang may have divisions in any of the less powerful classifications. For example, the gamemaster may decide that the Inferior gang you just destroyed is actually a division of a Superhuman gang that was looking to move into the player characters' turf. The player characters just made a powerful gang leader very, very unhappy … .

As with player-character gangs, the size of the turf should determine the size of the gang. The minimum number of gangers is one per city block; there is no maximum.

GANGS IN SHADOWRUN

The following five examples represent Seattle-based street gangs of various power levels. The information provided appears in the format used in *Gang Creation* (p. 120), with the following additions.

Leader: Refers to the gang leader and lieutenants (if any), with a brief bio for each.

Gang Rating: Inferior, Equal, Superior or Superhuman.

Head Count: Represents the number of members in the gang.

Foes: Other gangs and/or organizations that the gang considers their primary enemies.

These gangs can be used as gang archetypes or as is. Gangs are mentioned in the *Underworld Sourcebook* as well as *New Seattle.* More gangs will be highlighted in various upcoming *Shadowrun* products, presented in this format. These descriptions supersede all other information published about these gangs.

THE HALLOWEENERS

Gang Focus: This gang started as a small group of humans out to rob the rich folk of downtown Seattle of their cred and trinkets. Renraku Security eventually decided that enough was enough; they sent operatives to follow the Halloweeners and their then-leader, Funky Errak, to the gang's hideout. The ensuing gun battle left the hideout in flames and most of the original Halloweeners dead. Only the current leader (known as Slash and Burn) and two other founding members survived. Slash has decided that all megacorps will pay for Renraku's crime, and has opened the ranks of the Halloweeners to anyone willing to take on the corps. This gang has a reputation as one of the most psychotic in the sprawl.

Leader: Slash and Burn, human. An incredibly skinny freak, he likes to burn those who oppose his gang.

Lieutenants: 5

Zazz, a human mage and an original Halloweener who survived along with Slash. Zazz still suffers nightmares about fire and has a mental block against using any kind of fire spell.

Zany Janey, a human razorgirl and another original member. She just loves to cut people—the more blood the better. Janey is Slash's girl.

Honest Jack, a dwarf. He rescued Zazz, Slash and Janey from the fire, which also destroyed his home. He became the first new member of the Halloweeners, and he wants every corper dead. He loves to shoot guns.

Sister Love, a female elf and a rigger. Sister is Zazz's main squeeze.

Bobby Blue, a troll. He likes to hit people—any people.

Gang Rating: Superior

Head Count: Approximately 25–40 members.

Initiation Rituals: The Halloweeners use two rituals. The first is the Circle of Fire, in which the gangers build a fire around the recruit. The recruit remains in the middle of the fiery circle for about as long as Slash remembers being in the burning building during the Renraku attack (approximately 5 to 10 minutes). The second ritual is to break into a megacorporate office and bring something back as proof.

Uniforms: The colors of the Halloweeners are orange and black, befitting their name. Most often they wear black clothing, with orange bandannas tied to their arms, legs or neck. They dress up to commit their crimes and almost always wear masks. Ever since the fire, Slash prefers to wear a big ape head when having his fun. Zazz favors a hellhound mask that looks freakishly real in the lights of the downtown arcologies.

Symbol: Originally a pumpkin with an evil leer, the gang's symbol has evolved to the now-familiar vague representation of a pumpkin (usually a circle with eyes and mouth) smiling demonically against a fiery background. The eyes and mouth seem to be coming out of the fire.

Territory: The Halloweeners consider all of downtown and every arcology their turf (that's where they fight their never-ending war, after all). Their headquarters is just outside the downtown area, in the docks south of the Renraku Arcology. They control and patrol the docks up to and including the ones behind the Renraku Arcology, plus the entire area west to the river (including half of Kobe Terrace Park) up to the border of downtown.

Operations: The Halloweeners make their nuyen in straight crime sprees. Most of what they sell goes to the Triads or the Seoulpa Rings.

Foes: The Halloweeners rarely fight other gangs. They prefer to concentrate on their main enemies: Renraku security forces, Lone Star and (surprisingly enough) the Yakuza and the Mafia. The Halloweeners will steal from anyone they think looks corporate enough, and the yaks and the Mob fit that bill. The Halloweeners sometimes run into

trouble with other gangs because they tend to ignore turf borders. Several gangs in the downtown area and south of downtown Seattle have fought with the Halloweeners at various times.

Uniqueness: Aside from Slash's weird fire fetish, the Halloweeners have no specific modus operandi. They attack those they perceive to be corporate wage slaves, make the occasional hit on the Renraku docks, and every once in a while pull a run on Renraku or some other downtown corp. Their crimes tend to be brutal: multiple deaths, plenty of property damage, fires and so on. The Halloweeeners like to set fires. From fear of their bloodthirsty reputation, no one hits them very hard or for very long. Certainly no one wants to be on Slash's hit list.

THE SPIDERS

Gang Focus: More than anything else, this multiracial gang is characterized by its members' implacable hatred of bug spirits. This loathing is personal and visceral. Every one of the original Spiders fell into the hands of the Universal Brotherhood at some point in his or her life, and none of them have gotten over the horrors they experienced. Living to destroy bugs, in the company of a like-minded "family," is their way of dealing with these traumas. Their links with the Spider totem, which each gang member meets as part of his or her initiation ritual, reinforces this fiercely anti-bug mindset.

The gang is extremely violent, but keeps a relatively low profile. Unlike other violent gangs, they never leave "calling cards" or other clues to their presence. Like the spiders they emulate, these gangers prefer to strike silently and lethally. They recruit new members by snatching likely prospects off the Seattle streets and brainwashing them into joining the gang over the course of several days. Their methods are brutal and effective; most prospective recruits become true believers in short order.

Leader: Widow, a human Spider shaman. She wears black all the time, to set off her pale skin and gray eyes. She could be anywhere from 20 to 35 years old—no one can tell for sure. She is incredibly vain about her hands, which are long and narrow and extremely graceful.

Lieutenants: 5

Tarantula, a young ork recently promoted after singlehandedly killing two roach spirits with a jerry-built contraption that she refers to as "my Raid can." Barely out of her teens, Tarantula is Widow's protégé; the gang leader treats her almost like a daughter. Tarantula repays this regard with fanatical loyalty, imitating everything Widow says or does.

Fiddler, an elf and founding member of the gang. Skinny and undernourished, with piercing black eyes, Fiddler is a city dweller down to his toenails; he claims he can't breathe if he goes too far away from the concrete jungle. His arms are covered with puckered scars, about which he refuses to speak.

Trapdoor, a dwarf. He hates wasp spirits above all other bugs, though he'll glady kill any bugs he can get his hands on. Trapdoor plays incessantly with a cat's cradle, and can make more shapes with it than anyone alive ever knew existed.

Wolf, a human who escaped from the Chicago Containment Zone just a year ago. He is convinced that his Spider totem led him to Seattle, the one place on Earth where he could hope to find people capable of "casting out" the fly spirit that he believes was attempting to possess him. The Spiders picked him up in the Redmond Barrens within weeks of his arrival in Seattle, sized him up as a potentially powerful magician, and made him their own in record time. Wolf believes that Widow is divinely appointed to rid the world of bugs, and that she will ascend into Heaven on spider-silk wings when her task is finished.

Recluse, a troll and Fiddler's squeeze. She rarely talks to anyone except Fiddler, and even to him rarely uses more than two or three words at a time. She's deadly with almost any kind of blade, but is especially partial to a jagged-edged hunting knife that she's named "Sweeney." Somewhere, Recluse picked up detailed knowledge of anatomy (though she doesn't remember where anymore), and so she supervises the bulk of the gang's organlegging activity.

Gang Rating: Superior

Head Count: Approximately 50–100 members.

Initiation Rituals: Each prospective recruit goes on a vision quest to meet Spider and receive his or her gang name (always the name of a spider). Those who survive this ordeal become gang members; those who don't generally die raving within a day or two of the quest's end. Once a new ganger receives a name, he or she is assigned a specific task as part of "guarding the Web." In practice, this usually means a specific building to protect, area to patrol, or other job to do that somehow relates to keeping the gang's territory bug-free. More experienced gangers explain carefully to each newbie exactly what their assigned task is, how best to do it, and why it's important in the Scheme of Things.

After proving themselves by satisfactorily fulfilling their assigned tasks, new gangers move on to part two of their initiation—kidnapping a potential initiate. They usually also take part in the brainwashing of their victim, sometimes even assuming the leading role. Once they accomplish this, they are eligible to become lieutenants.

To become a lieutenant, a ganger must kill a bug spirit singlehandedly. The ganger in question seeks out a nest of bugs and informs at least five fellow gangers of his or her intent to kill one. These witnesses accompany the gang member to

ground zero, where they watch the ganger attempt to kill the bug. They do not intervene unless their fellow ganger looks likely to lose the fight, in which case they will jump into combat to save the ganger's life. The ganger does not become a lieutenant, however, and must spend at least a year living down the disgrace before being permitted to try again.

Uniforms: The Spiders wear synthleather jackets in the gang's colors: black or dark brown and red. Most often, black or dark brown is the background color, with a red design on the jacket in synthleather, embroidery, paint or (occasionally) colored tape.

Symbol: Each Spider makes (or finds) his or her own variation on a web—anything from the classic spiderweb to a butterfly net to a schematic representation of a Matrix network. These symbols may be painted or embroidered on jackets, worn as shoulder patches or jewelry, tattooed on the ganger's body, or anything else the ganger desires. All gang members wear web tattoos on their shaved scalps.

Territory: The Spiders claim all of Redmond as their territory, which they refer to as "the Web." According to rumor, their headquarters is an abandoned warehouse in a particularly god-forsaken section of Redmond known as Brain Heaven.

Operations: To finance their bug-hunting expeditions and pay for their living expenses, the Spiders most often serve as couriers, fences and other types of criminal middlemen. They also frequently resort to petty theft. The most lucrative of their activities is organlegging, as they have a steady supply of failed recruits to carve up for spare parts.

Foes: The gang considers bug spirits of all types as its primary foes, and will go out of its way to attack bugs or anyone the gang perceives as being somehow "in league" with the bugs. (This definition can be fairly loose, depending

on who's making the call.) The Spiders also have occasional run-ins with other gangs in Redmond, generally when another gang "refuses to accept the Spiders' protection from the evil bug spirits."

Uniqueness: The Spiders pride themselves on acting like their namesakes—moving silently and striking so swiftly that the "enemy" is immobilized or dead before he knows what hit him. They mark their territory with signs rather than patrols; an intruder into Spider turf will suddenly find himself surrounded by gangers who seemingly materialized from thin air, and will shortly afterward be unconscious or a corpse. This "guerrilla warfare" approach has made the Spiders a force to be reckoned with, against bug spirits and in more ordinary criminal activities. Spider couriers have a reputation for being able to deliver the goods in record time; Spider fences are known for webs of contacts so dazzlingly vast that most attempts to trace the sale of illegal goods back to the gang end in failure.

THE SPIKES

Gang Focus: Once a run-of-the-mill go-gang, the Spikes (formerly the Spike Wheels) have recently come under the leadership of a charismatic troll named Lord Torgo. Torgo became the gang boss after singlehandedly destroying one of its major rivals, the Silent Ps; after the victory, he changed the gang's name to reflect its improved status. Always anti-elf, the gang has stepped up its operations against Tir Tairngire under Torgo's control.

Leader: Lord Torgo, a troll of awe-inspiring dimensions with a bloodthirsty streak to match his size. Though as poorly educated as any other lifelong resident of Seattle's slums, he is fantastically intelligent, and reads everything he can get his mitts on. His favorite books—actual paper books with battered covers and dog-eared pages—are Sun Tzu's *The Art of War* and Machiavelli's *The Prince*. Though no one dares mock him for his interest in reading

ELVES MUST DIE

MIKE·N·86

(though many consider it a waste of time and energy better devoted to survival), the information contained in his best-loved books allowed him to dispatch the Silent Ps in the spectacularly messy and unquestionably personal manner that solidified his fearsome reputation throughout Seattle.

Lieutenants: 2

Goddess Ursula, an enormous female troll and Torgo's main squeeze. She can barely write her own name, but has an instinct for fighting tactics that won her Torgo's respect. She loves to ride at full speed toward large armored trucks, firing away with an Uzi in one hand and a rocket launcher in the other.

Manny One-eye, only half Torgo's size but fanatically loyal to him. Manny has not a brain in his head, and is so hideous that his appearance alone will intimidate almost any enemy. He claims to have lost his eye in a brawl with a Tir Ghost patrol, of which he was the only survivor. Current rumor among the Spikes says he actually lost it in a poker game with the gang's previous leader, and that Torgo won it back for him. Torgo is said to keep the eye in a lock-box under a floorboard in the gang's HQ.

Gang Rating: Superior

Head Count: Approximately 15–25 members.

Initiation Rituals: To join the Spikes, a prospective recruit must kill an elf. He can accomplish this any way he wishes, but must have at least two witnesses to the killing and must bring back a "trophy" for Lord Torgo to put on display. Favorite trophies are ears and scalps—the latter especially if the victim had hair of an unusual color.

Uniforms: All gang members wear camo fatigues, in keeping with Lord Torgo's conceit that the gang is actually a disciplined private army. Gang members also wear gold bandannas, most often tied around their heads or upper arms.

Symbol: Usually spray-painted on the sides of vehicles they've trashed, the Spikes' symbol is a crudely drawn elf head with Xes for eyes; the head is pierced by a spike, which frequently (though not always) has blood dripping from it.

Territory: The Spikes claim Interstate 5 and the neighborhoods surrounding it, from just south of downtown Seattle all the way to the Tir Tairngire border—this area includes Fort Lewis, Puyallup and Hell's Kitchen. Their HQ is rumored to be in Fort Lewis, though no one knows exactly where.

Operations: As the "tollkeepers" of Interstate 5, the Spikes are perfectly placed to indulge in their favorite activity—attacking anything and anyone going into or coming out of Tir Tairngire. Any vehicle on the road is fair game, but favorite targets include shipments of goods with potentially high value in Seattle's shadows. In addition to (literal) highway robbery, the Spikes are known for particularly vicious hate crimes against elves.

Foes: Lord Torgo's personal ambition is to destroy the Ancients, Seattle's best-known elf gang. He and his fellow gangers love to use Tir border patrols as target practice. Because the gang's primary enemies are elves, they rarely bother ork or human or dwarf gangs unless provoked.

Uniqueness: One of the few all-troll gangs in the Seattle sprawl, the Spikes are known for their unorthodox mode of attacking their chosen targets. Like the ancient Mongol hordes

who galloped across the steppes of Central Asia, the Spikes ride down their victims en masse; the sight of a posse of troll bikers thundering toward a truck or armored car, howling all the way, has given more than one driver heart failure.

THE RED HOT NUKES

Gang Focus: The Red Hot Nukes prefer to think of themselves as a neighborhood association rather than a gang, despite their clearly illegal activities. They regard their primary mission as protecting and aiding residents of their neighborhood any way they can. Though membership is only open to dwarfs, the Nukes display no prejudice against other races; they will defend their people against any threat, and define "their people" as being everyone who lives on their turf.

Leader: Grinder, a young black dwarf and ex-runner with an anarchist bent. Grinder is an adept, and is personally training every member of the Nukes to be as talented an adept as he is. On the rare occasions when Grinder gets tipsy, he hints at his deep dark reason for founding and training the gang—he claims to have discovered some horrible future event while on an anti-megacorp run a few years ago, which he is grooming the Nukes to prevent. He refuses to tell anyone exactly what this future is; the mere mention of it gives him nightmares.

Lieutenants: None.

Gang Rating: Equal

Head Count: Approximately 15–25 members.

Initiation Rituals: Each new recruit must prove himself by disarming a bomb built by Grinder. Those who fail this test are blown to smithereens.

Uniforms: The Red Hot Nukes wear gray and red, and each of them sports a baseball-style cap.

Symbol: The gang's insignia is a mushroom cloud, which commemorates both their name and their skill with explosives. The symbol appears somewhere on every ganger's clothing, often painted on their jackets or worn as a patch on the jacket or cap.

Territory: The Nukes claim Redmond as their turf; their headquarters is in the Hollywood neighborhood.

Operations: The Nukes specialize in jobs that require expertise with explosives. In addition to demolitions, they build small bombs for use in protection rackets and insurance scams; local businessmen who need ready cash frequently call on the Nukes to destroy their businesses so that they can then pocket the insurance money. Part of every ganger's training involves bomb-building with a wide variety of materials; the Nukes go out of their way to avoid "signature" bomb-making styles so that law enforcement can't trace explosive devices back to them. The gang also pulls the occasional theft, or even wetwork if the price is right.

Foes: Perhaps reflecting their leader's ex-runner background, the Nukes are anti-corporate to the point of paranoia. Though they do most of their demolition work for pay, they carry out a certain number of sabotage runs against corporate research installations, the more obscure the better. They regard most of the other gangs in Redmond as "enemies of the people," and fight them when they must; however, they don't go looking for trouble. The Spiders and the Rusty Stilettos are the most frequent targets of punitive action by the Nukes, as they are more likely than other gangs to challenge the Nukes' authority.

Uniqueness: As far as anyone knows, the Red Hot Nukes are the only gang composed entirely of dwarf adepts. They're also the only ones who specialize in bomb-making to the virtual exclusion of any other moneymaking activities.

THE NIGHT HUNTERS

Gang Focus: The skinheads of the 2050s, this human-only gang and its various like-named splinter groups live to hassle and intimidate metahumans. Unlike their twentieth-century counterparts, the Night Hunters don't discriminate based on skin color or gender; only metahumans are the targets of their hatred. They lean toward the Humanis policlub party line, and proudly act as front-line thugs in the policlub's war "to make the world safe for true humanity." They are often violent, but actually kill their victims far less often than most people believe. Most gang members are much younger than thirty; many of them are heavily into body-piercing and chains.

Leader: Stiv (main group; the various splinter gangs have their own leaders). Stiv grew up in a respectable middle-class home, ruled by his father's iron hand. Father was a preacher of the fire-and-brimstone variety, and as the oldest child Stiv got the lion's share of harsh paternal attention. He is a classic sociopath—highly intelligent and completely lacking in empathy or conscience. When under extreme stress, he burns himself with cigarettes as a way of proving himself impervious to pain.

Lieutenants: 2 (main group; splinter gangs vary)

Splitter, a stocky half-Amerind woman with vicious knife scars on her cheek and throat. She claims to have gotten the scars on the Night of Rage, when a rampaging band of trolls broke into her home and murdered the rest of her family. The trolls left her for dead, but she managed to drag herself to the household PANICBUTTON and call DocWagon. Orphaned and homeless, she survived as best she could on the streets of Seattle until the Night Hunters took her in when she was ten years old. She has never tried to challenge Stiv's authority; she considers it a waste of time as long as there are metahumans around to hurt.

Shank, a skinny mulatto of nineteen who has been Stiv's right-hand man for the past five years. Shank hails most recently from Redding in Northern CalFree, and has an especial loathing of elves (though other metas aren't much better, to his way of thinking). Abandoned by his mother at a young age, Shank doesn't know who his father is; lately, though, he's been fantasizing that Daddy is really Kenneth Brackhaven. Shank would never presume on the relationship, however; he merely wants to admire his "father" from afar. Right now, the Night Hunters are all the family he needs.

Gang Rating: Equal

Head Count: Approximately 20–30 members.

Initiation Rituals: Each new recruit must brand a metahuman with the Night Hunters' symbol. Some Hunter gangs will accept painting the symbol on a metahuman's skin, but most gangs prefer more painful methods. The favorites are burning (like cattle branding) and carving the symbol about a quarter-inch into the skin with a rusty knife. Particularly sadistic gangers follow up the second method by sprinkling salt into the cuts.

Uniforms: Night Hunters favor head-to-toe black leather ornamented with chains and studs. All of them, male and female, wear their hair in mohawks dyed bright green. Every Night Hunter sports three hand razors on one hand, which they use to make their distinctive slashing mark.

Symbol: A talon slashing the moon. They wear the symbol most often on clothing or as a scalp tattoo. Many of the gang members like to draw the symbol on their jackets in glow-in-the-dark paint; that way, their intended victims can see them coming and feel the appropriate terror.

Territory: The Hunters claim all of Renton, but lack enough members to patrol the area. Countless splinter gangs exist, all but one of whom continue to call themselves the Night Hunters; the single exception is the group known as the Werewolves, which split from the main band of Hunters three or four years ago and has managed to share the gang's turf relatively peacefully.

Operations: The Night Hunters trade in BTLs for money; aside from that, they commit whatever crime seems like it might be the most fun way to kill a slow afternoon. They are partial to vandalism—there's nothing most Night Hunters like better than making lots of noise and smashing things, especially if they can terrorize some metahumans in the process. They rarely kill their metahuman victims; for most Hunters, the thrill is in humiliation and torture. A corpse doesn't cringe or beg for mercy, and so is no fun any more.

Foes: The primary foe of all Night Hunter gangs is the entire metahuman population of Seattle. From the high-level elf corporator to the ork janitor down the street, all metas are equally fair game (though they prefer the very old and the very young as the easiest to intimidate).

Other Night Hunter groups, formed when one lieutenant or another tried and failed to unseat Stiv, are hostile to the main gang (and to each other). Each splinter group sees itself as the "true" Night Hunters to a greater or lesser degree; the various groups act out this belief by assaulting each other or else refusing to acknowledge each other's existence. On occasion, one Night Hunter gang declares war against another; these wars invariably fizzle out after the first couple of casualties, however.

Uniqueness: More than any other human-only gang, the Night Hunters are obssessed with humiliating metahumans. If a ganger's day goes by without his at least being able to spit on an elf or trip up a troll, that day has been an utter waste of time. Night Hunters love to collect trophies from their metahuman victims, especially elf ears, troll and ork tusks, and dwarf beards (complete with the layer of skin that used to cover the unlucky dwarf's chin). The gangs' distinctive triple arrangement of hand razors is highly unusual.

ACTIONS

The following actions are described in *SR3*, *Rigger 2*, *Virtual Realities 2.0*, *Magic in the Shadows* and the *Critters* book in the *SR3 Gamemaster Screen*.

FREE

General
Activate Cyberware
Delay Action
Drop Object
Drop Prone
Gesture
Observe
Speak a Word

Combat
Call a Shot
Change Smartgun Fire Mode
Eject Smartgun Clip

Critter
Cold Aura
Corrosive Saliva
Fading
Flame Aura
Magical Guard
Shadow Cloak

Decking
Allocate Utility Pool (SKs and AIs Only)
Analyze IC or Icon
Jack Out
Maintain Monitored Operation
Notice New Icon
Retrain Bandwidth
Terminate Download/Upload
Unload Program from Active Memory
Unsuppress IC

Magic
Allocate Spell Defense/Reflecting/Shielding dice
Centering (Metamagic)
Deactivate Focus
Drop Deliberate Masking (Metamagic)
Drop Sustained Spell
End Manifestation
Missile Parry (Adept Power)

Rigging/Vehicle
Activate/Deactivate Rigged Autonav/Sensors/ECM/ECCM/ECD
Arm/Disarm a Rigged Weapon System
Call Up a Status Report
Suppress CCSS Automatic Alarms

SIMPLE

General
Change Position
Observe in Detail
Pick Up/Put Down Object
Use Reflex Trigger (Activate/Deactivate Wired Reflexes)
Use Simple Object

Combat
Change Gun Mode
Fire Weapon (SS, SA or BF)
Insert Clip
Quick Draw
Ready Weapons
Remove Clip
Set Up Bipod/Tripod
Take Aim
Throw Weapon

Critter
Concealment
Magic Sense
Materialize/Dematerialize
Mimicry
Sense Link
Telepathic Link

Decking
Analyze Security or Subsystem
Attack
Decrypt Access, File or Slave
Download Data
Edit File
Improvise Attack
Monitor Slave
Perform Combat Maneuver
Relocate
Scan Icon
Swap Memory
Upload Data

Magic
Activate/Deactivate Focus
Call Nature Spirit
Command a Spirit
Deliberately Mask the Aura (Metamagic)
Issue Mental Command (Control Manipulation Spells)
Manifest Astral Form on Physical Plane
Observe Spell for Design Inspiration
Read an Aura
Rooting (adept power)
Shift to/from Astral Perception

Rigging/Vehicle
Activate/Deactivate Non-rigged Autonav/Sensors/ECM/ECCM/ECD
Affiliate/Disaffiliate a Drone
Jump into a Primary Drone
Monitor Radio Traffic
Perform the Same Free Action on Multiple Drones
Return to Captain's Chair

COMPLEX

General
Use Complex Object
Use Skill

Combat
Attempt to Break Free from Grapple/Entanglement
Fire Automatic Weapon (FA)
Make Spotter Test for Indirect Fire
Melee/Unarmed Attack
Reload Firearm

Critter
Accident
Aid Power
Animal Control
Animal Form
Animal Gateway
Binding
Blindness
Compulsion
Confusion
Desire Reflection
Dispell
Empathy
Engulf
Essence Drain
Fear
Glamour
Guard
Human Form
Hypnotic Song
Influence
Innate Spell
Mist Form
Movement
Noxious Breath
Paralyzing Touch/Howl
Petrifying Gaze
Possession
Psychokinesis
Search
Silence
Sonic Projection
Spraying
Storm
Wealth
Weather Control

Decking
Analyze Host
Change Deck Mode
Control Slave
Crash Application or Host
Decoy
Disinfect
Dump Log
Edit Slave
Graceful Logoff

Invalidate Passcode
Jack Out Under Attack from Black IC
Locate Access Node, Decker, File, Frame, IC, Paydata or Slave
Logon to Host, LTG or RTG
Make Comcall
Null Operation
Purge Hog Virus
Redirect Datatrail
Tap Comcall
Use Medic or Restore Utility
Validate Passcode

Magic
Activate Sustaining Focus
Astrally Project or Return
Banish Spirit
Call Elemental/Ally
Cast Spell
Cleansing (Metamagic)
Divination (Metamagic)
Conjure Spirit
Control Spirit
Create Wards
Dispel a Spell
Erase Astral Signature
Heal Spirit
Link Spell to Anchoring Focus
Move Area of Effect of a Sustained Illusion/Manipulation Spell
Possession (Metamagic)
Quicken a Spell (Metamagic)
Remove Self from Ritual Team
Ritual Sorcery
Struggle to Change Course of Action (Dog Shamans Only)
Suppress Astral Barrier
Use Expendable Spell Focus

Rigging/Vehicle
Accelerating/Braking
Break Missile Target Lock
Conduct Signal Interception
Conduct MIJI
Control a Room through CCSS
Disengage from a CCSS System
Engage a Security Rigger in CCSS Combat
Fire Mounted or Vehicle Weapon
Hiding
Issue a Command
Make a Sensor Test for Gunnery Target Lock
Observe through a Secondary Drone
Operate a Drone
Positioning
Ramming
Reconnect a Lost Carrier
Reduce Footprint
Regenerate Channel Degradation
Turn On/Off Device through CCSS

CHARACTER RECORD SHEET

SHADOWRUN®

NAME

RACE   SEX   AGE

DESCRIPTION

NOTES

ATTRIBUTES

Body _____   Reaction

Quickness _____

Strength _____

Charisma _____   Initiative

Intelligence _____

Willpower _____

Essence _____

(Magic) _____   Matrix/Rigging

CONDITION MONITOR

	Light Stun	Moderate Stun		Serious Stun			Deadly Stun
Stun	+1TN # -1 Init.	+2 TN # -2 Init.		+3TN # -3 Init.			Unc.
Physical	+1TN # -1 Init.	+2 TN # -2 Init.		+3TN # -3 Init.			Unc. Maybe Dead
	Light Wound	Moderate Wound		Serious Wound			Deadly Wound

Physical Damage Overflow

KARMA

Karma Pool

Good Karma

Karma Spent/Lost

SKILLS

Name	Rating

DICE POOLS

Combat Pool

_____ Pool

_____ Pool

_____ Pool

ARMOR/GEAR

Type	Rating

EDGES & FLAWS

Type	Rating

CYBERWARE

Type	Rating

WEAPONS

Name	Type	Concealability	Reach	Mode	Ammo	Short	Medium	Long	Extreme	Damage	Modifiers

EQUIPMENT & GEAR

CONTACTS & INFORMATION

CHARACTER NOTES

VEHICLE

TYPE _____

Handling	_____
Speed	_____
Acceleration	_____
Body/Armor	___/___
Signature	_____
Autonav/Pilot	___/___
Sensor	_____
Cargo/Load	___/___

Light Damage   Moderate Damage   Serious Damage   Destroyed

NOTES

NAME

RACE SEX AGE

MAGICIAN RECORD SHEET
SHADOWRUN®

DESCRIPTION

NOTES

ATTRIBUTES

Body _____ Reaction
Quickness _____
Strength _____
Charisma _____
Intelligence _____ Initiative
Willpower _____
Essence _____
(Magic)

Astral

CONDITION MONITOR

	Light Stun	Moderate Stun		Serious Stun		Deadly Stun
Stun	+1TN # -1 Init.	+2 TN # -2 Init.		+3TN # -3 Init.		Unc.
Physical	+1TN # -1 Init.	+2 TN # -2 Init.		+3TN # -3 Init.		Unc. Maybe Dead
	Light Wound	Moderate Wound		Serious Wound		Deadly Wound

Physical Damage Overflow

KARMA

Karma Pool

Good Karma

Karma Spent/Lost

SKILLS

Name	Rating

DICE POOLS

Combat Pool	
_____ Pool	
_____ Pool	
_____ Pool	

ARMOR/GEAR

Type	Rating

FETISHES & FOCUSES/ ADEPT POWERS

Type	Rating

SPELLS

Name	Force	Type	Range	Target	Duration	Damage	Drain

CYBERWARE

Type	Rating

EDGES & FLAWS

Type	Rating

CONTACTS & INFORMATION

NOTES & GEAR

VEHICLE

TYPE _____

		Light Damage	Moderate Damage		Serious Damage		Destroyed

Handling _____
Speed _____
Acceleration _____
Body/Armor ____/____
Signature _____
Autonav/Pilot ____/____
Sensor _____
Cargo/Load ____/____

NOTES

INDEX